GOOD TIMES

GOOD TIMES

JUSTIN Lee COLLINS

EBURY
PRESS

1 3 5 7 9 10 8 6 4 2

Published in 2009 by Ebury Press, an imprint of Ebury Publishing
A Random House Group company

The Random House Group Limited Reg. No. 954009

Addresses for companies within the Random House Group can be found at
www.randomhouse.co.uk

A CIP catalogue record for this book is available from the British Library

The Random House Group Limited supports The Forest Stewardship Council (FSC),
the leading international forest certification organisation. All our titles that are
printed on Greenpeace approved FSC certified paper carry the FSC logo. Our paper
procurement policy can be found at www.rbooks.co.uk/environment

Mixed Sources
Product group from well-managed
forests and other controlled sources
www.fsc.org Cert no. TT-COC-2139
© 1996 Forest Stewardship Council
FSC

Designed and set by seagulls.net

Printed and bound in the UK by CPI Mackays, Chatham ME5 8TD

ISBN 9780091932916 (hardback)
ISBN 9780091933739 (paperback)

To buy books by your favourite authors and register for offers visit
www.rbooks.co.uk

CONTENTS

ACKNOWLEDGEMENTS

I'd like to thank Mum, Dad, Gran, Grandad, Karen, my baby boys
Archie and Harvey, Boyd Hilton, Tim Hurford, Daniel Goater, Dylan
Burnett, Duncan Hayes, Lisa Toogood, Ruth Larkin, Katie Phillips,
Liz Matthews, Peter Bennett-Jones, Robert Kirby, Claire Nightingale,
Stuart Murphy, Richard Ackerman, Richard Woolfe, Giles Pike, Noleen
Golding for telling me "remember it's not about you" and Dean
Nabarro for telling me "do less" – the two greatest pieces of advice
I've received in TV, Andrew Phillips, Andy Ashton, Karl Pilkington.
Ricky Gervais, Clive Tulloh, Nicky Waltham, John Gilbert, Claire Slessor,
Derek Hallworth, Simon Tucker, Simon Irwin, Graham Stuart, Katie
Crawford, Simon Welton, Anna Blue, Emma Hardy, Henrietta Conrad
and Sebastian Scott, Zai Bennett, Claire Zolkwer, Paul Jackson, Andrew
O'Connor, Lee Hupfield, Tom Beck (the nicest man in telly), Nathan
Eastwood, Greg Bower, Andrew Newman, Julian Bellamy, Kevin Lygo,
Danny Cohen, Andrew MacKenzie, Andy Auerbach, Andrew O'Connell,
Andi Peters, Fleur Fekkes, Gary Monaghan, the lovely Will Yapp, Doug
Brazier, Nick Benson, Tina Noble, Marie Baker, Shaun Nicholas,
Richard Cadell, Panache (aka Zara Mason), Mark Denton, Steve Lount,
Richard Bacon, David Owen, Jay Pond-Jones, Andrew Goodfellow,
Liz Marvin, Mari Roberts and finally, Alan Carr, the air that I breathe.

INTRODUCTION

eWOK SOAP

I sat there in the Cannon Cinema, Frogmore Street in Bristol with my gran. The lights went down. And I burst into tears. I was petrified, quite frankly.

It was 1977. I was only three years old, admittedly, and no one told me it would suddenly get pitch black in the room. I was an easily scared child. But I soon recovered, and when C3PO and R2D2 walked across the sandy desert on Tatooine in bleached-out sunlight, the incredible brightness of that image calmed me down instantly. I completely forgot I was frightened of being in a dark room with a load of strangers.

Star Wars was the first film I ever saw in the cinema and to be honest the only thing about it I really remember is that shot of R2D2 and C3PO making their way across the sandy landscape.

I've seen it since then, of course, and I'm pretty sure I enjoyed the rest of the film too though not much about the intricacies of the battle between the Empire and the rebels sank into my three-and-a-half-year-old brain. But that day was all about that one stunningly bright image. It was burned into my retinas.

Thirty years later I was sitting in the bright, sunlit garden of Princess Leia herself. I was about to interview Carrie Fisher at her home in the Hollywood Hills. It was a classic LA mansion, previously owned by Bette Davis, among others. Before the interview, Carrie showed me round the house. Star Wars merchandise and memorabilia were everywhere, including a statue depicting Princess Leia with her breasts exposed. George Lucas sent it to her, she told me.

It was a pinch-me-am-I-dreaming moment. Ever since I saw Star Wars as a little boy, I'd been obsessed with it. I collected the toys, I competed with my friend Andrew Jackson to collect stuff, every birthday and Christmas I asked for more Star Wars-related items, I re-enacted scenes from the film on my own at home. I loved it.

And there I was, as a grown man, making a television programme about the film saga that had meant so much to me throughout my life, hearing from the woman who played the stunningly sexy Princess Leia herself about how she had to tape down her breasts underneath her white toga-style costume because they wobbled around too much and George Lucas the director wouldn't let her have any underwear on. He told her straight: 'There's no underwear in Space.'

Not only that, she revealed that she had flirted with Harrison Ford throughout the shoot, and, she hinted, maybe more than flirted with him.

Carrie was still beautiful, she was totally honest, funny and she gave me a big hug. And a bar of Ewok soap. I'd never seen that merchandise before. And I've acquired a lot of Star Wars merchandise in my life, as you've probably gathered. I've still got the Ewok soap in its box at home. It would be worth loads on eBay.

But I'll never sell it and probably never open it.

Carrie Fisher was fabulous. I loved everything about her. It was the best interview I've ever conducted.

*

The thing is, although I still can't quite believe I ended up doing a job that entailed meeting so many of the key figures in my favourite film and turning it into a TV show which I got to present, I have to say it's only one of a number of mind-blowing experiences I've had which relate directly to the things I loved when I was growing up.

I'm not boasting. I'm as stunned as anyone by the ridiculous route my life has taken and by the absurd number of my lifelong dreams that have somehow ended up coming true. I guess that's what this book is about, if it's about anything other than a bunch of silly stories from my increasingly absurd existence.

Now that I come to think about it, I'm stunned and amazed that any of these dreams have come true, because until fairly recently every time I thought I was about to fulfil my ambitions, it all went horribly, sickeningly, but in retrospect quite entertainingly wrong.

That's what this book is about too – the long, long, extremely bumpy and badly signposted road to becoming a reasonably successful professional TV presenter, which is, for as long as I can remember, what I always wanted to do. It's the story of how I've had so many good times I can barely believe it, because along the way there were so many bad times.

I'm not going to moan about the bad times, don't you worry. I'm just telling you about them because they happened and because I can laugh about them now. Hopefully we can all laugh about them together and learn something about ourselves along the way. Or at least learn something about me and my daft life.

Good times ...

CHAPTER 1

MUCUS AND PEE

Welcome to my book. This is the first chapter, about my childhood and that.

My name is Justin Lee Collins. You can call me JLC. Or Justin. Or just Just. I don't mind. Really, call me anything you want.

The first thing you should know about me is that I'm an only child. I think that's very significant. (Every now and then in this book I'll signpost something that I think is highly significant by saying that it's significant. That's an advance warning. I hope I don't repeat myself too often. Apologies if I do.)

I think it's important to know I'm an only child because it meant I had to amuse myself from as early on as I could remember.

My dad, on the other hand, was one of fourteen children. Yes, they were Catholic. But my dad isn't really very religious. I think he's lapsed.

My mum also has two sisters and a brother. She's a bit more religious but not born again or anything. She goes to church regularly, but bear in mind her local church in Bristol is the nicest place. It's very laid-back and relaxed. They don't try to force anything on you. They don't really preach as such. I love it there.

Anyway I was born in Southmead Hospital, Bristol in 1974, the year

of Goodbye Yellow Brick Road by Elton John, Living For The City by
Stevie Wonder and The Night Chicago Died by Paper Lace.

Our first house was in Teresa Avenue, Bishopstown. A couple of
people claim that house was haunted. But we never experienced any
hauntings. We weren't haunted – can I just say that here and now?
Despite what you may have heard, we were not haunted.

We lived there from 1974 until 1981. Then about two months
before my seventh birthday we moved to Kingswood. That was also the
year Charles and Di got married. I won't give the full address in
Kingswood because my mum and dad still live there.

My dad was a self-employed electrical engineer and he was often
away from home working in Saudi Arabia, laying marble flooring. He's
also a plumber. In fact, my dad can pretty much do anything. He's a
proper handyman. He can do heating, plumbing, electrics, lay marble
floors and many other things. The exact opposite to me. I cannot bang
a nail into a wall. I'm useless.

I think he laid marble flooring on and off in Saudi Arabia for about
three years. He wasn't around in my formative years an awful lot
because of those working trips to Saudi when he'd be away for around
three months at a time.

Later on, when I was older, he'd be away from home again when
he worked at Kodak shops in the London area from Monday to Friday,
fixing them up.

As for my mum, she has always worked and has had loads of
different jobs. When I was very small she worked in a bookies, behind
the counter. Then when I was in junior school she was a dinner lady.
Not in my school but another one in the area. She also worked in a
hairdresser's, a post office and a charity shop at weekends.

I was a long time coming. My mum was twenty-four when she
married my dad. And I took about seven years to come along. My

mum was thirty-one, and my mum didn't carry very well with me, as they say. I wasn't a very pleasant baby to carry. Even in the womb I was a trouble-maker. So that might be why they never had another baby and I'm an only child. Which, as I mentioned before, is very significant.

My earliest memory is from when we lived in the Bishopstown house and I remember being sat in my highchair and looking from the open-plan dining room into the kitchen where my mum was with her mum, my gran. I have nothing to say about that memory except that it's the first snapshot image I can think of from when I was very little. I must have been about a year old.

I do have lots of memories of that house. It was a large, three-bedroom terrace house. But my dad split one of the bedrooms in two so it became a four-bedroom house. I had a playroom. I had a rocking horse. Not a fancy wooden one. It was made of tin.

I've always had a lot of ear, nose and throat problems. I always had bad catarrh and coughs and a bunged-up nose. Often I would wake up and I couldn't open my eyes because my very long eyelashes would be matted together with sleepy dust. My mum would have to clean my eyes with a warm flannel so I could open them.

I produced a lot of mucus. An awful lot of mucus. I would be bunged up all the time. I still produce quite a lot of mucus to this day and am often bunged up now.

Back then, the doctor prescribed me some medicine and it made me very drowsy. I went into the back garden one day and locked the door behind me because I thought it would be funny to lock my mum in so she couldn't come out into the garden. But because I was on this medication I fell asleep on the lawn.

I was sprawled out, totally unconscious. So my mum was stuck there banging on the door looking at me fast asleep in the garden.

Eventually I woke up because I heard her yelling at me and banging on the door.

I remember another time we'd been out and my mum had left that back door open. She'd cooked a chicken and then left it on the worktop. When we got back, the chicken had gone and there were muddy paw prints on the worktop and all across the kitchen floor. A cat had nicked the chicken and eaten it. That story has no great significance apart from the fact that it mildly amused me at the time.

More importantly, I was circumcised at the age of four. For ages I had no idea why I was circumcised. I went through a period in my early teens of wondering if I was Jewish because I was circumcised. I had heard that Jewish men were circumcised and I was circumcised so I thought maybe I was secretly Jewish. I thought that because my parents are quite dark-skinned that they were perhaps secretly Jewish and just didn't tell me. Another theory, albeit short-lived, was that I was adopted. I considered all kinds of possibilities. Of course I'm not Jewish. And I'm not adopted. I just don't have a foreskin. And this is why.

When I was a little boy my foreskin wouldn't retract properly so when I went to pee it was a bit cumbersome and slightly painful. So the doctor said I needed to get my foreskin taken off. It was a medical condition.

I can vividly picture being in Southmead Hospital, the same hospital where I'd been born, waiting for this operation. My mum brought me my Uncle Bulgaria from the Wombles – he was my favourite cuddly toy. I also had an emu and a frog.

I was a Ribena freak at that age. I loved it. While I was in the hospital waiting for my foreskin to be removed, I was always pulling the cord to ask the nurse to bring me some Ribena. But you're only supposed to have about three Ribenas at that age, perhaps at any age, because they're so full of sugar.

My gran told me that when I was in hospital to have my foreskin removed, a day or two after the op, she took me for a walk through the ward and we bumped into the doctor who said, 'Hello, Justin, how's your willy?'

And I answered, 'It's okay, Doctor. How's yours?'

So I've got a circumcised penis. It wasn't really much of an issue at the time, because I had no idea that not having a foreskin was in any way unusual. I didn't know any better.

But I first noticed my willy was different to other boys' willies when I was in secondary school. It was all due to being forced to shower with the other boys. I don't think these days it happens so much. I think they have individual showers. At least I hope for their sakes they do.

But when I was at school we all had to shower communally, just at the precise point in our lives when we're most embarrassed by our bodies. We were all feeling self-conscious and unsure and we're all looking to see who's fat and who's got a big willy or a small willy and who's got pubes, like the horrible little boys we were. And if you didn't have any pubes, for example, you were going to get ridiculed. It was awful. We were forced into that situation of having to look at each other's penises, circumcised or not, by adults. It was just wrong. It was fuel for the bullies. It was a nightmare. I hated it.

But that was when I first noticed my willy was different. It looked very different, because, let's face it, when circumcised willies are flaccid they do look very different from uncircumcised ones.

While I'm on the subject of medical conditions, let me jump ahead to the next time I was in hospital overnight.

I was twelve and I broke my wrist in two places. Everyone said how brave I was. And I *was* brave, considering the agony I was in. And I didn't cry at all – not in front of my mum or anyone. My dad was working in London and rushed back to see me that night in hospital.

It happened on a Wednesday night, which was the night I used to do karate. The classes took place on Stapleton Road in Bristol at a community centre called the Mill. It was quite a rough place. In fact, it was the place where David Blunkett chose to go a few years back when he was trying to publicise his latest crackdown on crime, surrounded by security staff, of course.

Anyway, I started doing karate from the age of eleven, mainly because my dad wanted me to. I was into it initially.

Before that my dad took me to judo when I was six. I went to one class in Hanham folk centre. I was there with my little white suit and my little white belt and I was forced into sparring with a ten-year-old blonde girl who was very pretty and had a basin haircut. She was much taller than me and just as I was thinking that I quite liked this judo thing and that it might be for me, she threw me over her shoulder and I hit my head on the mat and it hurt and I thought, 'Actually, I don't think I do like this judo after all. I'm not going to do this any more.' So that was my last judo lesson.

A few years later I got into Bruce Lee and, especially, Chuck Norris. Luckily, there was a video shop that stocked all the Norris films: Breaker! Breaker!, Good Guys Wear Black, The Octagon, A Force Of One, Lone Wolf McQuade, and obviously Missing In Action – the trilogy. So when my dad wanted me to start doing karate, I liked the idea because of the Chuck Norris connection.

So I started karate lessons every Wednesday night at the Mill and for about the first year I quite enjoyed it. Then when I ended up enjoying it less, I really only carried on doing it to keep my dad happy. Eventually I made the decision to stop going and I told my mum and she backed me up, but when we told my dad he went ballistic. I think like many dads he thought I was in danger of becoming a mummy's boy and of being mollycoddled. So I carried on going in spite of the fact that I didn't really like it.

Anyway, this Wednesday night, I'd come home from school and had my tea – six corned beef sandwiches. That was my tea that night.

After I'd had my tea, Jason McAuley came knocking on my door to see if I wanted to come out and play.

I said I would go out for a bit of a play and my mum pointedly reminded me that I had karate later. But I thought it would be fine to have a bit of a play with my friends before karate. I should have just let my tea go down and wait for karate. But I didn't.

So we went to play in the school grounds, which we often did because the gates were always left open. There was this bay where they kept all the bins and there was a big wooden box in the corner. Inside the box was some kind of generator, and you could stand on top of this box and above you would be two green iron girders and what you could attempt to do was stand on the box and jump up onto the girder and swing.

You could do that if you wanted to. It was pointless but we did it.

That night Jason did it first and then I tried to do it. But I didn't really commit to the jump properly. My fingertips just brushed the edge of the iron beam, then I immediately slipped off and fell to the ground in a seated position and I fell forward onto my hands. All the weight fell on my wrists.

I sat there and thought, 'Ooh, this feels quite painful.'

Jason said, 'Oh shit! Mate, are you all right?'

I told him yes, but then I looked at my hand and my jaw dropped to the floor. My right wrist was literally about 180 degrees from where it should be and it was hugely swollen. It was hideously disfigured.

I immediately ran across the road to my house to show my mum.

I walked in the back door and through the kitchen and I could see my mum sitting there in the living room with her dinner on a tray on her lap. By this point I was quite calm but I knew that if I showed my mum my hand in that state she would totally freak out. So I stood there in the living room and I hid my hand behind my back because I didn't want her to freak out, but I also knew I had to tell her what had happened. It was a quandary.

So I said, 'Mum, I've done something ... '

She said, 'Oh my god – what have you done?' She knew something was up.

I said, 'Well, I've done something but whatever it is I don't want you to be upset.'

I knew when I showed her my arm that it looked so freaky and horrible and beyond repair that she would freak out.

As I pulled my arm from behind my back, I said, 'I think I've broken my wrist.'

As soon as she saw it, she did of course freak out.

But the first thing she did, as soon as she saw this hideous sight of my disfigured hand, was to grab me, take me to the kitchen and run my wrist under cold water. I suppose she thought it could numb the pain and take the swelling down.

But it didn't help much.

Then my mum decided to run me over to my Uncle Dave's, because my dad was away in London working, and she wanted someone to be with us. Maybe she felt she should have a man around for this distressing incident.

We went in the car to my Uncle Dave's and he actually told me he thought it didn't look too bad – like I'd just sprained it or something. I think that was his way of trying to make me feel better. Because in fact it was an abomination.

On the way back, my mum decided for some reason that we should stop off at a chemist and see what the pharmacist thought of my clearly broken wrist. So first she ran it under cold water and then she decided we should show the pharmacist. That was her plan of action.

We stopped off at the chemist's on Lodge Causeway and by this time I had a wet tea towel wrapped round my wrist, and when I took it off to show the pharmacist, sure enough he said, 'You really need to take him to A&E immediately.'

Years later my mum broke her nose while she was getting a shovel out of her garden shed and a broom fell to the floor and my mum tripped over it and fell flat on her face. My wife Karen and I happened to be in my mum's house at the time and as soon as I saw her I could see she'd broken her nose, so I told her we had to go to casualty. But my mum said, 'No, let me go to the pharmacist first.'

I've no idea why. I've no idea what she thought the pharmacist could do about broken noses and wrists.

But sure enough, twenty years later, I did take her to the same pharmacy that she took me to all those years ago when I broke my wrist.

Funnily enough, this time round the pharmacist told us there was nothing he could do and that my mum should go to A&E.

Anyway, my mum and my Uncle Dave did eventually take me to the hospital.

When I got there, the doctor asked me when I had last eaten. I told him I'd had my tea a few hours previously. He asked what I'd eaten for my tea and I told him – six corned beef sandwiches.

He said, 'SIX corned beef sandwiches?!'

I told him, 'Yes, Doctor, six corned beef sandwiches.'

A few hours later, I was in the hospital bed and my arm was up in a sling and I'd asked if I could have a TV and they brought me a portable TV and I was watching Taggart. For the first time ever, as far as I could remember, I was on my own, and I had a little cry.

I'm not sure if that was because it was a particularly bad episode of Taggart or because it all suddenly hit home how much pain I was in, or just because I was on my own.

CHAPTER 2

GOTTA LOTTA BOTTLE

As usual, I was thirsty and I couldn't sleep, so I went down to the kitchen to get a satsuma and a glass of water, and as I walked through the kitchen, I just happened to peep through the crack in the living-room door. I could see my mum sitting on the sofa with the Millennium Falcon on her lap, in the middle of wrapping it.

She saw me. She knew that I'd seen her. And I'd seen it.

I said, 'I didn't see anything,' but I had.

It was Christmas Eve, and I knew right then that there was no Father Christmas. But I didn't really care. I was getting a Millennium Falcon from Star Wars.

I was nine years old.

The thing I remember most about being that age was that I loved watching films and TV programmes and almost simultaneously realising that I wanted to be in those films and TV programmes. Or that I wanted to do something akin to what the stars of those shows did. You could say I wanted to be on TV from a very young age. I know, it's a ridiculous cliché. But it's true.

After I saw Star Wars that time when I was three, I used to go to the cinema all the time, whenever I had pocket money. In the school holidays I'd go four times a week. If there was nothing new on I'd see the same film again.

My gran used to take me to the cinema during the summer holidays too. The three things we'd do were: 1. Go to Weston-super-Mare, for the Grand Pier, which burned down recently and is sadly no longer with us. 2. Go to the movies. And 3. Go to Bristol museum, which was brilliant. They had a stuffed gorilla called Alfred which I loved.

But the cinema was my favourite (partly because the trip to the Bristol museum was knackering because it was up a steep hill). When Return Of The Jedi came out, some cinemas had special Star Wars Spectacular events in which they showed all three films back to back – Star Wars, Empire and Jedi. My gran took me and had to sit through six hours of Star Wars. What a great woman.

Apart from Star Wars, I loved films like Young At Heart with Doris Day. Channel 4 launched when I was eight and I grew up watching the old films on Channel 4 in the afternoon. I also loved the old RKO horror movies. Bela Lugosi as Dracula. Abbott and Costello. Abbott And Costello Meet The Wolf Man. Abbott And Costello Meet Dracula. Dracula Meets The Wolf Man and even Dracula And The Wolf Man Meet Frankenstein. I loved them all!

Apart from watching the TV till all hours, I would also listen to Brian Matthews late at night on Radio 2. And I loved Steve Wright on Radio 1. But Dave Barrett on GWR was my favourite. His phone-ins. Late-night radio was a big thing for me. I loved it so much that I soon knew I wanted to be on the radio and, equally, I loved Abbott and Costello so much I knew I wanted to be a comedy actor.

And the one thing I never ever ever ever had any inclination to do my entire life was stand-up comedy ...

The first comedy person I ever remember liking is Harold Lloyd. They'd show Harold Lloyd films on BBC2. And Monkey would be on straight afterwards. I would have been about three when I first saw Harold

Lloyd. I adored him. I also loved Laurel and Hardy on Saturday mornings. Bilko was huge for me. Then there was Morecambe And Wise and Tommy Cooper.

Then a little bit later I used to stay up till about eleven at night and watch Rhoda and Taxi and Laverne & Shirley. In my teens I moved on to Happy Days, Mork & Mindy and The Garry Shandling Show.

Then when I was about fifteen it was all about Vic & Bob.

But if you asked my mum what my favourite programme was as a little boy, if you called her right now and asked her that question (although I doubt very much you've got her number), she would answer without missing a beat, and she'd say, 'Come Dancing.' The original ballroom dancing show.

I'm not talking about Strictly Come Dancing – that came much later, of course. And I love that show too. But when I was a little boy, the original Come Dancing was going strong on BBC1. And that was my favourite show. I loved the glamour, how the dancers looked, the music and maybe the element of jeopardy – that they might fall or have some kind of accident as they were attempting a particularly difficult paso doble. I just loved it all, to be honest. But it was mainly the glamour and the jeopardy I loved when I was a little boy. I used to sit there and cuddle up to my mum while watching Come Dancing.

The amazing thing about Come Dancing and ballroom dancing in general is that it has taken on an almost mystical importance in my life. Seriously. You'll see why when I tell the story of my first ever steps as a radio broadcaster. And my first ever moments as a proper live TV presenter.

I also became obsessed with darts at an early age. That was probably due to my auntie's ex-husband. He played county darts. We always watched Bullseye on a Sunday. If they ever brought that back again, I'd love to host it. My uncle was on Bullseye once, as the thrower. I watched the world championships every year at the Lakeside.

All this is by way of explaining that I had weird tastes. There's something random about it all. Darts. Ballroom dancing. Horror movies. And then there was showjumping and Jimmy Cagney films. I haven't even mentioned those.

People say to me, how can you like that but not this? Or, how can you like him but not her? But I don't see it like that. I just do like one thing and not the other. I like my little niches.

For example, I really like football but I'm not a die-hard fan. I support Bristol City and I've supported them all my life but I also like to see Bristol Rovers do well. I can't get that passionate about football because it's the number one sport in the entire world and it's too big for me. But the darts world championship – I'm there!

I also have to admit, not that I'm in any way ashamed of it, that I stayed in a lot and watched a lot of TV. I didn't ever do that teenage thing of hanging around on street corners, and when I saw all these local kids doing that I would assume that it couldn't be very nice for them at home, because instead of staying in and watching Mork & Mindy they preferred standing on street corners, gobbing.

As well as our Come Dancing habit, Saturday nights as a kid for me meant staying in and staying up late watching TV with my mum. We'd watch Columbo, wrestling, The Rockford Files ... all sorts. I loved it.

Where was my dad? you're probably wondering. Well, he'd go out with his mates on a Saturday, down the pub, which was fair enough when you consider he'd been working all week plumbing or sawing or grouting or whatever, including often working during the day on Saturday itself.

The Saturday routine was always the same.

My mum worked in a charity shop on Saturdays but she'd always prepare Dad's tea for him so when he got home he'd just have to heat it up. Then he'd have a shower and come back down with his hair still soaking wet. He never blow-dried it. He would lie on the floor in front of our awful wall-mounted four-bar gas fire and dry his hair with it, while Tosca was playing on TV. He loved opera. Well, he loved two operas in particular, Tosca and La Bohème, because they were the two he had on video cassette. He'd put one of these operas on while he was drying his hair by the gas fire and I just wanted to watch The Muppet Show.

One time I was sitting there wondering if I could get away with turning the opera off when I looked over to my dad and saw steam coming off his head. Plumes of smoke!

'Dad! Your hair's on fire!' I yelled.

He darted across the room. I'd never seen my dad move so fast in his life.

But his hair wasn't on fire at all. It was just the condensation from drying his soaking-wet hair in front of the gas fire.

After he'd dried his hair and watched some opera, Dad would go out for the night with his friends Doddsy and Tony Morrison. Meanwhile, my mum and I would sit at home, get a Chinese takeaway and watch TV. Eventually I'd go to bed and stay awake and listen for when my dad came in and then, and only then, I'd be able to go to sleep.

Sometimes he'd come back just after pub closing time, armed with a prawn curry, and I'd come down and have a few prawns with him. But other times I'd be up till 3am waiting for him. I used to think, 'Where's he gone? What's he doing till 3am?'

In fact, it was only very recently that I found out. I asked him where he used to go and he just said, 'Oh, we used to go back to Tony Morrison's.'

He didn't have many hobbies or anything but for long periods Dad did have an organ in the living room, which he loved to play, especially using the wah-wah pedal. He'd have organ lessons at home while my mum took me to karate. Or the TV would go off and he would announce, 'Right, I'm going to play the organ!' I'd go upstairs. I couldn't stand the bloody thing and nor could my mum.

To make matters worse, our house had very thin walls. My dad would leave the toilet door open and we could all hear him having a pee. So I certainly couldn't escape the wah-wah organ sound anywhere in the house.

He even tried to get me to play the organ because apparently I had the right kind of long and thin fingers for it. But I had absolutely no interest in organs whatsoever. I hated the organ. He dragged me to a class one night but afterwards I told him there was no way I was going to come back ever again. The organ was not for me.

Apart from his organ, my dad had a few other interests, though I wouldn't really call them hobbies as such. The only piece of exercise equipment he ever had was his Bullworker. He used it every now and then, although he was a pretty fit man anyway, what with his constant manual work. Well, he hardly *ever* used it actually. Did anyone ever use one of those things?

Actually my mum and I used it. As a security device. When my dad was away on work business and my mum and I would be left on our own, my mum would wedge the Bullworker down between the door and the wall at the foot of our stairs. She would say that if anyone did try to break in and force the door open to come upstairs, the Bullworker would come straight through the door and whack them in the shins.

My dad didn't like playing the family man; he's never worn a wedding ring. I once asked my mum why he never wore a ring, and she said, 'Well, he's a jack the lad, isn't he?' She didn't mind. She knew what he was like.

Similarly, he never really liked family holidays, which most of the time meant going down to Brean Sands to stay in our caravan. In the days leading up to one of these trips he'd start complaining about his back. He often went on about his bad back, which was fair enough when you consider all the manual labour and bending down and banging things into other things he was doing. But when a holiday was approaching, mentions of the back would suddenly be more frequent. My mum and I would laugh about it, especially when we'd suddenly see him lying down flat on his back on the floor in the living room, with one of his operas on the TV, stretching out that bad back of his.

His bad back was very real, though. He had to have a separate bed with a tough, hard mattress because of his back. So my mum and dad had two single beds in the same room, which I think was actually quite common for married couples in those days.

My mum and dad didn't show each other a lot of affection in front of me. I'd never see them kissing or cuddling or anything, but I guess that was quite usual at that time. To this day I've never seen them properly kiss each other.

But they both gave me an awful lot of love.

All the time my mum used to tell me, 'You're my life ... I don't know what I'd do without you ... you're my life.'

My dad was temperamental. I think that's what happens when you've experienced a tough time growing up, which he most certainly did. He was born in Southmead, a rough estate in Bristol. His dad died when he was ten after drinking himself to death. My dad has memories of the police standing outside his house while his dad stuck his head out the window telling the police to fuck off.

But even though my dad had a temper, he never took it out on me. He never laid a finger on me at all. He was never a violent man. But he didn't have to smack me or anything anyway. If he told me off, I'd stop. My hair would stand on end and I would run upstairs or into the garden. I was definitely scared of him and his temper, but at the same time I loved him dearly. He was very firm with me. But he also made sure I had everything in life that he never had as a kid. My upbringing was totally the opposite to his. He helped with anything I ever needed or wanted. I never went without.

I certainly had all the toys I could ever want.

Particularly the Star Wars toys.

But when I started getting them, and slowly built up quite a collection, I wasn't into them just to have them sitting around my room as inanimate objects. I wasn't collecting them for the sake of it. I didn't leave any of them in their boxes. I didn't care about the boxes. I loved actually playing with them. I was re-enacting Star Wars with them. I was putting myself into Star Wars. (I'm not an obsessive kind of fan at all, by the way. I loved the first three films because they were brilliant fun to watch. I hated the more recent ones. They were shit.)

I'd also imagine that I was staging a TV show, complete with me doing the continuity announcements. I had my soft Emu puppet, which we bought at Brean Sands, for example, and I'd do an Emu show, and I'd introduce it with a menu.

'Coming up tonight on Children's TV, we've got the Emu show, we've got Star Wars ...'

I'd always do it as if I was putting on a show. If I was playing with my Star Wars toys I'd build in cliffhangers that would come at the end of my play-time as if it was a proper film. So maybe one episode would revolve around the AT-AT Walker, and the end of this five-minute bit would feature one of the main characters falling out of the side of the AT-AT and that's when I would stop, and I would say, 'Join us next week for more Star Wars.'

But I was just talking to myself as if I had an audience. There was no 'us'. I'd disappear into my own world.

My favourite character was Luke Skywalker. Luke represented me. The young boy who wants to leave home and cut his ties and achieve all he can in the wider universe.

As you know, Andrew Jackson, my best friend at Chester Park Junior School, was as much into Star Wars as I was. Every birthday and Christmas we both got Star Wars stuff. One Christmas I wanted the Rebel Transporter, which Andrew had already received for his birthday, then the next birthday I wanted the Millennium Falcon. Which I eventually got for Christmas, as I just told you. At the height of my Star Wars toy banjoree, I had a Scoutwalker, a Speeder bike, a Tauntaun, and maybe thirty action figures.

The only one of all these toys I don't still have is the Rancor Monster. As I'm sure you know, when Luke goes to Jabba the Hut's palace to try to get Han Solo out of the cryogenic chamber and Jabba drops him down into the pit, there's a monster in the pit which he fights – and that was called the Rancor Monster.

My Rancor Monster was the pride of my collection. It was a huge toy and I loved playing with it.

But a while later, when I was really skint, I took a lot of stuff to a car boot sale and I put the Rancor Monster in there. I don't really know why – it was a rash decision. Maybe I did it because it wasn't a ship and I mainly enjoyed playing with the ships. So I thought I could live without the Rancor Monster. I sold it for three pounds.

But in fact my Auntie Carol bought it and told me I shouldn't have sold it. I thought, 'Brilliant – the Rancor Monster is in safe hands. It'll stay in the family, and maybe one day, when I have some money, I can buy it back from my auntie.'

Then a couple of months later my Auntie Carol sold it herself at a car boot sale. So she obviously thought the same thing: she could live without it. But I really wish I still had the Rancor Monster. I bitterly regret to this day that I haven't got it. It would be worth about forty quid now I reckon.

So I spent a lot of time playing by myself as a kid, amusing myself, keeping myself excited. But I also learned that I could entertain others.

At weekends my dad would take me with him to see his friends and I'd often do impressions in front of them. I was only five or six and my dad loved me doing them. I'd do Frank Spencer, as you had to do if you were an impressionist at the time, and I did Ruth Madoc from Hi-De-Hi! 'Hello campers!' and all that. I also did Groucho Marx, which was a bit odd for a little boy, I suppose. I think he was featured in a TV ad at the time. I used to memorise stuff I saw on TV. Silly stuff. I had a great memory for daft stuff – jingles and ads. I would get a jumbo stick of rock and use that as a cigar and I'd do Groucho saying, 'I used to smoke a cigar until I found out this was better value.' I also did the Hunchback of Notre Dame because there was a TV ad which featured Charles Laughton as the Hunchback saying, 'The bells! The bells!' I guess it was a weird mixture of impressions for someone to do. Mike Yarwood never did the Hunchback as played by Laughton. I'd mix it up! I did Groucho Marx, Ruth Madoc, the Hunchback of Notre Dame and I'd also do bird impressions. I'd do a big gulp, which was a swallow, and I'd quickly bend down as if something was flying overhead and that was me doing a duck.

My dad and his friends lapped it up.

Throughout my childhood I was surrounded by adults and I quite enjoyed it. I think that meant that I became quite advanced in terms of interacting with grown-ups and then reading and stuff. But from an early age I was quite happy talking to and hanging out with grown-ups. Because that's what I knew.

I was ten the first time I performed to a proper audience.

It was 1984, and I went on holiday with my mum and dad to the Devon Coast Country Club in Torbay. My Auntie Liz and her husband Keith and their kids Lita and Christopher and my Uncle Dave and my Auntie Sue and their little baby Sam were also there.

To this day it was the best holiday of my life, because my family was there, my little cousins were there, and because of the competitions. (My dad took me to Disney World that same year, which I'll get to in a bit, but it wasn't as much fun as the Devon Coast Country Club.)

They held a lot of competitions at the Devon Coast Country Club. When he was young my dad had singing lessons so he fancied himself to have quite a good singing voice. But he was known by his mates as 'One-Note Collins' because whatever he sang he only ever hit the one note, in a kind of semi-operatic, big booming style. My mum would say, 'It's the same old note every time!' as soon as he started to sing.

So he entered the talent contest and sang but he didn't win. He only placed.

My Uncle Dave entered the ape man contest in which you had to pretend to be an ape and make ape noises and beat your chest and pick up one of the Yellowcoat staff and run around with her like something out of 2001: A Space Odyssey, and he won.

That holiday was an endless series of contests.

They also held competitions for children, including a talent competition and a Bionic Man competition. (The Six Million Dollar Man was huge on TV at the time.) The competitions were sponsored by the

Milk Marketing Board, whose slogan at the time was 'Gotta Lotta Bottle'. So the prizes consisted of lots of Gotta Lotta Bottle merchandise, including a Gotta Lotta Bottle T-shirt and a Gotta Lotta Bottle floatable dinghy and a Gotta Lotta Bottle mug.

I entered two competitions that week. First, I entered the Bionic Man competition in which you had to run round the outdoor swimming pool in slow-motion like the Bionic Man. I wore trunks and trainers. No shirt. I was topless. And I won that. It wasn't much of an achievement to be honest, but I was excited to win it. There was a brilliant-looking guy in charge with a big Afro and beard and glasses and he presented the prize to me and said, 'Well done, Justin, you're our winner,' and he put the microphone up to my mouth and I gave a big thumbs-up and said, triumphantly, 'Fans! Fans!'

That was my acceptance speech: 'Fans! Fans!' And a thumbs-up. I was ten, remember.

That was the first time in my life that I won anything and the first time I felt I could be a winner.

My triumph in the Bionic Man competition inspired me to enter the talent show. I got cocky. My dad and my Uncle Keith were super-keen that I did the talent show, and essentially they were my managers. They thought I could get an act together. Something more ambitious than running around in slo-mo in trunks. They'd seen me do my impressions, and they encouraged me to form them into some kind of act.

My dad even gave me some jokes to do. He didn't write them. I remember doing one joke which he must have seen on The Comedians.

It went like this: 'I was driving my car the other day' – again, bear in mind I'm doing this act and I'm only ten years old – 'and I saw flashing lights in my rear-view mirror. I pulled over to the side of the road and this policeman came up to the door and asked me, "Sir, have you been drinking?" and I said, "No, I haven't been drinking," and the policeman said, "Well, can you just blow into this bag, please, sir?" and I said, "Why do I have to blow into that bag if I haven't been drinking?" and the policeman said, "Because my chips are too hot."'

That was an example of the material in my act. My dad also had the brilliant idea of referring to one of the Yellowcoats by name. He knew I had a bit of a crush on one of them, who was called Sue, so he told me to mention her at some point, so during my Ruth Madoc impression, when I impersonated one of her very Welsh Hi-De-Hi! announcements, I said, 'The Miss Lovelylegs competition will take place round the pool tomorrow. If you want to take part go and see Sue.'

So I had jokes, mainstream impressions, obscure impressions ... and this was what I used to enter the talent show.

I was nervous and I don't think I really wanted to do it. I've carried that feeling through to this day. Whenever I'm about to perform, I think, 'I want to do it, I like the idea of doing it but when it comes down to the reality of it, I'm not sure if I can really do it and I'm not sure if I can really go through with it.'

I was tenth on the show so I had to stand there watching the nine other acts before me, during which time all these doubts swam around in my head.

But my dad and my uncle were both really keen that I did it.

I was standing on stage. My family were sitting just to my right in this huge family ballroom which must have sat a few hundred people. I watched the other contenders. The competition was open to fifteen-year-olds and under. There was a fifteen-year-old chap who was very well turned out. He looked considerably older than me and he was much more mature, and he sang 'Zip-A-Dee-Doo-Dah' from the Disney film Song Of The South. I have to say, he was brilliant. I remember thinking, 'We're all just competing for second place because Zip-A-Dee-Doo-Dah guy has got it in the bag.' He was brilliant. My other main competition were two ten- or eleven-year-old boys from Liverpool – a comedy double act. They were pretty good too.

So afterwards there we were backstage and a voice was announcing the top three in reverse order. Third were the young comedy double-act guys from Liverpool. In second place was ... Zip-A-Dee-Doo-Dah guy.

I thought, 'My goodness, well, whoever has beaten Zip-A-Dee-Doo-Dah guy must be absolutely brilliant because Zip-A-Dee-Doo-Dah guy was amazing. Who's won? Who on earth has won?!'

And then this voice booms: 'Number ten!' and I looked around to work out who number ten was. Then I looked at my wrist and saw the number ten band on it. I had no idea I was number ten. And just then the announcer shouted, 'Justin!'

I had definitely won. There was no other explanation.

I was stunned. I couldn't believe it. I'd beaten Zip-A-Dee-Doo-Dah guy. Eventually I gathered myself and walked out on to the stage and my dad and my uncle leapt out of their seats and cheered, and my mum had tears in her eyes. It was quite a moment. Don't forget it was sponsored by Gotta Lotta Bottle so it was quite a prestigious event.

I was given a Gotta Lotta Bottle T-shirt, three Gotta Lotta Bottle tumblers, an inflatable Gotta Lotta Bottle dinghy, which I didn't really know what I was going to do with, and some Gotta Lotta Bottle stickers.

But the really significant thing for me, the really important thing and why it was such an incredibly significant moment in my life, is that the main prize was another five-day holiday later that year so I could return for the big end-of-season final when they would bring all of the winners back for a big final competition.

But my parents decided that we wouldn't go back.

And let me say unequivocally that I'm totally happy with that decision.

That's what my parents were like. Totally un-pushy. They never forced anything on me, including religion or anything like that. They didn't force me to get christened, which was great of them, and they didn't push me to become a little showbiz kid.

So we never went back so I could take part in the end-of-year Devon Coast Country Club talent show. It's all part of the same philosophy. My mum used to say, 'I'd never care if you became a dustbin man. I'd love you just the same.' Maybe other parents might have made sure I went back to take part in the final, because it was the obvious thing to do, but I don't think I was particularly bothered one way or another. My parents didn't even entertain the thought of taking me back. And I love them for it. I think that's helped make me who I am. Whatever that is.

Anyway, immediately after the talent competition and flushed with my success, I entered the fancy dress competition. I went as World Of Sport. My costume consisted of me carrying a snooker cue, a table tennis bat, a tennis racquet and a golf club. And I had a sign round my neck saying 'World Of Sport' written in felt-tip pen. But on the way from the chalet to the family ballroom, the rain made it run. So no one could read it. Needless to say, I didn't win the competition. It was the first of many disappointments in my life ...

I got cocky, I guess, because I'd won the talent show. I got carried away. I thought I could win everything. I even thought I could win the fancy dress contest just by carrying too much sporting equipment. It was a disaster.

My next performing experience was at Barry Island Butlins where we went for a few days the following year. They had a junior variety show, which you could audition for, and then at the end of the week the kids would put on a show for the mums and dads. So I auditioned with pretty much the same act – Groucho Marx, bird impressions, Hunchback of Notre Dame ('The bells! The bells!'). After I did my act for a few minutes, I noticed this redcoat who was standing backstage laughing his ass off. When I'd finished, he said to me, 'You were brilliant!'

The guy who judged and picked the acts was called Malcolm the Magician, and he was also the compère for the junior variety show. He picked me to take part and I loved it.

The following year we went back to Barry Island Butlins and I auditioned again. But I didn't get through. And I think I know why. I had developed my act and by that point I was including a bit I did from Rambo: First Blood Part II, where I impersonated Sylvester Stallone. There's a speech he does at the end where he comes back with the POWs and he gets out of the helicopter and he knees that guy from Cagney & Lacey in the nuts. Martin Kove, that was his name. He knees Martin Kove from Cagney & Lacey in the nuts. He's carrying a big gun. He goes in to get Murdoch and then he comes out and Richard Crenna, as Colonel Trautman, says, 'What do you want, John? What do you want?' And Rambo says, 'What I want is for our country to love us as much as we love it. That's what I want.' Well, I incorporated that speech from Rambo into my act.

So I'd got a bit older and I felt I needed to mature and develop my act, and I remember thinking clearly as I was on stage auditioning for the variety show that Malcolm the Magician, the head judge, also known as Uncle Malcolm, was distracted.

I stood there, reciting John Rambo's climactic speech from First Blood Part II in my best Sly Stallone accent, and just then, someone walked into the hall and approached Uncle Malcolm to tell him something – I've no idea what; maybe they gave him an important message of some kind – and Malcolm there and then just got up and left the auditorium!

In the middle of my act!

He'd left the room by the time I got to the end of my Rambo speech. I was amazed. I felt like a dick. I was in the middle of what I thought was a pretty decent Rambo impression and I thought, 'This isn't working. That guy Malcolm who's supposed to judge my audition isn't even here. This isn't right.'

When he eventually came back I somehow knew I wasn't going to get through.

Sure enough, a few days later we checked the notice board and I wasn't on the list. I hadn't made it. I was gutted. One of the parents of one of the other kids auditioning that day told me she couldn't believe I wasn't picked, so I just said, 'Well, the judge left the room while I was on.' Maybe it was a protest at the nature of my act. Unlikely. I think he was just distracted.

That was my first big knock. Aged eleven. It all seemed most unfair.

But before that disappointment, I experienced one of the great surprises of my young life ...

I arrived back home from school one day and my mum seemed a bit upset. I could tell from the look on her face that something was up. She looked disappointed about something. But I could tell my dad was really excited. He just looked at me and came out with it: 'How do you fancy going to Disney World, Justin?'

I immediately ran out into the garden and ran around with my hands in the air yelling 'Yippee!'

The reason my mum was upset was because she suffered from quite bad travel-phobia. There was no way she was going to be able to come with us, so she was going to be missing her little boy and her husband for over two weeks.

You see, apart from that eventful, perhaps historic, trip to the Devon Coast Country Club, our main holidays in those days were to Brean and, a couple of times, to Barry Island Butlins. It was rare that we went anywhere else mainly because of my mum's travel-phobia. She didn't like travelling on trains and boats and coaches, let alone planes. The longest journey she could cope with was the ninety minutes or so it took for us to drive to Barry. Brean was about an hour maximum. Even Devon Coast Country Club was only about ninety minutes away. We never went to Cornwall because that would have been a two-and-a-half-hour drive.

So my dad and I and a few of his friends all went to Florida together.

My mum came with us to the train station to see me and my dad off to the airport. She got on board the train to kiss me goodbye and she didn't look happy. It was the first time I'd been anywhere without my mum. I didn't want to leave her but on the other hand I did really want to go to Disney World. So in the end I told her, 'Come on, Mum, you've got to go – the train's about to leave.'

Disney World was amazing, as you can imagine, but the main event of the trip wasn't the chance I had to see Donald Duck or Mickey Mouse or any of those characters, it was my introduction to the sensual wonder of Ms Sylvia Kristel.

Sure, my dad took me on all the rides, and Big Thunder Mountain was amazing. I loved it there. We spent the first week in Orlando going to all the amusement parks, then the second week we settled down for a more relaxing time at the hotel by the pool. I got massively sunburnt – huge blisters on my shoulders. It was awful.

One evening my dad decided to go for a quick drink with his friends who we'd travelled with and left me to amuse myself in our room on my own. And by the way, I was absolutely fine to be left on my own. My dad knew I'd be absolutely fine. He told me to lock myself in the room, which was on the ground floor, and he'd check on me every now and then.

In his absence, the main way I kept myself amused was to watch the hotel TV, which had loads of channels, maybe sixty, which seemed amazing to me, coming from a country that had at that time a paltry four TV stations. So I was twisting the knob on the TV and soon stumbled across something that caught my eye. A beautiful woman. In a film. It was called Private Lessons and the sexy woman was Emmanuelle herself, Sylvia Kristel. After the success of the Emmanuelle films she'd obviously gone to America, probably with Ian McShane, and made this film – this sex comedy.

In fact, the blurb on the movie's poster was 'The bedroom is a fun classroom ... Emmanuelle's star is the teacher.' Private Lessons, you see, wasn't a proper porno or anything. It wasn't even a soft-core film at all, even though it starred Sylvia Kristel. It was a legitimate film. But I do have to say, it was a film which had a very sexy premise. Especially to a ten-year-old boy. It was about a schoolboy, who I think was about fifteen, from a well-to-do family, and his housemaid, played by Sylvia Kristel, decides to help him with his sexual awakening. As I sat there watching this film, which was being shown on the Playboy Channel, it soon became clear that the story was going down an interesting path. And then suddenly there was this scene where Sylvia Kristel starts taking her clothes off in front of the boy.

Bear in mind, I didn't really have any idea of what sex was at this time. I'd had no kind of birds and bees conversation with either of my parents and never did. I'm sure most kids by the age of ten have some conception of sex and where babies come from, but I really didn't.

I was a very late developer. I was late about a lot of things. I didn't actually masturbate until I was about fifteen. See? Very late.

I never listened to the other boys at school when they started talking about sex stuff, and my best friend, Andrew, who was also an only child, and I never talked about any of that. We just talked about Star Wars and compared our Millennium Falcons.

Now at that point in the film, as Kristel was disrobing, I was mindful that my dad said he was going to check on me from time to time. So, feeling that what I was doing was not quite right, knowing that a little boy shouldn't really be watching that raunchy film, I kept running from the TV, where Kristel was slowly taking her clothes off, to the door to check if my dad was coming.

In the film, as Kristel started taking her blouse off, the kid was feeling nervous and intimidated and of course stimulated. But at the same time he was feeling kind of nauseous and sick. And that was exactly what I was feeling too. I was feeling stimulated but also naughty and sick. I'd never seen anything like that before in my life. I didn't think I should be watching it but I couldn't stop myself from watching it.

Then Kristel asked the boy if he wanted her to remove her bra and I was thinking 'Shit!' And just at that moment, at that key juncture, I thought I could hear footsteps. I ran to the door. And sure enough my dad was there in the distance, on his way back towards our room.

So I ran back to the TV and grabbed the knob on the telly to switch it over to the Disney channel or something. But I was so flustered and nervous that I grabbed the knob too hard and it came off in my hand. So I was standing there with this knob in my hand and on the TV there was Kristel taking her clothes off in a film I was clearly too young to be watching. And my dad was about to walk in.

I couldn't believe it. I tried desperately to shove the knob back in.

And somehow I did manage to get it back in place. I turned over to another channel, hopped into bed and tried to make everything seem normal. It worked. My dad didn't suspect a thing.

That night I didn't feel well though, due, I think, to the nerves of that situation and the feeling that I was doing something wrong by watching this titillating film. I felt sick all night.

About six years ago I finally told my dad what happened that night in the Orlando hotel room and he thought it was hilarious.

That was a very unusual, early memory of seeing something rude. I had no idea who Sylvia Kristel was. I didn't see Emmanuelle until we got Sky TV in 1989. I think I first watched it on RTL in those days when several of the German channels would show soft-core films at night.

My parents never had any kind of naughty material in the house.

I'd have friends who would find their dad's porn stash. One mate of mine at secondary school once snooped round his parents' bedroom and found his mum's drawer of sex toys and even showed me her dildo.

I never had any experiences like that.

I never went looking for that kind of stuff either.

I was a very naïve young boy. For me, anything sexual was wrong. Sex equalled Wrong when I was growing up. And I mean for the first twenty years of my life.

I don't know why I felt it was wrong because I don't remember anyone actually telling me it was wrong, although I did grow up in the era of Aids and all those ads telling you that sex could equal death so I suppose that didn't help.

I do remember reading an agony aunt column in one of the tabloids soon after that, when I was still ten years old, and someone had written in asking a question about oral sex and I had absolutely no idea what this term oral sex was. So I asked my parents what oral sex was because I'd just read it in the paper.

My mum said, 'Ask your dad.'

So I asked him and he said, 'Ask your mum.'

Neither of them answered the question. And they never did. I never got an answer.

So to this day I'm still in the dark about oral sex.

On the flight back from Florida to England, at the end of our Disney World holiday, I had an unfortunate accident. I fell asleep in my seat on the plane and woke up the next morning in a puddle of piss.

The other thing you should know about my childhood at this point is that I was a big bed-wetter. Huge. I was wetting the bed way beyond the age when you're supposed to be wetting the bed. In fact, I was still regularly wetting the bed at ten years of age. So that incident on the flight back from Florida was no one-off.

For years I slept on a rubber sheet underneath my regular sheets. Bed-wetting is weird but what would happen was that I would have a very vivid dream about having a pee and then sure enough in the morning I'd wake up in a puddle of piss. I also used to drink a lot when I was a kid. I would stay up late and drink a lot of water or squash or whatever and so I always wanted to pee. My mum would implement a cut-off. So after about 7pm I wouldn't be allowed to drink any more. And hopefully as a result I would have a dry night. This cut-off plan did work for a while, but I would still regularly end up breaking the cut-off and invariably end up wetting the bed.

Eventually, when I was ten, my mum resorted to desperate measures and tried to inspire me to stop me wetting my bed by using my favourite show, The A-Team, as some kind of encouragement. You see, there were these A-Team action figures available at the time, five of them: Hannibal, BA, Murdoch, Face and Amy. And I wanted all of them because it was my favourite show.

So my mum said to me, 'Right, I'm going to buy you the A-Team figures, but here's how we're going to do it: if you can go one month without wetting the bed, I will buy you one A-Team figure. Then if you go another month, I'll buy another action figure ... ' And so on.

So if I could go five whole months without wetting the bed, then I was going to have the full set of A-Team figures. I thought this was a pretty good deal. Not only did I have the chance to own all the A-Team action figures but I would also have gone five months without wetting the bed, and if I achieved that, then effectively I would have conquered my bed-wetting habit. The problem would be gone. It was an exciting opportunity on both fronts.

But I only managed to get BA and Murdoch.

Luckily they were my two favourite characters.

Years later, when I made my TV documentary Bring Back ... The A-Team, I told all the cast members my bed-wetting story. I don't think they were that impressed.

Most of the time, if I woke up after wetting the bed, my mum would come and rescue me from the wet bed and give me dry sheets and sometimes I'd climb into bed with her. One time I even climbed into my dad's bed and I don't know what possessed me to do so, but I did. I think it was the only time I ever did it. My dad was already asleep in his bed on his tough, hard mattress, and I climbed in his bed and lay there spooning him.

The next day he woke up on his side. 'Hold on,' he said, confused and bewildered. 'What is that wet sensation on my back?'

He'd been woken up by a sudden wetness.

It was me pissing on him.

I'd urinated on my dad.

How many people can say that?

Unbelievably, that wasn't the last time I wet myself, although in the end I did manage to stop the habitual bed-wetting. It just kind of died out gradually. I don't still wet the bed. Honestly. And I like to think the A-Team perhaps played some part in my eventual triumph over bed-wetting.

CHAPTER 3

FROM KEENER TO CLOWN

I got a massive whack across my leg.

From a teacher. Those were the days when teachers could hit you and leave a huge red throbbing welt down your leg. I don't even know what I'd done to deserve it. I wasn't a naughty boy at that time, in Ashley Down Infants. I was a naughty boy at every school after that, but at that time I hadn't yet learned how to be naughty.

I think the teacher who gave me that whack across my leg just wasn't a very nice person.

Ashley Down in Bishopstown was my first school – and the only other notable thing that happened there was that I had a crush on Katy Rimmer. And the only notable thing about that was that it was my first crush.

There were many more to come.

At Chester Park Junior School I had a crush on Suzanne Wilcocks.

I never even held the hands of these girls. I would cycle my bike up and down Suzanne Wilcocks' street deliberately, in the hope that she would come out and see me. I think one time she did see me, and decided to stay inside. She thought better of it.

One time in assembly I was sitting cross-legged on the floor and I noticed that my trouser leg had risen above the top of my sock. So between the end of my trouser and the top of my sock was about two or three inches of white flesh. Just as I was pondering this fact, Suzanne Wilcocks walked into assembly with the rest of her class. She looked down at me and stared at those two or three inches of flesh between the end of my trouser and the top of my sock with complete disgust. She had this expression on her face of total disgust. But it was just my leg. Then I looked down at my own leg and I thought, 'Yeah that is quite disgusting: my bare bit of leg.' Because really you always want your trouser leg to come down as far as your sock and your sock to be pulled up as far as your trousers. Both sock and trousers, if they're doing their jobs properly, should be covering your legs. But they weren't. Which suggests that either my sock wasn't pulled up enough or that my trousers weren't long enough. Most likely it was the latter, so I think Suzanne thought that I was this boy who clearly fancied her and whose trousers were too short. Which is pretty disgusting.

So at that moment I realised there was no future for me and Suzanne Wilcocks.

Years later she came to the video shop where I worked in Bristol to drop a film back and I thought, 'Wow, you're Suzanne Wilcocks.' Luckily she couldn't see my trousers, which were probably still too short, because I was working behind the counter.

My first proper girlfriend in the sense of someone I actually had a couple of dates with was in the last year at Chester Park. Her name was Jenny Prescott. She was originally from Derby and then lived in Downend.

She was my girlfriend for maybe about a week. She came to our house one day for tea and my mum gave her a lift home. The following Saturday I was adamant that I would ride my bike to her place, which was about three miles from where we lived. When you're eleven years old that's quite a long way.

But I did cycle the journey. We went to a video shop and we hired Footloose, and Jenny and I watched it together at her house. Nothing else happened. There was no hand holding or kissing or anything. No attempt to do anything like that, because that was never going to come from me. That was never going to be initiated by me. I was far too scared to instigate any kind of actual contact with a girl. I was terrified of it. And she certainly didn't initiate anything either. So we just enjoyed Footloose together. Which I loved. But that was the end of it. That was our last ever date. The relationship fizzled out after that.

The big story with Jenny Prescott is that she was the real reason Daniel Perritt broke my nose. You may have noticed that my nose is a bit squashed.

In the playground one day, Daniel Perritt was play fighting with Jenny Prescott. But even though I knew it was play fighting, I regarded myself as a man of honour so I entered the play fight to defend her honour. I was a play man of honour. So then me and Daniel and Jenny were all play fighting. I know it doesn't make any sense, but the play fighting soon got a bit out of hand and I swung my arm in the air completely by accident and I caught Daniel on the side of his face.

Mortified, I dropped my hands to my mouth and said, 'Oh my god! I'm so sorry – I didn't mean it!'

But his face was already contorted with anger.

In that split second, he reacted by hitting me really hard on my nose. He knocked my head back and I put my hands to my face and saw a massive pool of blood in my hands. So of course I reacted to that and tried to attack him. At that point, a school lunchtime playground attendant intervened to split us apart.

Now by that time at school, I was already considered a naughty boy. But Daniel wasn't. Inevitably I was frogmarched to the nurse,

Mrs Golding, who tried to stop the blood and put a bandage on my nose. It really, really hurt and I could tell it was already swelling up so I asked the nurse whether it was broken. She said, 'No, it's not broken.'

But it clearly was. By the time I was twenty I had to have a septo-rhinoplasty operation because I had breathing difficulties due to that broken-nose incident at the age of ten. So when I was growing up my nose was even more squished and bent than it is now.

That was all down to Daniel Perritt and my decision to play defend Jenny's honour in a play fight. I should never have got involved even if it was only a play fight.

What made it all worse was that I was brought out into the playground and I was made an example of in front of the other kids, for fighting. Even though I was the one who apologised to Daniel for accidentally hitting him. Then I saw Daniel over by the wall and I was thinking, 'I can see you and I'm going to come and get you because you're not getting away with this,' so as soon as my lecture was finished and the teacher walked away, I ran over to him and I attacked him all over again.

A letter was sent to my parents saying that I was a danger to other kids and a danger to myself.

From that point on, Daniel was very concerned, especially when I became friends for a brief period with Pete Daggert. Pete was the tough kid that everyone was scared of. So Daniel was terrified. By that point I wanted to move on. I wanted to leave it. But Pete Daggert was very keen. He said, 'No, we're going to get him and you're going to have a fight with him and if it looks like you're losing then I'll get involved and I'll do him.'

The problem was, there was no way I could just tell Pete that we shouldn't bother because he was a bit of a nut-job.

So I did try to provoke Daniel into doing something against me but he didn't take the bait because he was scared of Daggert and he wasn't an idiot.

That was the end of that.

My next schoolboy crush was Kirsty Rowlands. She told me she thought my broken nose was sexy.

By the time we got to Speedwell, my secondary school, she had blossomed and was regarded not just as being one of the nicest-looking girls in our year but in the whole school. When we were in the second year the boys in the fifth form fancied her and she went out with a few of them.

We had a couple of classes together, including maths. She sat behind me in maths and the thing about Kirsty, as well as being very pretty, was that she was also one of the first girls in our peer group to develop breasts. So everyone fancied her.

And for some ridiculous reason she decided she fancied me. She told me I made her laugh and that the bump on my nose was cute.

In class, boys would go on about her boobs and try to touch her boobs. All deeply inappropriate behaviour. But that's what the kids were like at Speedwell. It was a tough school.

One time when she was getting this unwanted attention about her breasts, she suddenly said, 'You can't touch them, they're Justin's!'

You can't touch them. They're Justin's.

'Christ,' I thought, 'this is pressure I don't need!'

I wasn't ready for that.

I really thought she was lovely but I was clearly out of my depth. I wasn't ready to be the custodian of her breasts. I wasn't ready for her.

Nevertheless I did pluck up the courage to meet up with her one evening after school. You see, her best friend was Janine Wilding and

Janine was going out with David Outhwaite, who was in my class. So Outhwaite came to call for me, and Outhwaite and I went along the Kingsway where we'd arranged to meet Janine and Kirsty round the back of the Gateway supermarket.

Which was a bit odd. Why did we think we'd get any enjoyment out of gathering at the back of a supermarket? It was just the way it was.

I was sick with nerves. I was terrified of the whole impending event. But what put the fear of god into me even more was an incident that had occurred earlier that day.

I was walking across the quad in the playground and Jed Thornton, the kid who was regarded as the toughest lad in school, was there with his mate Richie Carter. They were both fifth-year boys, older and much scarier than me. I wasn't scary at all, yet somehow I'm kind of going out with this gorgeous girl who the whole school is in love with.

Anyway, Jed Thornton and his mate stopped me dead in the quad.

Jed looked me up and down and said, 'So are you going out with Kirsty Rowlands?'

All I could think to answer was, 'Yes, I suppose I am.'

They both stood there looking at me. Then they burst out laughing and pointed at me. They were literally laughing in my face.

And the reason they were pointing at me and laughing is because it was indeed so ridiculous that I could even be considered to be going out with Kirsty Rowlands. Obviously, I was relieved that Jed and his mate just laughed at me rather than beat me up for my insolence for even considering myself worthy of Kirsty Rowlands.

This incident brought home to me even more that I was completely out of my depth with her.

So in the whole build-up to the night of this date when I was meeting up with her behind the Gateway, I was a wreck. I was terrified. I was scared of girls anyway, and was naturally of a nervous disposition. So I was feeling physically sick. We were at the back of the Gateway but all I was thinking was, 'How long do I have to stay here for? How soon can I reasonably leave, without the others thinking I'm pathetic and frigid and weird?'

Weirdly, I ended up sitting on Kirsty's lap while Outhwaite and his girlfriend were kissing. I was just sitting there on her lap, trying to stay calm. But I didn't really stay calm.

Instead, I started to break wind.

I was sitting there on the lap of the loveliest girl in the school and all I could do was fart. I couldn't help myself. It was my nerves.

Perhaps to try to distract her from my farting, I did at least touch her breasts. I say I touched her breasts but all I did was very lightly with an open hand very gently make the slightest of contact with them. With an outstretched palm, fingers out, I established an almost imperceptible contact with her breasts, and then we kissed with open mouths (but no tongues) and we cuddled a little bit. Throughout all of this physical contact I was still farting the entire time with nerves.

I decided I had to tell Kirsty I had a funny stomach so I could leave. In a way, I did have a funny stomach because I was breaking wind all the time. So I used the flatulence to make my excuses and leave.

Looking back on it now, I should have told her the truth and said something like, 'Kirsty, I think you're lovely and beautiful but I'm just really nervous and I can't take being with you like this because it's making me feel sick.' And I think that would have been quite endearing. But of course when you're twelve or thirteen you don't think to simply tell the truth. You want to at least try to appear cool even if you're farting on this lovely girl round the back of the Gateway.

In fact, the great thing about Kirsty, even though she was more or less the same age as me, was that she was so lovely, she could tell that I wasn't quite capable of dealing with her.

That night I walked back to my mum's church and I got a lift home from my mum and in the front seat was her friend Iris Bowyer. I felt guilty. I felt guilty because I'd been in this situation with this girl and put my palm on her breast and kissed her and even those tiny first few steps on the road to sex were preying on my mind. So after my mum had dropped off Iris, who was about eighty, I decided to confess all to her. My mum, not Iris.

I told her that I'd had this date with this girl and sat on her lap and did some vaguely naughty stuff and my mum interrupted me and just said, 'It's all right. Don't worry about it.'

I think she just didn't want to know. But I was feeling the weight of the world bearing down on me. I felt bad about what I'd done with Kirsty because in my mind anything to do with sex was wrong. So I confessed to my mum, and she absolved me. And then my mum drove us to the local Chinese takeaway and we had some nice chicken balls.

Confession. Absolution. Chicken balls. That was how the night ended.

The next day, when it was sports day, Kirsty came to sit next to me and she put me out of my misery. She could tell I was petrified and completely out of my depth. So she looked at me and said, 'Just? Do you still want to go out with me, or would you prefer if we were just friends?'

And it was a huge weight off my mind. She was being so sweet.

I looked straight at her and said, 'Oh, can we just be friends, Kirst?'

And she said, 'Yeah, of course we can!'

At that moment I wanted to kiss her more than ever because she was being so lovely to me. Of course I didn't. That would have been madness.

A few years later there was one more classic moment between Kirsty and me, when we were fifteen, and I was sitting next to Kirsty on a wall watching some of our classmates playing tennis.

She was still beautiful. Even more so. And we were just having a nice relaxed conversation and I thought, 'Now I'm a bit older and wiser and I feel relaxed with her so I'm going to ask her whether she's going out with anyone at the moment.' And sure enough, I just looked at her and asked, 'So, Kirst … are you going out with anyone at the moment?'

'Yeah,' she calmly replied. 'He's twenty-two and he's coming to pick me up in his car after school … '

Twenty-two. With a car. There you go.

Years later I got a friend of mine to check out Kirsty Rowlands on Friends Reunited. Turned out she was belly-dancing all over the Bristol Moroccan restaurant scene.

There was even a photo of her, in full belly-dancing gear. She was still wonderful.

Eventually I did have some proper girlfriends at Speedwell. Kind of. But there were a lot of mis-steps on the way.

The first one was a girl called Becky who I found out lived on Gorse Hill in Hillfields so I cycled up and down her street in that slightly stalker-ish way of mine. But nothing ever happened.

Then there was Michelle Tully who was my girlfriend for about two weeks. For our first date I took her to see Haunted Honeymoon with Gene Wilder, Gilda Radner and Dom DeLuise. Now I had no money for this date. But luckily it was the day of the local St Joseph's car boot sale. So that morning I made about four pounds twenty by selling some old toys and records (including my beloved Rancor

Monster, as I told you about earlier). I had just about enough money to pay for my own ticket and maybe her and my bus fare or else a cheeseburger at McDonald's. I had to decide which bit to pay for. Why I didn't just ask my parents to lend me a tenner for the date, I don't know. But I didn't.

I decided to pay for her bus fare so we went to the Odeon on Union Street and we watched Haunted Honeymoon together.

Of course, again I was feeling sick and nervous and uncomfortable. So there was no hand holding or kissing or anything. We just watched the film in silence.

That was our one official date. But another time, she invited me round to her house and, knowing that I was a big Bruce Lee fan, she gave me some Bruce Lee magazines and a Ninja Star toy weapon.

She only had this Ninja Star because Stephen Hand had given it to her before when he was going out with her. And then she gave it to me. But that was our final get-together of any kind.

A few weeks after that I started to go out with a girl called Simone Hepworth. She was as close to a proper girlfriend as I had at school.

I'd liked Simone for quite a long time. She was in the same year as me but not in my class so I'd seen her from afar in the playground and in assembly and stuff. She was really petite and had very blonde hair; super-blonde hair.

Our first date was to a roller-disco at Kingswood Leisure Centre. It was a Friday night and we watched people rollering. I didn't skate, of course. I was petrified. But we just sat there enjoying the disco vibe. They played the song Requiem by the London Boys. So Requiem by the London Boys became our song.

I ended up going out with her for a total of five weeks. But that included a family holiday when she was away for two weeks. I include that holiday because while she was away, I received this lovely gatefold postcard thing on which Simone had written a lovely letter telling me how much she loved me and everything.

So Simone and I used to meet up and walk around holding hands. We'd walk the streets of Bristol together chatting. Or probably mostly not chatting. Then I would walk her home and I would try to do a proper kiss to say goodnight, and then I'd walk home and watch Roseanne.

And that went on for five weeks.

But again I did feel nervous about the whole situation. I started to worry about whether she wanted me to do anything more than just kiss with no tongues. But we just carried on walking around hand in hand.

Then after about five weeks there was a knock on my door and it was Lisa Rich, who was Simone's best friend, and Lisa told me that Simone didn't want to go out with me any more.

I just said, 'Oh. Okay.'

I think I just assumed she didn't want to go out with me any more because she thought I was frigid. Because all I would ever do was kiss with mouths open but no tongues and hold her hand.

I considered myself to be a bit rubbish because I wouldn't take it any further. So god knows what she thought; it certainly wasn't a relationship that was going anywhere. Lisa never actually told me the reason why Simone didn't want to go out with me any more. I just kept thinking, 'It's because I'm frigid. And I *am* frigid. Frigid is what I am.'

I was thinking this because at school all I would hear were sex stories from my friends. They'd talk about how they were fingering girls, left, right and centre. This girl was being fingered. That girl was being fingered. People were fingering. I knew this was happening because they were talking about it. I was hearing that people were being fingered and I assumed this was going on all over the place. Lots of fingering. I even remember stories of fingering dating back to my junior school. It had been going on for years. But not for me. I'd never fingered anybody. I'd never gone anywhere near that. So I assumed because I hadn't fingered Simone or even French-kissed her, that must be why she didn't want to see me any more. We hadn't had an argument. So she must have dumped me for a boy who would finger her.

Fifteen years later I was sitting behind the console in a studio at Xfm in London hosting my radio show and I received notification on my screen that there's an email from a Simone Hepworth who was listening to me on her radio. In the email she said, 'Hi Justin I don't know if you remember me but we went out at school and I dumped you ... because I fancied Graeme Doon and wanted to go out with him more.'

I thought, *'Graeme Doon?!'* He had nothing. He was just a guy with a bit of a quiff. I was outraged.

I suppose at least she didn't dump me because I wouldn't finger her.

Throughout all these ridiculous encounters with members of the opposite sex, I suppose the only information I did actually learn about sexual matters came from watching TV.

I loved the Red Triangle season. This was an idea of Channel 4's when I was in my early teens, where they'd show an adult film, most of them arty foreign films with subtitles, and they'd put a red triangle on the screen to warn people that these films had sex in them. Well, I loved that. Luckily, I was allowed to stay up every Friday night (and Saturdays) anyway, but only in the company of my mum or dad. Usually my mum.

I would stay up watching telly with my mum on a Friday night, stuff like The Last Resort with Jonathan Ross and Vic Reeves' Big Night Out, and eventually she'd invariably nod off. By midnight she'd be fast asleep. Half an hour later Channel 4 would plonk its big red triangle on the screen warning me about the imminent scenes of a graphic sexual nature and I thought, 'Brilliant!' and for the next two hours I'd watch these sexual films while constantly looking back towards my mum to check that she was still asleep. I watched one Red Triangle film which had a black man having sex with a white woman when she had her period. And there was blood everywhere. Another one was set in a weird, freaky circus and there was one which had a dildo attached to a tank! I saw all sorts. I kind of wish they'd bring the Red Triangle films back.

But weirdly, I wasn't actually *doing* anything while watching these sex scenes in the Red Triangle films. I suppose I was getting aroused and of course it would have been wrong to act on that when my mum was still in the room. But the simple fact is, I had no idea about masturbation at that age.

As I mentioned before, I was fifteen before I did that, and it was all down to Sky TV.

We were quite early adopters of Sky TV, thank goodness, because they showed quite adult films, and by that age I was allowed to stay up on my own at the weekend and watch TV.

The film which encouraged me to masturbate was Nine And A Half Weeks.

My dad would be out with his mates on a Saturday and my mum would go to bed and then I would be left on my own to watch TV. The first sexy film I saw on Sky was Lifeforce, which had naked busty vampires.

But that was nothing compared to Nine And A Half Weeks. By that time I had started getting aroused by these scenes I'd be watching, but I'd not actually touch myself. I'd be aroused and just fidget in my seat, feeling a bit hot and bothered between my thighs. But I never touched my penis. I still felt there would be something wrong and perhaps a bit unhygienic if I touched myself down there.

I was scared of the unknown, I guess.

But Nine And A Half Weeks was so erotic, so much sexier than anything I'd ever seen, that I just exploded in my pants.

But I had no idea what had happened. It was just the end of this sexy feeling I'd had for about ninety minutes.

When I went to the toilet to have a wee and took my trousers down I saw that there was some sticky, smelly substance down there all over my pants. I thought it was sweat! Some kind of sweaty goo. I had no idea I had produced that substance from out of my penis. And I was fifteen years old. I think you'll agree by now that I was a late developer.

Apart from spending my entire time developing pointless, chaste crushes on girls, most of my school years were marked by my commitment to consistent naughtiness. From Chester Park Junior School onwards, I was a naughty boy.

I started junior school a week later than everyone else because my family had just moved house. I had to be specially introduced to the class, which is never good.

I would get sent out of classes all the time because I would disrupt them so often.

For instance, I had a temporary teacher called Mrs Turpin who decided to institute a new disciplinary procedure. She brought in a Naughty Book. Anything you did wrong would be noted down in this book. If you had three comments in the naughty book then you'd be sent down to see the headmaster.

Mrs Turpin was a stand-in teacher and she was taking our class one day and she was teaching us about textiles and arts and crafts, and she was trying to get us to make frogs out of felt. But I thought it was rubbish and I didn't want to make a frog so I was being disruptive and I started singing 'Pick your nose and eat your bogies' repeatedly. I wouldn't stop singing 'Pick your nose and eat your bogies'. So she put a note in the Naughty Book and as she was writing the note she said out loud the words she was writing in the book.

'Right – Justin Collins sings "Pick your nose and eat your bogies"!'

I thought that was really funny.

But then a weird thing happened and I started to think about how much shit she was getting from the rest of the class and I suddenly realised I had caused a lot of that shit and that I wasn't being very nice to this lady who was just trying to get us to make a felt frog.

So I decided I would, after all, make a felt frog.

In the end she was pleased with me for making the frog and she decided to cross out the entry in the Naughty Book about me singing 'Pick your nose and eat your bogies'.

What a nice lady Mrs Turpin was.

When I neared the end of my junior school days, my mum asked me to make a big promise that I would be good in Big School. I did want to make a concerted effort not to create any problems for my mum. Every day my mum sent me to school with the maxim, 'Be good and kind to people.' Every day she said that to me. And it made sense to me.

But the really big challenge for me was to be a good boy at Speedwell School, because it wasn't a very nice place. But I did try my best, at least to start with.

It was inevitable that I went to Speedwell, even though it didn't have a good reputation, because it was located quite literally opposite my house. We used to live in a nice, middle-class area of Bristol called Bishopstown for the first seven years of my life. But my mum hated it there because the rest of her family was on the other side of town. So in 1981 we moved to the house on the Speedwell/Kingswood borders, much closer to her relatives, where my mum and dad still live now. And the house was directly opposite this school.

But it was a bad school. It was a big, ugly place, half of which had been burned down in a fire in the 1970s. I would have been quite happy if it had all gone up in smoke. My class was based in E Block (it even sounded like a prison) – the new red-brick bit which had been rebuilt after the big fire. It was a mind-numbingly routine-looking school. I hated it.

The only incident I really remember from my first day at Speedwell was that I met Sophie Gordon, who instantly became the object of my affection. She was sitting directly behind me next to her friend Jen. I put my satchel on the back of my chair and Sophie knocked it on the floor. But she didn't do it in a horrible way. She was just trying to get my attention, I think. I turned round, picked it up, looked at her and turned back round again and she knocked the bag off again, so I would go through the same rigmarole again. I rather enjoyed it.

At first I did make a concerted effort to be good and in fact I became a gold star kid. I was getting merit marks for attendance and for my work. I was considered a bright kid by my teachers. I was getting top marks in all my classes. Even French!

Mr Stoneman, our French teacher, gave us all alternative French names and would take the register by reading out all our French names. We had to respond by saying '*Présent!*' ('Here!' in French.) I was called Marcel, and Marcel became quite good at speaking the language.

(Mr Stoneman was a bit of a funny one. He'd suddenly go ballistic and his face would go red and then he would slap his hand on his forehead and say, 'Silly Stoneman!' And he would calm down and apologise because he was annoyed with himself for having got angry.)

But I couldn't keep it up because it made me really unpopular and meant I didn't really have any friends. I was regarded as a 'Keener'.

A Keener was someone who was just there at school to work and get merit marks. Imagine that! A pupil who was primarily interested in learning stuff. That's what I was and for my pains, they called me a Keener. And this school was a completely impossible place for Keeners.

By the end of the first year I was sick of being a good pupil because I was so unpopular. I'm ashamed to admit it now but I did want to be liked and have friends. I wasn't able to do that because I was a Keener. They would literally shout 'Keener! Keener!' at me in class. Some boys would even want to fight me because I was getting merit marks. I would just ignore them as best I could. But I thought, 'This has to stop.'

So it all went out of the window at the end of the first year.

Let me say now that I hate class clowns. I hate the whole idea of them. I think they're intolerable. I wanted to be one of the genuinely funny, clever kids who sat at the back making fun of the class clown. But somehow, instead, I just became the class clown. Not that there were any of those clever, funny kids in my class. It was the kind of school where you had to fall into one of three categories. You could be a diligent, hard-working pupil, and everyone would hate you and make fun of you and probably bully you. There weren't many of those – but there were a few. You could be a sporty kind of kid and everyone would leave you alone or even look up to you. Or you could be the one who made everyone laugh. The clown. And you weren't making them laugh by being clever and witty, you were doing it by acting like an idiot.

Then there was the issue of fashion. Let me say right now that I was not a cool kid. The annoying thing was that before my big school days, when all of that suddenly becomes important and you start worrying about the way you look and noticing that everyone else looks better than you (at least that's what I thought), I was actually quite a trendy little boy. From age two up to the age of about ten, I looked great. I had my long, blond hair, sheepskin coats, roll-neck jumpers and flared slacks and dungaree suits and cowboy hats. Then, by the time I got to Speedwell, it all went to shit. I wore nondescript, grey slacks that were a bit too short for me, boring shirts and dull jerkins. And, worst of all, rubbish trainers.

Kids would take the piss out of my BMX canvas trainers. They had a little BMX sticker on the side with a kid riding a BMX on it. They were rubbish, shit trainers, which came from FK Walkaround, which was a linen and bedding and net curtain specialist. This was where I was getting my trainers!

So I went home one day and complained to my parents that I had rubbish clothes and that they hadn't bought me any new clothes for ages and that I wanted to get some better clothes, and some cool trainers.

I said, 'Dad, I've got rubbish trainers!'

To make me feel better, my dad took me to Foster's one Saturday and bought me some chinos. Then we went to a sports shop and he bought me a pair of Puma Match. They were my first pair of decent, brand trainers. I wore them out after a few months because I never took them off. So my dad took me back there and bought me a pair of Puma Super-Match, which were essentially the same as Puma Match except they had a red trim around the Puma stripe.

I wasn't happy with my hair either.

I had a double crown and as a result a portion of my hair would always stick up.

To remedy the situation, my mum took me to a Kingswood salon which was owned by a guy named Shaun. They gave me a great modern, spiky hairdo which made my double crown look okay. That was my first good haircut. My mum took me back there regularly. Even though after a couple of days I could never recreate what the style looked like when I left the salon.

Then Shaun closed the Kingswood salon to focus on his central Bristol enterprise, and my mum was not the type of woman to drive all the way into town and park the car just to get her hair done. Or my hair done. I started going locally and then this mobile hairdresser would come to our house. My mum encouraged me to get highlights one day – and they looked terrible. Patchy highlights. It looked rubbish.

I always wanted long hair. I did have quite long hair as a boy but my gran would say, 'He looks like a girl. Get his hair cut.'

So when I was about fifteen, after I got into WWF Wrestler Hulk Hogan and his lush, long hair, I vowed that when I was old enough and no one could tell me how to dress or how to look, I'd grow my hair long. And sure enough, when I was eighteen I did grow my hair and I went back to see Shaun at his central salon called Maximum FX, and from that day to this, I've never let another soul touch my hair.

Shaun still cuts my hair now. That look you can see on the cover is all down to Shaun at Maximum FX.

The beard came later. Much later.

But back when I was a Keener at Big School, I had a shit haircut, shit trainers and shit clothes until I moaned about it to my parents.

You could, of course, go too far the other way. You didn't want to be *too* image-conscious. In Speedwell, there was a boy called Kevin Thomas, who told me I stank of piss, because I did (I was wetting the bed! I had no defence!), and so I called him Kevin Boghouse, which was a rubbish comeback. Anyway, Kevin wore Benetton and had curtains for a hairstyle and for his pains he was called a Yuppie by the other kids. He looked *too* smart. Relaxed and cool was always the ideal.

*

Towards the end of my early, deeply uncool, Keener period, the only thing that I was really interested in at school was drama. I enjoyed putting on plays and performing for my classmates.

But in my second year they took the decision to axe the drama department. They decided drama was surplus to requirements. PE and Games – that we had to do, and I couldn't stand it. I hated games. Especially winter sports – it was cold and wet and I was the smallest boy in the class and I'd have to try to tackle the bigger, scarier boys and if I did have any effect on them then afterwards they'd threaten me and challenge me to a fight because I'd dared to show them up in football or rugby or whatever. Why would I want to play games with the big boys and tackle them so they'd then be horrible and threatening to me? I did my absolute best to avoid games at all costs. I'd forget my kit, I'd get sick notes, and for much of the time it worked.

They say these days there should be more games and PE at school but I say sod that. I say there should be more drama and song and dance and musical theatre and less games and rugby and football and less of that showering together when you have to get your little mysteriously circumcised penis out in front of the much bigger, uncircumcised ones!

So I had to go through years 2, 3, 4 and 5 with no drama. But there was one exception: Mrs Platt, who was my English teacher when I was in the fourth year, started her own drama group and she decided to put on a pantomime. And I was Buttons in our production of Cinderella. So that was my only outlet to perform during those four long years. I'm not saying that as an excuse, but I have to say I think the lack of any creative outlet whatsoever may have contributed to turning me into an annoying little shit. Okay, maybe I am using it as an excuse.

*

It was at Summer Camp at the end of my first year that I sealed my role as class clown.

In the run-up to this trip, I'd started to sing silly songs at school. I'd formed a one-man band by myself, obviously, called Justin And The Ethiopians. I think I was inspired by watching Live Aid and by the Dead Kennedys and their song Holiday In Cambodia. I sang that song in drama class, as part of a little sketch I did where I was pretending I was flying in a plane to Cambodia. While singing the song. It was all a bit random, as the working of my mind always was, but I still got a few laughs. Not from the teacher. I made up my own Justin And The Ethiopians theme too, which went like this:

'They're cold ... they're dying ... they're hungry ... there's no food ... there's no water ... Justin and the Ethiopians! Dah dah dah dah dah!'

I would also sing songs in my music classes too, in front of Mr Windass, who looked like Papa Smurf and was quite a cantankerous man. Justin And The Ethiopians would sing songs in Mr Windass's class. (He wouldn't let me carry on in his music class the next year because he'd had a gutsful of me.)

Then I made up some songs inspired by a short-lived comic book at the time called Oink! I loved Oink! The first issue came with a flexidisc which had songs on it that were about pigs. One was based on the first rap song by Grandmaster Flash And The Furious Five called The Message, which went 'Don't push me, cos I'm close to the edge ... I'm trying not to lose my head ... ' But the Oink version went:

'Don't eat pigs cos they're made from ham ... eat the nasty butcher-man ... '

So I started incorporating these pig-based songs into a Justin And The Ethiopians a cappella act.

When the school year came to an end, I went on a school trip to a summer camp at the Fort in Plymouth, and by that point I'd become more destructive and was more concerned about making my schoolmates laugh than being keen. But at least there I had a legitimate chance to show off my performance skills. They held a talent contest at the camp. I did my Justin And The Ethiopians songs, my pig-based songs, and the class loved them, and I won.

I think it was a bit of a foregone conclusion that I'd win because the teachers knew my act was based entirely on pigs because they'd seen me perform that in class. Some of the teachers clearly liked me. I amused them. While others hated me. I divided opinion even then, just as I still do!

So I was announced as the winner and was presented with a china pig. That's what I mean when I say it might have been a foregone conclusion. They obviously decided I was going to win in advance and bought this pig for me. There was no other explanation. So the talent competition at the Fort in Plymouth was essentially a fix. At least they were trying to be nice to me. I was flattered.

I was also the star of Summer Camp. To the extent that singing those pig songs even made me popular with girls. Kirsty Rowlands and Sophie Gordon, who was the unrequited object of my affection for my entire time at school, even wanted to hold my hand when we went on a walk up Lovers' Lane. Both of them held my hands at the same time! One hand each. I couldn't believe it.

On the same walk, we came across a Mini which was bouncing up and down with steamed-up windows. When we got closer we realised there were three naked people in there – a man with two women. But I had no idea what they were doing. Miss Lowe said, 'They're just having a bit of fun. Keep walking ... '

The bloke wound down the window and yelled, 'It's just a bit hot in here.'

I believed him.

On the last night at Summer Camp, I had an incredible experience with one of the sixth-form girls who were there as camp supervisors. She was seventeen.

That night some of us boys almost became the pets of these sixth-form girls. It was all harmless fun. The girls were being lovely to us and making us feel special.

And that night those girls told us boys that we could kiss them.

We paired off, and I ended up with this lovely girl called Shirley. She was much taller than me because I was the shortest kid in my class, plus she was considerably older than me.

I had never properly kissed anyone in my life and Shirley was about to let me kiss her. I was mortified. I was terrified. I had no idea what to do so I really didn't want to go through with it. But I also thought that if I didn't kiss her I would be letting myself down, letting this amazing opportunity go. So I went in for the kiss and put my open mouth next to Shirley's open mouth and opened and closed it like a fish. I had no idea what I was doing. I did this opening and closing of my mouth on top of hers for about twenty seconds.

Shirley pulled away from me, looked at me, and said, 'Ohh ... You don't know how to do it ... '

She said it perfectly sweetly, and to underline how sorry she felt for me, this little boy who couldn't kiss properly, and she picked me up and carried me back to my room.

For years after that event with Shirley, I was haunted by the fact that I didn't know how to kiss (and you've heard how rubbish I was at kissing Kirsty Rowlands behind the Gateway). It stayed with me. The shame.

After that Summer Camp experience, when I learned that I really could make my classmates laugh, and could even arouse some interest from girls, even older girls, that was it for me as far as being keen at school was concerned. I'd never be a Keener ever again. What would be the point? It would only ever lead to ball-ache and pain. I acted up for the rest of my school career. I threw myself into becoming the clown. And I didn't have any legitimate outlet for my acting up, because they cancelled all the drama classes after that first year and Mr Windass wouldn't let me into his music class.

I would start thinking of silly things to do in class each day. It was almost as if I was preparing material.

I was eventually told that the mantle of being the funniest person in the school went between me and Martin Neeson. But Martin never developed his act. He did the same things week in week out. I got better and sillier. I would love to have been able to quietly take the piss and get recognised and appreciated for that, but it would never happen. I only took the piss out of myself. I never bullied anyone or made fun of anyone else. I just wanted to get laughs by being silly. It was just a way of getting by.

I think some of my teachers quite liked me even after I'd become a bit of a trouble-maker. I once had to go and see Miss Lowe, who was the head of year. I was summoned to see her in the staff room because I'd been behaving particularly badly. She asked me if I wanted a drink, which seemed quite unusual. I said no thanks.

She said, 'I've got juice … do you want juice?'

And I said, 'No, I'm okay.'

She said, 'Now, Justin, I know you're not one of those spiteful kids. You're not one of those who would come to school at night and smash the windows. You're not malicious. You're just daft. You spend your entire time mucking around. Your entire time. All I hear about is you mucking around constantly … being disruptive and ruining lessons with silliness. So here's the thing: it's got to stop. And if it doesn't stop, I will suspend you. Is that clear?'

And I said, 'Yes, that's clear, Miss. I understand.'

After that talk from Miss Lowe I did make a concerted effort to tone it down a bit. A little while after that talk, when I'd been a bit naughty, Miss Lowe reminded me about the talk and said, 'Remember what I said to you that time you were being naughty?'

I said, 'Yes, Miss, you said if I didn't stop being disruptive then I'd be gone.'

But she replied, 'No, I didn't say you'd be gone, I said you'd be suspended. And you will be if you carry on being silly.'

Now, my form teacher for most of those years was Mr Lowe, who was no relation to Miss Lowe, although they did used to joke that they were brother and sister. I really liked him, but in our penultimate year he put me on the list he kept of kids that were disrupting his class, and he had quite a few disruptive pupils, the poor man. By that time he'd had enough of me. That list put the fear of god in me because by then I did like my schoolmates and I was used to entertaining them and I'd carved myself a little niche. I didn't want to be thrown out or sent to another class. Mr Lowe was also our art teacher. But he was so sick of me that when it came to art class, which was the last lesson of the day, he would allow me to go home early and just not attend the class. That's how sick he was of me! He'd rather send me home early than put up with me. At the time I thought he was being brilliant to me and I loved it. But now I just think, wow – he must have been really sick of me.

If you're wondering what kind of thing I used to get up to in these classes that so annoyed my teachers, I'll give you this example.

During Mrs Tennant's religious education class I got up and stood on a table and saluted and attempted to sing the Russian national anthem.

Why did I do this?

It was purely because I had a silly, absurd and daft and completely random sense of humour. I suppose I still do. To this day I'm still standing on the table trying to sing the Russian national anthem. Anyway, the slightly random explanation of the thought processes that led up to the Russian national anthem incident is this: I went to the pictures with my dad and saw Rocky IV and in it Rocky fights Ivan Drago, played by Dolph Lundgren, in Moscow on Christmas Day, and of course before the fight they play the Russian national anthem and they all stand up and sing it. So I thought, 'Well, wouldn't it be funny if I tried to sing that national anthem?' I didn't know the words of course so it was me standing there saluting and singing 'Dolore spalusco malare badusco ... ' Just made-up nonsense which I thought sounded a bit like Russian.

At the precise moment when I was singing my version of the Russian national anthem in my class, Martin Neeson, that chap who was supposed to be my rival for funniest boy in school, had been sent from another class with a message for our teacher and he opened the door to see everyone sitting there looking up at me singing the Russian national anthem with Mrs Tennant standing ten feet away desperately trying to get me to sit down.

So that's what I would do: sing songs, make noises, just silly noises, and generally do silly things. I wasn't being nasty and throwing shit or anything. I was just messing about. It was just nonsense.

In Mr Stoneman's French class Tony Adams would sit in front of me and I'd make a silly noise like *wooooeeeough!*, and then I'd get Tony Adams to make the same noise, *wooooeeeough!* Mind you, Mr Stoneman did have that habit of slapping his head and saying 'Silly Stoneman' if he got something wrong.

I also used to talk constantly in class. If you looked at my exercise book you'd see the date single underlined, then the title double underlined and then nothing. I'd write the date and the title then distract myself by just talking. So there were pages of dates and titles of projects and essays but no actual writing or anything.

I was also a bit of a serial best friend-er. I must have had seven or eight best friends at school. I'd have one best friend, then six months later there'd be another. Jason Macauley was one best friend. Stephen Chard was another. Mathew Packer. Chris Simpson. Wayne Morgan. Darren Lynch. I was prolific at getting best friends.

I was a very straight kid. What I mean by that is while I was silly and disruptive in class, I was weirdly grown up for my age. Is that a dichotomy? Yes, I think it is. So outside of the classroom, I would be honest and straight with my friends. I didn't hang around smoking and drinking or taking drugs or having sex. (And a lot of that was going on in my school. Remember when I told you about all the fingering?)

One time a few of my friends knocked on my door and they had cigarettes in their hands and they said, 'Do you want to come with us? We're trying smoking.'

I thought, 'You look ridiculous ... you all look ridiculous.' And I stayed indoors and let them try smoking without me.

So in many ways being the Keener was more the real me. I was essentially a decent kid, I think. My situation at school was probably best summed up by Mr Lowe. He said to me at one point, 'Never in my teaching career have I seen a pupil go so far downhill as you ... '

From Keener to (insufferable) Class Clown. That was me. That was my way of dealing with my big school. That was my way of getting through it.

This is going to sound arrogant, but I also felt there was nothing they could teach me there. I could read really well. In my English class I would read all the books aloud. Mrs Platt would get me to read entire books like Kes and Joby to the class. She said I was a better reader than she was herself. And that was all I needed really.

I still mucked around even while I was reading.

In the fourth year, my mum went to the first parents' evening and she met Mrs Platt and Mrs Platt told my mum, 'Justin's the best in the class at English; if he keeps this up he'll get an A in his GCSE.'

So my mum came home really quite pleasantly surprised that evening. She walked in and told me, 'I wasn't expecting that!'

Then six months later there was another parents' evening and this time Mrs Platt said, 'B – he could get a B ... '

Then the year after that, she was saying, 'At best he could get a C, if he stops mucking about.'

Of course I got a double D.

Years later Mrs Platt saw me when I was working at M&S and I was on the till and she told one of my colleagues, 'He was the brightest kid in my class, but he would *not* stop pissing about the entire time.' And she asked me, 'What did I give you in the end? C for English?'

I had to tell her, no, she gave me a D for English language and literature.

As far as maths was concerned, I was put into a large group for the final two years with all the troubled kids. This was a class full of kids who were just not very bright, or were very naughty, or who had particular trouble with maths. It wasn't a special needs class but it was one notch above it. This class was so big and was such a difficult class that it had two teachers – Mr Bottomley and Mr Lance.

They decided to split the class into two sections. So they set a test in general maths. The kids who did well in the test would be in the top group which would end up with Mr Bottomley and the other group would be with Mr Lance. Now this test was so absurdly easy that it was almost embarrassing to take it. It was train times and apples.

I sat there thinking, 'This is ridiculous ... this is where I am.' Train times and apples and plums. But I did the test. A week later they read out the results and I got ninety-seven per cent. I sat there thinking, 'Bloody hell, how did I get three wrong?!' But it was the highest mark in the class. This girl Lucy looked at me and sneered at me. For doing so well in the test! There was a look of contempt in her eyes. She thought I was being a Keener. All over again.

Anyway, Mr Lance came up to me very quietly in the class and said, 'It's quite clear to us that you should not be in this class.'

To which I said, 'Well, move me out of it then!'

'It's too late now,' he told me. 'You're here because of your constant mucking about for the last three years.'

But this class was so low in standard that we weren't even going to be entered in for the GCSE. So Mr Lance did at least say that if I did well in the end-of-year test then they might consider entering me into the GCSE re-sit. But in the end I wasn't entered into the GCSE because I couldn't be bothered. I left school at fifteen with no qualifications. Nothing.

But that was the story of my school. If you did well it was frowned upon by your peers. But if you acted stupid, then they liked you. So while I might have started out doing well, I inevitably ended up acting stupid.

And in a way acting deliberately stupid was a key part of my act for years after that. I played the idiot. I would get things deliberately wrong.

But I hate the idea of being the class clown. I think of myself then and want to shoot myself in the face.

CHAPTER 4

WALKING FASTER

My tutor Mr Lowe practically fell off his chair when he read it.

I did a work experience week at John Lewis in my final year. It went really well. The people at John Lewis liked me, and they wrote a report on me and I was considered outstanding in every category.

Mr Lowe told me he took this absurd report to the staff room and passed it round and none of the other teachers could believe that the John Lewis people were talking about me.

I spent the first few days of the placement in the catering department, in the café, and the second few days I was in the Christmas decorations department. And I loved it, because it felt grown up. It was a proper workplace, full of adults, and I didn't feel I had to perform or impress them to make them like me. I liked the fact that I felt grown up.

I never worried about what I was going to do when I left school, because my parents never put any pressure on me.

So when I was about to leave school at fifteen, without any qualifications, I went to see the careers officer and she asked what I wanted to do and, based on the fact that I spent a lot of time in my bedroom listening to late-night local radio phone-in shows, I told her I wanted to be on the radio. She looked at me and said, 'Yes, but what do you *really* want to do?'

After my startlingly positive John Lewis experience, she encouraged me to apply to other shops and there was a scheme that John Lewis was part of called the YES, the Young Employees Scheme, designed to attract new young staff to the company. So I applied to that scheme at John Lewis and to another similar one at Marks & Spencer's. I had an interview with M&S and by pure coincidence another girl from my school was also being interviewed that same day. My interview was with a lady who asked me what my expected grades were and I said, 'Well, not very good, to be honest. The best I could hope for is maybe a C in English.'

But Marks & Spencer's required three passes in GCSEs.

'I will probably get a C in English lit. and language and aside from that – maybe I'll get Ds and Es,' I told her.

But she liked me and the interview went well and I had a good recommendation from John Lewis. In the end I was offered a job at both M&S and John Lewis.

At this stage I knew I wanted to perform but I had no idea how to go about doing it. So all I knew was that I was sick of school and I didn't want to go back or go to college.

My dad had heard about a media studies course at Soundwell College and took me to meet one of the tutors and I told him I wasn't going to do well in my GCSEs and that was the end of that.

So I thought, 'Well, I enjoyed the work experience at John Lewis. It was easy. I know this isn't what I want to be doing for the rest of my life. Maybe I'll save up some money to go to drama school or something like that.'

I didn't exactly know. But I thought I'd work in a shop for a year maybe. It wasn't a career decision. So I went to work at M&S.

I'm sure you're wondering why I chose Marks over Lewis, I'm sure you are. The M&S starting salary was £138.50 a week as opposed to

John Lewis's £65 a week (though John Lewis had better prospects, apparently). So there I was – sixteen years old and I had to decide between earning 65 quid and earning £138.50. I chose the latter.

As soon as I earned my first weekly wage I thought, 'I'm rich! I'm earning £138.50 a week!' I bought new trainers, a new tracksuit, a Sega Megadrive, some CDs ... It was brilliant.

I started working in the food section of M&S on the Horse Fair in Broadmead on August 10 1990.

I was sixteen and I was the youngest person in the store.

I was thrown into Produce, the busiest, most hectic part of the whole store. There were people running about all the time; it was loud and lively, which meant, to start with, I didn't stick out. Of course we all had to wear the standard M&S uniform, which, back then, meant a grey and white striped shirt and grey Sta-prest trousers. It was horrible.

One of the first people I met was a young girl called Serena Smith, who'd been there a while. I secretly fancied her. She was a few years older than me. She was like my unofficial sponsor in Produce. She showed me the ropes. There was also a guy called Tom Phillips who was on the same YES scheme as me but he'd done it the year before and he'd finished the scheme and now had a job on Foods. Oh, and there was a part-time girl there called Tina who used to work Thursday night, Friday night and Saturday who I liked. I thought, 'Ooh she's nice.' For three years. Eventually I took her to see Robin Hood: Prince Of Thieves. That was our one and only date.

But apart from those relatively youthful colleagues, I felt like a kid in a very grown-up world.

There were some people there who were okay with that – mainly older ladies who had their own kids. But others had a problem with me. I was this sixteen-year-old who walked round the place singing and laughing.

In fact my laughing was a big problem. They must have thought, 'Who is this child, laughing? Why is he laughing in our workplace?' I must have been intolerable for them.

But as far as I was concerned, I had my whole life ahead of me and being in this new world of retail was quite funny. Laughing and singing was my way of dealing with the fact that I was working in M&S and not broadcasting to Bristol and the South West on my own radio show.

The supervisor of Foods was a lady called Kathleen Harris. She was known to be a bit of a dragon. She had a fierce reputation. She was hard.

She once told me off for not walking fast enough.

At the end of every day I had to account for the waste in Produce. There would be rotten peppers, mouldy tomatoes, produce that had gone off that would be dumped or sold off at the staff shop for a discounted price. I would have to account for all that waste on a Psion personal organiser type of gadget. So I'd enter 'tomatoes x 20' or 'cucumbers x 32' and so on.

One evening I had just dealt with some mashed-up old manky tomatoes and I was walking across the sales floor looking at my hands, which were covered in rotten tomato juice. I stank. I was reeking of stale produce. You know that damp, slightly off smell you get at the greengrocer's? I smelled like that.

So I was looking at my hands and thinking: 'What am I doing here? What am I doing with my life?' My rotten smelly hands were a symptom of the state of my life.

And just as I was staring at my hands I heard Kathleen the supervisor barking, 'Justin! Justin!'

I looked up and, pleasant as you like, said, 'All right, Kathleen?'

She looked like thunder. 'What are you DOING?' she asked incredulously.

'Oh, I've just been doing produce, Kathleen ... '

She looked at me and said, 'Let me show you what you're doing.'

And I had to stand there while she proceeded to do an impression of me walking across the floor with my hands in front of my face. She looked like she was imitating Frankenstein's monster doing a death march.

She finished her impersonation of me and said, 'Right?'

I just stared at her. I didn't know what to say.

Then she said loudly, 'Walk *faster!*'

Again, I just looked at her blankly, thinking, I suppose, of the rotten produce all over me. So she said it again, even louder.

'Justin, walk FASTER!'

I just looked at her and said 'Okay, Kathleen, I'll walk faster.'

So I was sixteen. I was working in Marks & Spencer. I was covered in rotten produce. And I was being told off for slow walking. It had come to this.

Another time I was on the freezer section. And the freezer section had just been moved to just outside Foods office door where Kathleen and her deputy supervisors used to sit. On this particular day I was called in to Kathleen's office where there were three or four deputy supervisors looking at me and trying not to laugh.

But Kathleen looked at me sternly and said, 'Justin ... '

I said, 'Yes, Kathleen?'

'We're all in here trying to work and all we can hear is you laughing. That's all we can hear.'

I could tell that although she was telling me off, this time there seemed to be an element of affection in the way she was doing it, and her deputies were sitting there smiling.

The truth is, I did spend most of my time on Foods just walking around laughing and singing. I sang old songs like Amen Corner's If Paradise Is Half As Nice, Build Me Up Buttercup by The Foundations ... and the ladies would ask how I knew such old songs. Songs that were in the hit parade when they were young. Those were just the type of songs that I'd always loved, going back to when my mum and dad played them while I was growing up.

For a while there, even though I had to walk faster and deal with many tomatoes, I was comparatively happy in Produce, singing and laughing. It was the busiest section of the store so I didn't stand out too much, even though I did manage to annoy and irritate Kathleen Harris.

But she seemed to have a soft spot for me. When it came to my appraisal on Foods, even though she had told me off quite a lot, for slow walking and the like, she did give me quite a nice write-up. She said I was good with the customers. There were various categories on the appraisal: ratings from A to C in Cleaning, Punctuality ... all that nonsense. I always scored highly for customer service. Other stuff not so good.

The real problems began when I moved to Menswear.

Menswear had an entirely different vibe. It was grey, like our uniforms, and quiet and had a whiff of oldness. Men like to shop for clothes quietly, especially while they're being measured for suits or trying on shoes. It was like Are You Being Served?, but quieter and a lot less fun.

So if you saw a young man walking along the floor laughing or singing, you'd notice it much more than in the hectic whirl that was Produce and Foods. I was that young man.

The atmosphere could be summed up by something I noticed on my first day in Menswear ...

Two female colleagues, Sylvia and Joan, were doing a move and shifting around some shoes. Sylvia was happily talking to Joan and they were just having a normal conversation while they were working. I noticed the store manager was walking across the shop floor, and I clearly saw him clock these two women talking, and he stopped dead in his tracks. He was rooted to the spot, watching them chatting away. He obviously wanted them to notice him and stop. He wanted them to work and not even acknowledge each other. But they didn't notice him so he just walked away, shaking his head.

I thought, 'Bloody hell, that's what it's like up here ... It shocks people if you even speak!'

The Menswear supervisor was a woman called Janice Morley. If the shop was like Are You Being Served?, then she was like its Captain Peacock. She made Kathleen Harris seem like a pussycat. She hated me. She tried to get me the sack.

Every little thing I did seemed to get on her nerves. Especially when I was challenging the routine. Fighting, in my own tiny and, in my opinion, thoroughly harmless way, against the boring system.

For example, there was my attitude to the Cyclic Count ...

Every day I had to place my menswear order on a handheld Psion. But there was this curious system called the Cyclic Count which meant that once a week one department couldn't place an order at a specific time because they'd be doing a stock take on that particular department in the warehouse. In the Cyclic Count system, that department was known as being 'in Cyclic Count'.

I started my Menswear stint in section To3 – which was Footwear. I'd go in on the Monday and I'd look at the Cyclic Count sheet in the cupboard and on that sheet it would have a drawing of a matchstick man on a matchstick bicycle cycling – thus Cyclic Count – and there would be a column next to the matchstick cyclist which said, 'This week do not order from these departments on these days ... ' So for example it would have Monday T03 (Footwear) ... Tuesday T15 (which was Suits), Wednesday T83 (Slippers), Thursday (T18) Leisure-wear. And so on. So every day I would go into the cupboard to download my organiser to place the order for my footwear department.

Stay with me, this is leading somewhere.

That process would take three or four minutes. Now maybe there was something useful I could be doing in those three or four minutes while the organiser was downloading the Cyclic Count information. Maybe I should have been grabbing a J-cloth and going to my department and cleaning my mirrors, which was another thing I was always being told off for – not cleaning my mirrors often enough. But the thing is, they had cleaners in every day whose job it was to clean the mirrors! Why did I need to clean the mirrors?

So while I was waiting for the organiser to download, I'd take my pencil out of my breast pocket and draw a little face on the matchstick man on the matchstick bike and I'd write my friend Paul Gammon's name above him. I'd maybe draw a little nail on the front of the bike and I'd draw air coming out of the tyre and I'd write, 'Oh no, Paul's got a puncture.' I drew lots of silly drawings on the Cyclic Count sheet.

It turned out that my supervisor was taking down every one of these drawings I'd made, all the Cyclic Count sheets that I had been defacing, and she put them in a file. She was compiling a dossier.

Now I only discovered this dossier months later when she called me in for an appraisal and showed me the file with all these old defaced Cyclic Count sheets in it. I was almost proud to be the subject of a dossier.

Paul Gammon was the one friend I made in Menswear. He was a rare, decent, friendly bloke at M&S not too far away from my own age.

Most of the older staff regarded me as a stupid kid, an annoying stupid kid. Some of them were quite vocal about what they thought of me. One guy called Fred Balls, for example, who was a warehouse man, hated me.

I would see him in the staff canteen. All the men in the canteen would sit together at the same table. The management would sit at a nicer table with high-backed chairs and a bowl of fruit. Supervisors would sit together. The regular staff ladies would sit anywhere.

I would grab some lunch, and just find somewhere, anywhere, to sit, and often I would sit there laughing about something or other I'd seen or maybe chat to one of the other younger people. One time Balls just looked at me after I'd laughed out loud and shouted, 'Shut up!'

If I passed Balls during the morning on the shop floor, he would ask me, 'All right, Justin, what time you on lunch today?'

'Ooh, I'm early today, Fred, 1 to 2pm,' I'd tell him.

'All right, well, I'll make sure I go from 12 to 1 then.'

He said that to me every day for a long time. He was horrible to me.

It was my laughter that he hated. My laughing was the primary problem for a lot of people at M&S.

As if dealing with the general everyday grey dullness of M&S menswear was not enough, I also had to take part in a retail course that first year at the store, which was part of the scheme that got me the job in the first place. So not only did I have to deal with Cyclic Counts and shoe displays but I also had to go to a college twice a week at the Victoria Rooms in town, and we had to sit there in a circle and discuss the finer points of retail with a woman called Debbie who ran the class.

It was mind-numbing.

I took the opportunity during one session with Debbie to be really honest. She was asking how we were doing and I told her it was really getting me down and making me miserable.

She answered quite flippantly, 'Well, why don't you just walk out the door?'

I didn't think that was a very helpful answer! I was making a cry for help and she wasn't bothered.

Another part of the course was an outward bound course. I kid you not.

All the YES employees from across the country had to go away to Dove's Nest in the Lake District for five days.

It was the first time I had ever been away on my own without either of my parents for any length of time. So the first thing I did before I left was to hide my stash of porn mags.

By that time I'd built up quite a collection. I used to go to the all-night garage round the corner from my parents' house and buy copies of Razzle and Escort and 40 Plus and Men Only. Magazines like that. (Obviously I now had a new hobby after that night when I watched Nine And A Half Weeks.) I stashed the mags away under my bed, but before I left on this Lake District trip, I shoved them beneath the mattress just to make sure my parents wouldn't stumble across them. Not that I expected them to spend much time in my room or anything.

So off I went, with huge reluctance, on this outward bound course in the Lake District.

And I managed to leave my suitcase on a train.

We had to change trains halfway through the journey. The train was packed and I'd put my suitcase in a luggage rack about three carriages away from where I found a seat. When we arrived at this station, I was on my way to getting my bag when the whistle went to indicate the train was leaving. I had to get off that train, which was heading for Edinburgh. Otherwise I'd miss getting the other train to the Lake District. But I hadn't reached my bag. It was too late.

I pulled down the first window I got to and pulled myself out of the train and jumped onto the platform.

A conductor shouted, 'What the fuck are you doing?!'

I said, 'My bag's on the train! You didn't wait for me to get off the train!'

The train sped away behind me to Edinburgh with my bag on it.

I spent the first two days in the Lake District on this outward bound course without anything to wear in the freezing cold, with people I mostly couldn't stand, to enable me to take part in a course for a job I hated.

The people running the course told me not to worry about my bag and that it would turn up eventually, but I had to borrow rubbish old clothes from them.

We had to do ridiculous activities like abseiling. Obviously a key skill when you're working in Marks & Spencer's. I refused to do the abseil. I was the only one who refused. I was on a guide rope, tied to a tree and the guy running the outward bound course was saying, 'You can do this. Do you trust me? Come on! Do you trust me?'

I said, 'No, I don't trust you!'

I was thinking, 'He told me I'd have new clothes after I left my bag on the train, and I don't have new clothes ... so no, I don't trust you!'

Eventually after a couple of days my bag did arrive, but I was still miserable.

Needless to say I never finished the retail course in that first year at M&S. Another qualification I didn't get.

When I got back from the Lake District, I walked through the door and my mum told me that they had a surprise for me. My parents led me upstairs, and we stood outside my room and they opened the door.

They'd secretly decorated the whole bedroom while I was away, and given me a new bed.

It was a surprise!

So I was looking at my lovely new room through gritted teeth, thinking, 'Oh my god! Where are my pornos?'

I decided I had to confront my mum about my porno mags. I knew they must have found them. But I couldn't speak to her face to face about it, so I waited for her to be in the bathroom and through the door I said, 'Erm ... Mum? Did you find my magazines?'

And my lovely mum, who was so cool, casually replied, 'Oh yes, I put them in your bottom drawer ... '

She didn't make a thing of it at all. I was so grateful.

But within a few years, I had so many porn mags that I was running out of space for all of them. I didn't know what to do with them. There was no recycling in those days. I couldn't put them in the bin because my mum or dad would see them, which would be embarrassing even though my mum at least knew I had them. So I was stuck. I couldn't burn them. I couldn't start a fire.

Then I remembered that round the corner of our house was a gossie, a bit of unused, overgrown land full of brambles and stinging nettles and trees. I thought what I could do is put all the porn mags in bags and go to the gossie and chuck them down there. I waited till my mum and dad were out of the house, put all the mags in two or three big plastic bags and carried them round the corner to the gossie.

But there was a terrible, gusting wind that night.

So I had to really give these bags of magazines a big swing as I hurled them down into the gossie. But the wind caught them as they came out of the bags and blew them all over the street. I ended up running around the road trying to catch my porn mags – I was floundering while dozens of copies of Fiesta, Escort, Razzle, 40 Plus and Men Only blew all over the neighbourhood. All I could imagine was that my neighbours could see me desperately flailing around, trying to pick up these porn mags blowing in the wind.

Eventually I managed to pick most of them up and I did dump them in the gossie.

Years later they built a block of flats on the land where the gossie was. So presumably some builder or other got lucky and found all my porn mags.

But perhaps my most frustrating M&S experience involved the vexed art of shelving and displays.

By this time I was eighteen and quite experienced in footwear.

Now one of the weird things about M&S at that time was that every week they'd move the products around. Nothing could be left in the shop in the same place for more than a few days at a time. I think it came down to the philosophy that everyone has to be seen to be doing something all the time. So moving stuff around was one way to make sure people were busy. Entire sections would be moved from one side of the floor to the other. It was all about moving!

One time I was given the task of moving footwear from one bit of the store to the other. I was supposed to use some slanting display shelves that were up against a feature wall. I was meant to put shoes and slippers on these shelves and maybe mix it up a bit by putting a nice turtleneck next to a pair of suede brogues or maybe a dressing gown next to the slippers. You know, create some attractive shoe and clothing displays.

But I discovered a problem as I was putting these shelving displays together – there was one piece of the shelving which didn't have the right end piece. It should have had a Profile 90 Perspex end. All the shelves were supposed to have this unique Perspex end that fitted perfectly on to the shelf.

But this particular shelf was missing the Profile 90 Perspex end.

I should add at this point in the shelving story that I think the bosses wanted me out by this time in my career at M&S. I think they were looking for ways to get rid of me. So I felt under some degree of pressure to do everything properly.

As I pondered my Perspex-end quandary, I thought, 'I must cover all the bases here.' I knew I couldn't placate my supervisor if I hadn't explored every avenue and ticked every box in the search for the correct eight-inch-long piece of Perspex.

I looked everywhere round the store from top to bottom.

I checked other departments and other sections. I thought about taking a Perspex end from another section and using it for my shelf. I checked the warehouse at M&S Broadmead, Bristol and I spoke to Steve Fulton who was in charge of checking for equipment and he said there might have been a spare Profile 90 Perspex end at the Weston-super-Mare branch of M&S, which had a lot more equipment, but that there wouldn't be a delivery for a few days anyway so there was no way of getting hold of a Profile 90 at such short notice.

So this is the situation I was faced with: I either didn't use that shelf and left it empty or else I took the shelf down but that would look odd because you'd see three shelves in a row and a gap at the end, or the other option was to use a different size end to the shelf so you'd see a shelf with a bit of Perspex at the end which didn't quite fit.

In the end I went with the display shelf with a bit of Perspex at the end which didn't quite fit. So there were two or three inches of Perspex hanging off the end. To the untrained eye, I thought, this is fine.

So there I was putting some shoes on the shelf with the too-long

Perspex end and Auntie Val and Auntie Barb are on their knees helping me.

They weren't my real aunties, obviously, they were just colleagues of mine, ladies of a certain age who had a soft spot for me and would help me out from time to time.

They were helping me because they knew the pressure was on and that certain people wanted me out. See? I wasn't just being paranoid.

Barb, who's sadly no longer with us, was saying, 'Come on, we've gotta get this done, Justin, otherwise she'll be on you!'

I said, 'All right, Auntie Barb, it'll be fine.'

Then, as we were frantically filling up the shelves with shoes I heard a voice behind me ...

'Justin!'

I looked around and there was my supervisor standing there and she was just about to start reading me the riot act.

But just as she was about to give me what I, and I believe any right-thinking objective observer, would consider a totally unwarranted bollocking, by pure coincidence the floor manager – a young guy called Bob who quite liked me – was standing right behind her. So I was looking up at her, and she was already fixated on the shelf with the too-long Perspex end, and I could see Bob the floor manager behind her. And because I knew she was about to confront me, I decided to get in first with my explanation that I'd actually done everything in my power to find the right Profile 90 Perspex end.

'Yeah, I know, Janice,' I told her. 'The reason why there's a longer end on that shelf and it looks a bit odd is because I've been round the whole store, I've been to other departments, I've called other stores ... '

And then she interrupted me. 'Yes, but have you checked with Steve Fulton?'

I said, 'Yes, I've checked with Steve Fulton, Janice, and he informed me that they do have the right Perspex end in the warehouse in Weston but the next trip to Weston won't be until Monday and he assures me when he goes to Weston he will find me the right Perspex end and bring one here. In the meantime I thought I'd make do for now with this Perspex end then swap them over when the new one arrives.'

There was nothing more I could do. Apart from stealing one from another department and leaving them in the shit, I had done everything in my power and I was explaining this to my supervisor. In my opinion, I was covered.

But she looked at me and said, 'Now that' – pointing at the too-long Perspex end – 'is NOT good enough!'

In fact, she pretty much shouted that at me.

So at that point I was just thinking, 'Now this is just victimisation. She's just got it in for me. I did all that I could!'

I hadn't been rude, I'd told her I'd done everything possible on T03 (Footwear) and T83 (Slippers) to rectify the situation.

At that moment, Janice the supervisor was startled by a tap on the shoulder. It was the floor manager Bob. He'd been watching her and listening to what she said to me.

He said, 'Janice, can I have a word?' and he led her off the floor and had a quiet talk with her.

A few minutes later she was back on the floor. And she was bawling her eyes out. She'd clearly had a strip torn off her.

I should make it clear at this point that I took no pleasure in seeing her crying, no pleasure at all, but I did think she'd been totally out of order with me regarding the Profile 90 Perspex end.

After that first year, I just became a person who works in Marks & Spencer. I wasn't doing anything in my spare time in terms of radio or amateur dramatics or anything creative: nothing in the areas that I really wanted to work in. I was also living at home and I was working Monday to Friday and every other Saturday. It was pretty mind-numbing, and I must have been worried, perhaps only subconsciously, that my life was going to be about retail and not performing. My only form of creative expression would be to sing Build Me Up Buttercup on the shop floor.

Then Tom Jones rescued me from the dullness. Tom Jones and the power of karaoke helped me show myself and all my colleagues what I was really capable of.

We used to have fairly frequent work outings. Every other weekend, for example, there was a staff do at the Spaghetti Tree, a basement club which served pizzas and had a disco.

Then one week they all decided to have a night at Papillon's karaoke nightclub. This was my big chance. I liked to sing, and I thought I could cope with singing to an audience so I decided I would definitely take part in the karaoke that night.

On the day of the outing to Papillon's, I got quite excited about the prospect of singing and I also wanted to impress everyone at work. So I decided to buy a new outfit specially. I bought a really lovely pair of Gierre orange slacks from a high-end fashion boutique in Bristol called The Boulevard. These trousers were bright orange and pleated with turn-ups. I also bought a pair of black Doc Marten shoes and then – and this is perhaps where I went a bit wrong – I also saw a bright orange shirt in Ciro Citterio. I thought, 'This shirt matches my new orange trousers – brilliant!'

So I went to this nightclub looking like a giant satsuma.

Geoff Weston, who's sadly no longer with us, was running the whole event, because he was our boss. He was the store manager of

Broadmead M&S. I don't like to speak ill of the dead, but I have to say he wasn't a very nice man.

But that night he did do a duet with me on Delilah.

It came about because the supervisors who were there that night decided it would be funny for the big boss Geoff to be partnered with me, the young little shit from Menswear who was far too happy-go-lucky for his own good. So they put my name forward to sing with Mr Weston. Our song was Tom Jones's Delilah. We walked on stage together and Geoff sang the first verse. He was terrible.

Then came my big moment. I held the mic and belted out the second verse of Delilah like my life depended on it. The audience gasped. I could tell they were impressed.

As soon as we finished singing Delilah, Geoff said to me, 'Well, you're good at singing. Fuck all else. But you're good at singing ... '

I said, 'Thank you, Mr Weston.'

That was the first time I had ever sung in front of an audience. And it was a triumph.

All my colleagues came up to me afterwards to tell me how stunned and amazed they were by my performance.

I'd sung to the point of embarrassing the store manager, who couldn't sing a note. It was a big moment for me. I'd shown them there was more to me than being an annoying kid.

I was actually a good kid. I wasn't throwing shit through their windows. My sin was being too carefree.

But not only had I proved to myself that I could sing pretty well in front of dozens of people, I'd also shown my colleagues from this boring retail job what I was really capable of. I'd reminded *myself* what I was capable of. That was what I wanted to be doing – singing and performing to people. Not sorting out Perspex ends.

That night, that duet of Tom Jones's Delilah suddenly made me feel an awful lot better about my life, and I'll never forget it. Next day on the shop floor I had an extra skip in my step.

On the way home from Papillon's, I walked through a not very nice area of Bristol dressed entirely in orange and this drunk man spotted me from the other side of the street and yelled out, 'Hey, wanker!'

Then he said, 'Hey, hardcase!'

I've no idea who he was but obviously my orange outfit had provoked him. And I can't say I blame him for being provoked. I just walked a bit faster and went home.

Kathleen the Supervisor would have been pleased. That night I did walk faster.

Anyway, that was also the beginning of a bit of a Tom Jones obsession for me.

Barely a year later I went to see Tom Jones at the Bristol Colston Hall with my mum and my Auntie Liz and he blew me away. Just hearing that voice live for the first time was incredible.

Years later I found myself in a hotel on International Drive, Miami, Florida, preparing to go on stage as a Tom Jones impersonator at the world lookalike convention. And after that, there was the time I actually duetted with the real Tom Jones on The Friday Night Project singing It's Not Unusual. Tom Jones has played quite a role in my life one way or the other.

CHAPTER 5

AN EXPLOSION

My dad could tell something wasn't quite right.

He was waiting in his car, very kindly picking me up from work as he did most Saturdays while I was at M&S, and he could tell from the expression on my face as I slouched towards him that something was wrong with me.

He was quite correct.

I'd had a thoroughly miserable day, and as soon as I got in the car, he could tell.

'What's up, son?' he asked. 'Are you all right?'

I said, 'I'm not, Dad.'

'Why, what's wrong?'

'I've got to leave,' I said. 'I've been here too long. I hate it.'

The real killer for me was having to work every other Saturday at M&S. When it got to that Friday night before the Saturday, I'd be at home thinking, 'I have to be up at 7am tomorrow.' It was a bit soul-destroying for a nineteen-year-old.

So my dad just looked at me and asked, 'But what do you want to do?'

And it all flowed out of me ...

'What I've always wanted to do. Be on the radio. Or act. Or work in TV. Something like that. What I've always, *always* wanted to do ... '

So my dad quite calmly said, 'Okay, well, I'll look into it. I'll see if there are any courses you can do or anything ... '

True to his word, my dad did look for performing arts classes and drama courses, and it was he who found out about a BTEC in performing arts at Filton College. It was only in its second year. He sent away for a prospectus and he told me, 'I think I've found it. I think this is the one for you.'

The other nice thing that happened was that for the first time since Mrs Platt's Speedwell School production of Cinderella in which I played Buttons, I got a part in a play.

My friend Tony was a student at the University of Western England and he told me they were putting on a production of Daisy Pulls It Off and that they would be holding open auditions. He said, 'You're into stuff like that ... do you want to come along to the auditions?'

So we all went along to the St Matthias Fishponds campus of UWE and I auditioned for the part of the gardener. It's a pretty small part. He's only in three short scenes.

That was the first time in my life I ever auditioned for something. And I got the part. We did about three performances and I loved it.

I was getting the taste for performing, and I thought I'd better not leave everything to my dad to sort out, so I did get off my arse and do some volunteer work at Bristol Hospital Broadcasting Service – BHBS.

I helped out every Sunday morning on the Jim Brown breakfast show. Actually, come to think of it, my dad *was* involved. He'd heard about BHBS and he wrote a letter to them to see if they would be interested in me. I was told I could go along one afternoon and be shown how to do things with a view to helping out as a technical operator. I went there for three or four weeks and learnt how to log the albums and use the desk. I was with an old guy called John who was in his seventies and had done a lot of radio but was now retired, and a very attractive girl called Lizzie. Together the three of us were shown the ropes. Then we were given specific slots during which we could help out. I was given Sunday mornings to help with the Jim Brown breakfast show.

I don't think he liked me one bit. In fact I think he hated me. I think he thought I was lazy. You see, I wasn't really interested in the technical stuff and filling out lists and logging. I wanted to do what he was doing – host the show.

Soon I started to go into the hospital radio station on a Saturday too, but because I was working at M&S, I didn't really want to get up at the crack of dawn on a Sunday if I'd been working on a Saturday; I hate mornings at the best of times. So I gave up doing the Sundays because it clearly wasn't going to lead to me being on air.

I remember one day the older guy John left and Jim Brown looked up and said, 'Okay, John, thanks very much ...' then I left a few minutes later and he didn't even look up at me. The weird thing about the hospital radio was that they all took it desperately seriously. They were all volunteers for sick people but they were all so serious about it. I thought maybe they should just be trying to have fun and entertain the patients. Jim Brown's day job was in the furniture department of John Lewis, coincidentally.

One time Barry, who was Jim's assistant, was operating the desk and he hadn't put the DJ's fader up fast enough, so his mic wasn't working, and there was a delay of a few seconds before he could be heard after a record.

Jim stood up and ran into the booth and shouted, 'Barry?! What the fuck are you doing?!' As if it was Radio 1 or something. This poor guy, a volunteer, was being screamed at because he made a tiny little mistake. I thought, 'That's a bit much.'

They also used to broadcast the service every Sunday from the chapel in the hospital and Barry would take the equipment down to the church and make sure it all worked. I helped him one morning and as we were walking down the corridor the minister stopped Barry and called out, 'Martin! Martin!' We carried on walking. But the minister thought he was being ignored and carried on shouting. 'Martin! Martin! Martin!'

Eventually Barry stopped and turned to the minister and said, 'Yes, Minister,' and the minister asked him a question. But Barry didn't correct him. So I asked him if the minister always called him Martin, and Barry said yes he did. And it suddenly dawned on me that as soon as the minister started shouting Martin, Barry knew that he meant him. But he just let him carry on shouting Martin. This poor guy was volunteering and being shouted at and sworn at by the DJ and was being called the wrong name by the minister. I just thought, 'Sod this,' and I left.

But I never told them I was going to leave. I just didn't go back. The week I left was the week I was supposed to be sitting in for Barry and operating the desk. But I just didn't show up. I just realised I didn't like it there. And I never went back.

A few months later one of the guys who worked at the station saw me at M&S and asked what happened to me. 'One minute you were there and the next you just disappeared,' he said.

I just said, 'Yep. I left.'

I've always been like that. If I decide I don't want to do something any more, I'll stop there and then, and there's not much that anyone can say to change my mind. Often, I must admit, they end up being absolutely right.

I was still at M&S, though, and I wasn't enjoying it. At all. It was getting me down, to be honest. I was having a tough time on

Menswear and I knew they wanted to sack me and that Janice didn't like me.

It all came to a head one afternoon when I was taken off the shop floor and was told by Janice that the deputy store manager, George Costello, and one of the personnel managers, Myra Woods, needed to see me.

So I went to George's office and I was told they were going to sack me because of my poor performance in certain areas – basically every area except customer service – and because of my general attitude of not taking anything seriously. My general light-heartedness offended them.

They gave me a three-month probation period. Final warning time.

George looked at me and said, 'So at the end of that period of three months there will be a review and if you haven't made significant changes and turned it round and started to take it seriously then we will sack you. You will be sacked.' He paused. 'Do you understand what I'm saying to you, Justin?'

I said, 'Yes, Mr Costello. I understand what you're saying. I can hear what you're saying and I can understand it. You're saying that if I don't turn things round and start to take things seriously then at the end of this three-month probation period you will sack me ... '

'Yes, Justin, that is what I'm saying.'

'Yes,' I thought, 'I do understand what you're saying.' But what George Costello and Myra Woods didn't understand is that I was a child and that I didn't give a fuck about the job. Although of course I didn't want a sacking on my CV or anything. But I certainly wasn't looking to work there for the next forty-three years of my life. Then Mr Costello added, 'Do you want to speak to Paul?'

Paul Gammon, he meant, my sponsor and friend. So Mr Costello, thinking that I wasn't fully grasping the severity of the situation, wondered if I needed to get help and advice from my sponsor. But I didn't.

I think they were disappointed by my reaction. Or by my lack of a reaction. I think they wanted me to break down in tears and sob about the prospect of losing my job in Menswear at M&S Broadmead. Then it dawned on me that they were thinking I couldn't do it. They thought I was incapable. They thought that they'd employed a simpleton. A simpleton who couldn't grasp how to make sure his mirrors were clean every day and who couldn't grasp that the top-selling shoe of the day should be featured on the end of the island so the customers could see it first and think, 'Wow! What a great shoe!' They thought I didn't get it. They thought it was all beyond me.

But the thing is I was just a kid and I didn't care. All I knew was that I didn't want to work at M&S for the rest of my life. And I've got nothing against people who do work for M&S their entire lives, but I knew I wanted something else.

But I didn't want them to think I was a simpleton, so I made the decision to actually try my best during my three-month probation period. I just thought, 'I'll show them I can do this bloody work.' I wanted to show them I wasn't simple.

So during that three-month period I turned it round. I went from 'This is your final warning, after this we're going to sack you' to my deputy supervisor telling me, even before the three months were up, 'Keep this up and you're next in line for deputy supervision.' Ridiculous!

In between working at M&S and becoming a model staff member, I'd started going out drinking regularly with friends from work. The only problem was, I couldn't hold my drink. A couple of pints was enough for me to be fairly drunk. Well, totally pissed, to be honest. And I didn't deal with my lack of drinking capacity very well.

For example, there was the time I agreed to go to the Century club in Kingswood to have a drink with Marnie Long who worked in the M&S warehouse. We had a few beers and played snooker.

I can't hold my drink, as you may have realised, and I was walking home from Century's and I hadn't had a pee for hours. I should have gone to the toilet before I left Century's.

That walk was a good twenty minutes long. I was busting. Most people would have found an alley to piss in, but I hated that idea.

I've always had this thing where I really hate urinating in public. If I'm out I will do my very best to find a toilet. I'm not one for going up an alley or in someone's garden. I loathe people urinating in public. I also hate it when people spit too. There's no need for it!

So I got all the way to my mum and dad's house without having a pee. I stood there at the front door and wrestled in my pocket for the key. But I couldn't find it. I found another key. The wrong key.

Then it all came out.

I wet myself. In my Levi 501s. Standing on the doorstep to my parents' house.

I am proud to say, though, that this was the last time I peed myself, after all those years of wetting the bed. I'd achieved that much.

But I still hadn't mastered holding my drink when I went out one night a few months later with Paul Gammon and our other M&S mate Matt Paddon at the Artichoke after work.

As usual, I'd had too much. That is, for me, probably three pints of lager. I caught the City Dart bus to Staple Hill. The City Dart is a little single-decker bus.

I was wearing a big, oversized grey Gap jumper over a T-shirt. It was a size too big because I was into the big and sloppy look in those days.

I was feeling sick. I had to be sick. But I couldn't stop the bus to be sick. I had no kind of receptacle to be sick into and I knew I had to vomit right there and then.

So I grabbed my big jumper and pulled the bottom up to my head to create a kind of bowl made out of my jumper and I proceeded to be copiously sick into my Gap jumper.

I had a jumper full of vomit.

I looked up and realised that most people on the bus could see and hear what was going on. I turned around and realised that sitting directly behind me on the bus was Sheila Lovell, a lovely woman from my mother's church. There I was with a pullover full of puke with a friend of my mum's having to endure the whole sorry sight.

She didn't acknowledge me or look at me at all, thank goodness.

To keep my sanity in my M&S stupor, I decided to apply for that performing arts course my dad had told me about at Filton College. I had to audition, so I performed a bit from Daisy Pulls It Off. I was so nervous and I didn't know it off by heart so I had the book in my hand and I was shaking like a leaf. Because for me at that moment this audition to get a place on this course was the most important moment of my entire life.

This was the gig to get me out of M&S. This was the audition to get me on some kind of path towards what I wanted to do.

I didn't think the audition went well. I thought I was a bit shit, to be honest. But with the exception of one girl, who was like a proper actress and everything, we were all a bit rubbish. The only difference between me and the others auditioning was that I was a bit older.

After the audition I was interviewed by Phil Crane, the guy who ran the course. He seemed to like me. And somehow I was offered a place on the course. It was a two-year BTEC course and I had to pay, but I'd been saving £50 every month from my M&S salary.

I was thrilled, and as soon as I found out I got the place on this course I wanted to leave M&S immediately. I couldn't wait.

I'd gone straight from school to work with no travelling or being young and free and mucking about like a student. I wanted to take time out. People who go to university can take a whole year out. I had no gap year. No taking time out to go travelling. I'd never done that. Still haven't. I wanted a gap year. Or at least a gap three months. But my dad said, 'You'd be silly to leave, son. You'd be silly.' He advised me to save as much money as I could for college. 'That will be money you'll be glad to have,' he said. So I took his advice.

But the day did come when I handed in my notice. After I gave my letter of resignation in to the personnel office, I went back to the floor to tell Janice my supervisor, the woman who one year previously had given me a final warning and pretty much wanted to get rid of me.

She said, 'What are you going to do?'

So I told her. I had a place on a BTEC course in performing arts.

She looked me straight in the eye and said, 'I think that's brilliant. That's the kind of thing I've always wanted to do. How old are you?'

I was nineteen.

'That's great ... you're young. You've got the rest of your life ahead of you. Why would you want to stay in a place like this?'

I thought, 'Yeah, exactly! Why didn't you say that to me a year ago instead of giving me a final warning and trying to sack me?!'

But she was genuinely pleased for me. So we were all right in the end, Janice the Supervisor and I. We were all right.

Not long after I resigned from M&S, I got my first proper girlfriend.

She was called Chrissy and I met her at the Causeway video shop, where I'd just started working part-time.

I don't want to sound cruel or anything but Chrissy was a very plain girl. That's just the fact of it. But I really fell for her and I think I did so because she didn't intimidate or scare me in any way, which was quite rare. Most girls did scare me. Chrissy wore John Noakes-style jerkins but beneath them she had voluptuous breasts. I guess that was quite sexy – knowing there were those lovely bosoms concealed beneath her turtlenecks and other varieties of knitwear. She also wore glasses and had very long hair. She looked like a less attractive Nana Mouskouri.

My friend Jim also worked in the video shop and his brother had previously gone out with Chrissy and had reported back that she had very pink nipples. I thought that was intriguing.

So I liked her and she seemed to like me and so we got together and started to date. Her family lived quite near me on a big council estate. I never felt very comfortable going to her house and hanging out there, which is a bit embarrassing to admit but it's true. They were quite poor. It was a pretty rough estate. They had a washing line going across the lounge and that's where they would hang the washing.

(I think of my own family as being working class but we never went without and materially I had pretty much everything I ever wanted. There's a case to be made that I was spoilt – certainly I was never lacking in the love department from my family.)

Chrissy and I had also both gone to the same school but we didn't meet properly until Causeway Video.

Our first date was to the cinema of course.

We were together for about eighteen months but for the first three months of the relationship we hardly touched each other. And that was down to me because I was nervous and worried about sex.

As I explained earlier, I'd had a few quasi-girlfriends in school but it never went beyond kissing. In fact I'd only really kissed one or two girls properly ... intimately, with tongues and that, because going right back to my experience watching Sylvia Kristel on the TV in my Orlando hotel room, anything to do with sex made me feel a bit wrong and nervous. I was scared of it. Terrified, in fact.

So I told Chrissy quite early on in our relationship that I didn't know if I wanted to have sex before marriage. I had a lot of confused thoughts swirling around in my head, including some vaguely religious ones to do with some Christian books a friend had thrust upon me.

This friend was called Steven and he was a big Christian. He would lend me books by people like Benny Hinn – an American preacher with insane hair like M. Night Shyamalan, the film director. He used to yell 'Fire on ya!' and he wore a white suit. Hinn wrote books such as Good Morning Holy Spirit and He Touched Me. Steven used to lend me these books. He also gave me a book called From Witchcraft To Christ. It was the autobiography of a woman who was raised as a witch but then found Christ. It was fascinating, although another friend of mine told me that same woman later wrote a book called From Witchcraft To Christ And Back Again. But I don't know if that's true.

But my reasons for not wanting to have sex weren't really religious at all.

I was just scared of it.

Perhaps that was due to the fact that I am part of the Aids Generation, when we were constantly being told that Sex Is Dangerous. Forget the free love of the 1960s and 1970s. I grew up thinking that you could get a disease and die from having sex.

The thing to remember is that I watched Mike Smith from Saturday Superstore when I was on the cusp of puberty and he and his guests were debating on TV whether you could get this new disease from kissing. And there was this big advertising campaign featuring a tombstone and a voice saying 'Aids: Don't Die Of Ignorance'. It was scary. The only way to be sure you weren't going to die of bad sex was to not have any.

In the end, though, despite all my self-consciousness and fear, I just got too horny. I started thinking, 'What the fuck am I doing? What am I waiting for? I'm not a born-again Christian!'

I've never liked people who never seem to worry about anything. They're not my kind of people. And I worried about a lot of things. But when I was twenty and thinking about sex, I did suddenly realise that I was fed up with worrying about sex.

I was still a late developer, as ever, but now I wanted to do something about it.

So we were at Chrissy's house in her room in her bed. It wasn't like we were in the back of a car or in a layby or a field or in the back of a cinema. Which would have been wonderful – I'd still like to do that. (In the cinema I mean, not the layby or field.) I think we had the place to ourselves because her family was on holiday.

I was all nervous and fumbly, of course, and excited, too excited. But I had absolutely no idea what I was doing so there wasn't much room for romance. Poor Chrissy. She must have thought I was an idiot. In fact, it was all a bit reminiscent of the first time I exploded in my pants while watching Nine And A Half Weeks. Except this time I was with another human being. And the problem was, I didn't actually realise when I was in, so to speak.

Basically, as soon as I made contact, I immediately exploded. So just when intercourse had been achieved, it was all over. I wasn't even aware of what had happened. I think the sensation of entering had coincided with the climax. Good timing!

It was awful.

I had waited twenty years for that moment and it was a diabolical anticlimax. Chrissy was very sweet about it, considering. Perhaps she was just relieved I had got over my nervous reluctance to even *try* to have some sex with her. I was too embarrassed and confused to discuss it, that's for sure.

Somehow, my relationship with Chrissy lasted another year and a bit. But it wasn't a good relationship. It was bad. We were totally incompatible. She was a Cancerian. I'm a Leo. They should not be allowed to get together – Leos and Cancerians. She drove me nuts. I don't think I was very nice during that period. I wasn't a good boyfriend. I was always faithful but I just wasn't very nice. It was a completely new experience for me and we were totally wrong for each other but it took me ages to identify that. So I tried to make this poor person into something I wanted her to be. We were thoroughly miserable and I broke it off about a dozen times. These breaks would last a day or two and then we'd patch it up. In the end, when she'd had a gutsful of me and I broke up with her over something trivial I suddenly thought, 'Maybe she is the one because she's putting up with so much bullshit from me!' Just when I was thinking that maybe she was the one for this reason, she told me she couldn't put up with me any more and I got all upset.

If losing my virginity wasn't exactly a moment of glory in my life, getting to appear on a proper radio show most definitely was.

I always used to listen to Dave Barrett on GWR and he was kind of the King of Local Talk Radio at the time. He used to do this late-night phone-in every weekday, and Tuesday night's slot was called Fun On The Phones, with Dave and Hungry Howard. Hungry Howard's real name was Neil Greenslade. He was another local radio DJ who was basically Dave's sidekick on Fun On The Phones.

By this time I'd left M&S and I'd just started at Filton Technical College. And one night I was listening to Fun On The Phones and for a while I'd been thinking of phoning in. I'd been thinking, 'Should I phone in ... shouldn't I? Maybe I should ... Maybe I shouldn't.' I couldn't decide.

Then this one week, Dave Barrett was doing a phone-in on the subject of 'If you could go up in a hot-air balloon with one famous person, and one item – who would you choose and what item would you take?' That was just the kind of topic they dealt with on Fun On The Phones. And it was probably connected to the fact that in Bristol we have an International Balloon Fiesta and Cameron Balloons are here. We're on the international hot-air balloon map in Bristol. And I just thought, 'This is my chance. I can run riot, I can do something funny and surreal and let my imagination run away with me.'

So I was thinking: hot-air balloons ... helium ... I'm going to phone in and talk in a high-pitched voice as if I'm on helium and I'm going to call myself Harry Helium, and I'm going to say I want to go up in a hot-air balloon with Bob Holness, because Blockbusters was huge on TV at the time. And I'll say I want to go up with Bob Holness and some slippers. I wasn't going to do anything horrible to Bob Holness or throw him out of the basket or anything. I was going to be nice to Bob, and have a good time with him. It was going to be nice. That's why I was taking the slippers. Now bear in mind that at this time I was massively into Vic & Bob. They were comedy heroes. From 1990 right up to about 1996, I loved Big Night Out, The Smell Of Reeves & Mortimer, Shooting Stars. So I think Harry Helium was massively influenced by Vic & Bob. It's possibly the only explanation for the way I was thinking.

So anyway I phone in and right from the start I used this high-pitched voice. And I called myself Harry Helium. I didn't use my real name at all. So I was put through to Hungry Howard to vet me to make sure I wasn't going to swear or say something entirely inappropriate.

But I tell Hungry that I'm Harry Helium and he puts me through. So then eventually I hear Dave Barrett say, 'Okay, let's take our next call from ... Harry Helium! Hello, Harry!' And all he hears is this young lad speaking in a high-pitched Bristolian accent, saying, 'Hiya, Dave!' And he asks me who I'd like to go up in a hot-air balloon with and I say, 'Bob Holness, Dave.' And he says, 'Okay, and what would you like to take with you?' And I tell him, still in the high-pitched voice, 'A pair of slippers, Dave.' It was so rubbish! But he kind of laughs. And it seemed to go down quite well. So I proceeded to phone in to Fun On The Phones every Tuesday for the next three or four weeks. Always as Harry Helium. One week my mate Nick at college asked me the next day, 'Did you phone in to the radio last night?' And I told him it was me, and he said he recognised me even though I was using the high-pitched voice. Then after about the fourth week of this, Dave Barrett said to me after I'd done my Harry Helium bit, 'Harry, would you mind staying on the line for a minute?' And they went to commercials. But he spoke to me off air, and asked my real name, and I told him I was Justin and he said, 'I just wanted to say, Justin, that I think you're absolutely brilliant. How about one week you come into the studio as a guest, and we do something together because I think you're really funny.'

This was one of my big dreams, to be on the radio, and suddenly this presenter who I'd been listening to for ages, who was the King of Local Talk Radio, was asking me to go on his show. As a proper guest. A comedy guest. So I said, 'That would be amazing. I would love that, Dave.'

It was probably the best moment of my life so far.

I was thinking, 'This is brilliant. Dave loves me. He's the King of Local Late-night. He's gonna have me in. I'll be brilliant. And someone from GWR is going to be listening, and even if they aren't listening, Dave has the power to tell them how brilliant I am and soon I'll have my own show on GWR and it'll be brilliant. This is the first step to radio stardom.'

Now GWR had two studios, one in Bristol in town and one in Wootton Bassett near Swindon. All the late-night shows came from Wootton Bassett, which was forty-five minutes away. Luckily I had a car – a jade-green Escort Mk 3, so I drove to Wootton Bassett. They hadn't told me what they wanted me to do, so I just presumed I'd do Harry Helium again or maybe another funny character, yet to be invented.

Now I'm not mystical or superstitious but sometimes I do feel that there have been some pretty weird connections between events in my life, so I have to remind you at this point that my favourite show as a kid was Come Dancing. Just bear that in mind.

Anyway, I got to the studio in Wootton Bassett and I was met by Hungry Howard who took me to meet Dave Barrett. So we'd just met … and I was really excited because I've been listening to him for ages and now I was going to be on his show live with him, and I was sitting there with Dave Barrett and his sidekick Hungry Howard. And pretty much the first thing that Dave said to me, after I introduced myself, was that the main theme for the phone-in that night was … ballroom dancing.

I said, 'Great, I love ballroom dancing.' But I couldn't really believe the show was all about one of my very favourite things in the world.

Dave said, 'I was thinking maybe of introducing you as something like the fourteen-times World Ballroom Dancing Champion of somewhere like East Cheam, because East Cheam is a funny-sounding place.'

And then he asked me, 'Is there some kind of character you could do that would fit that idea?'

Now this was about forty minutes before the show was due to start, and he was asking me to make up a new character, and bear in

mind the only character I'd ever created before was Harry Helium.
Then he gave me a piece of paper and a pen and he really sweetly said
to me, 'Do you want to go into a room by yourself, so you can
concentrate and come up with what you're going to say?'

I said, 'No, that's all right, Dave. I'm all right here. I'll just sit here
and have a think.'

I was there on the spot trying to invent a ballroom dancing
character. So I thought, 'Okay, the ballroom dancers on my favourite
show Come Dancing ... what are the stand-out things about them?'
Well, there's the fake tan, that's one of the things, and the sequins
and their outfits and their big smiles, the very toothy, big white smiles
standing out against the fake-tanned skin. I thought 'pearly glow' ...
Pearly Glow, he's quick quick slow. And I decided that's how Dave
Barrett could introduce me – here's Pearly Glow, fourteen-times
ballroom dancing champion of East Cheam, he's quick, quick, slow.

Then I wrote some notes about how maybe he could be friends
with Rosemary Ford, who was the last host of Come Dancing, and so I
told Dave Barrett my idea and he said it's great. Then we went into the
studio and he selects a bed, which those of you who've never worked
on radio might not know is a piece of instrumental music they play
behind a bit of talking. And the really professional DJs make sure the
bed will finish as the talking ends. He found this very kitsch ballroom
dancing piece of music as the bed, and we went on air.

He conducted a two-minute interview with me as Pearly Glow,
and I used a bit of a camp voice and answered all his questions, and
as we finished the interview, the bed ended, and Dave Barrett said,
'Thanks, Pearly Glow, we'll be back after the ads.' Then Dave took off
his cans, looked at me and said, 'That was absolutely brilliant.' So I
had no radio experience in my life, no live improvisation experience
or anything, and Dave was telling me it was brilliant. And Hungry

Howard added, 'That was great,' but he was slightly off about it, and by then I was already thinking, 'I will be offered a job now ... someone will be listening and maybe I'll be offered a sidekick slot, like the next Hungry Howard, I'll be the next Hungry Howard.' It felt like a realistic ambition.

I drove home thinking that the night could not have gone better. Dave asked me to do something, and I did it, and he told me it was brilliant. So I thought, at the very least he'll ask me back next week ...

And he did ask me back the following week. I did Harry Helium again, and then I went back later another three times. I was on for a few consecutive weeks and the third week he said to me and Hungry Howard that the programme controller was listening in, so of course I then thought, 'Well, the programme controller is going to love me.'

Then on that third week of going on the show, Dave Barrett told me GWR was axing Fun On The Phones.

The programme controller decided he didn't like it. And I wouldn't be at all surprised if I was something to do with it. He could have been listening and thinking, 'Who is this young guy who's on Dave's show doing these stupid characters? What is this shit?'

So he axed me and Fun, and Tuesday nights became Your Problems and Dave became an agony uncle. The show went from Fun On The Phones to serious emotional problems. In fact the week after Fun On The Phones ended, the next topic was Abortion. Needless to say, I wasn't invited to take part in the whole abortion debate.

I have to say, though, Dave Barrett made a really nice gesture. He told me I could use an empty studio at the station and use it to try stuff out and record there, and maybe if he liked it, Dave would use some of it on air. But here's what happened: I used that time for a couple of weeks and on my own I tried to write stuff and record it but it didn't work. So I was happy coming up with material on the spot when

Dave asked me to, as Pearly Glow. But when I had to sit down and do it on my own, I couldn't. Well, I did come up with one character – an American newsreader called Bret Posteur, who read these comedy news stories. But it was shit. It didn't work. So I did learn a significant lesson there: I can do stuff on the spot, but when I have to think about it I just can't do it.

And that was the end of my first on-air radio experience. It lasted a few weeks.

CHAPTER 6

WEATHER-GLAZE MY BOTTOM

Great hair, but why am I dressed like an extra from The Sound Of Music?

I do like a hat at a jaunty angle. Actually, that's the last time I wore one.

Perfecting the Starsky & Hutch car bonnet bounce... in a bonnet.

Look how my lovely mum merged me into the yellow and orange colour scheme.

Me admiring my Dad's great facial hair.

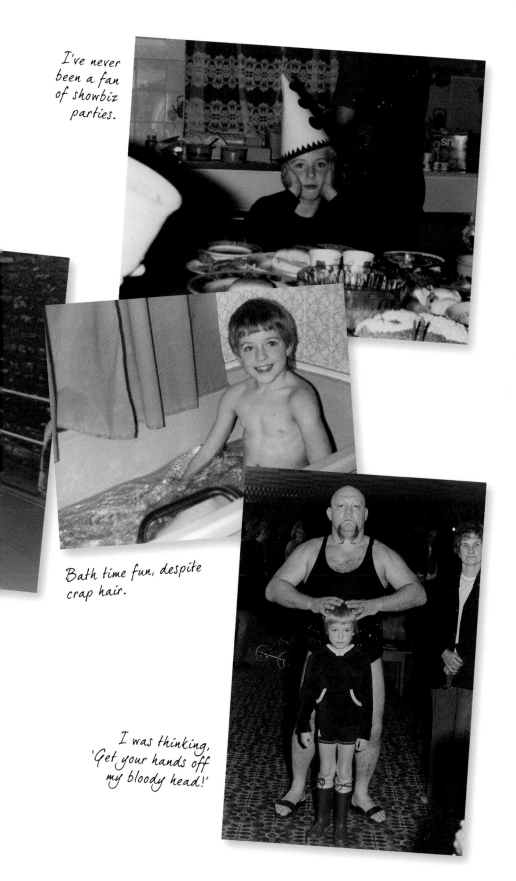

I've never been a fan of showbiz parties.

Bath time fun, despite crap hair.

I was thinking, 'Get your hands off my bloody head!'

I was so excited about the AT-AT walker that I didn't even get dressed.

Very proud of my presents, despite threat of Dad's organ in the background.

Very excited about my first transatlantic flight. And I hadn't wet myself yet.

The Orlando hotel bedroom. TV with Playboy channel on it not shown.

I was literally a star of tomorrow.

That's not my real hair, this is a fancy dress competition.

Having too much fun at
M&S, despite flowers
growing out of my head.

Me and lovely Karen having
a long-hair competition on
holiday in Spain.

'Look, MTV have only gone and given me a bloody TV job!'

Justin Lee-Collins

Luckily by the time I hosted Fat Nation on BBC3 I was actually fat.

I stood in the DIY centre by my pitch, which consisted of a UPVC stand with one white window, one wood-effect window and a door, and I started to hold out brochures and wave them in the direction of the passing shoppers. But I wasn't actually allowed to let them take a brochure. The idea was to reel them in and try to obtain their contact details. So I held out the brochures and they would try to take them, but I would not let them have the brochure. It was all about getting leads. As you can imagine, some of the customers thought it was a bit odd that they couldn't simply take a leaflet.

This was my new part-time job, working as in-store demonstrator for Weatherglaze PLC, based in DIY centres and shopping malls.

So as soon as someone touched the brochure, I had to pull it away. People would say things like, 'Well, let me take it then!' But no, they couldn't take it. Instead I told them to come closer to my pitch and I'd ask, 'Are you considering any windows or doors?'

If they said no, but admitted they might consider it in a few months or years, then I'd say, 'Well, can I have your name and number just for our records.' They'd be reluctant, of course, and they'd ask if they were going to start getting calls from salesmen and stuff. At that point I'd say, 'I can promise you this company does not cold call; they only come to the door if they have an appointment, so if you give me your name and number that looks good for me and you won't be disturbed too much.' They'd still be reluctant and some of them would say, 'Well, if I give you my name and number I will get a phone call, won't I?' In which case I'd then say, 'Yes, in all likelihood you will get a call, but you can just say you're not interested and put the phone down ... ' Which wasn't strictly true because they'd probably get another call. But I became quite good at getting those leads. On a good day, for example, when I was demonstrating in the gallery shopping centre in Bristol, I could get twenty leads from people who stopped by my stall. The average was five leads per day.

At that time I was also studying at my drama course at Filton College and also working part-time at the video shop.

To this day working in the video shop is one of the best jobs I ever had. I was a massive film buff so to get a job in what was effectively a film library was a dream for me. In fact if the video industry wasn't dying – in the old-fashioned sense of people going out to a shop to hire a video or DVD instead of sitting at home and getting them off the internet or whatever – then I'd probably like to own a video shop now. I loved it when someone would bring back a film they'd watched and they had a big smile on their face because they'd loved it and I'd say, 'Wasn't it good?' And they'd go, 'Yeah, it was great – thanks for recommending it.' Stuff like that happened all the time.

Films were my hobby. Going to the cinema, recording films off the telly, hiring films from the video shop. The great perk of working in the video shop was that we had free film hire provided the video was over three months old. But even then occasionally I would throw caution to the wind and take a video that was less than three months old.

As for my college course, I had a great time. At least for the first year.

At Filton College, studying for a BTEC in performing arts, I felt like I had finally found a place to go where I could do what I really wanted. Right from the start I was thinking that I needed to be in a place where I was doing and talking about and thinking about and learning about what I wanted to do: performing. I didn't want to worry about Perspex ends any more. It was a springboard to actually get out there and perform.

I liked the course, and my first tutor, Phil Crane, really liked me. I even managed to get good grades.

I was one of the oldest on the course. Most of the other students were sixteen or seventeen. I was nineteen.

The first thing we ever did at college was a pantomime.

Phil Crane split the class into two groups of ten or eleven and our first assignment was to write and produce and perform our own panto. After a week or so of all of us sitting around trying to come up with a clear idea or vision, I took it upon myself to just go home one night and write it. I wrote it one night, sticking to classic panto guidelines. I took home a copy of Babes In The Wood and based it on that. Next day I took the script to the college and suggested we performed it and the rest of the class agreed.

I called it Babes In Da Hood. It was a street version of the Babes/Robin Hood story. I played one half of the Cheeky Chappies. It was a small part. A girl called Kim who played Robin Hood felt that my street vernacular was pretty shit and she wanted to re-word her lines because they weren't accurate enough. We had a few words about it, but I let her do what she wanted.

Another student in the show was a bloke called Tim. He immediately seemed like my kind of person – funny but not too showy. There were all kinds of people on the course but quite a few of them were middle-class theatrical types. Tim wasn't. He seemed more like me. But we didn't become friends for a while.

In the panto Tim played the baddie, who was called the Boo Man. He had two big scenes, one in each act. And I didn't write his scenes because it was difficult to write for him. We were very similar in that way. We both preferred it if we were in control of our bits and we could let go and fly. We both wanted to fly.

Tim came up to me in the refectory a few months after the panto and told me that he thought if anyone was going to make it on our course it was going to be me and him. Then he suggested that we do something together. I loved the idea. Tim was an only child like me and when we became friends it felt like I'd found a brother. We were very similar. We spoke in a similar way. We had similar accents and we even looked a bit similar. People sometimes thought we were brothers.

As the summer break approached we decided to work together, though we had no idea exactly what we'd do.

Before the end of the year, we had to decide as a class what we would perform for our end-of-year show. We had a choice of Animal Farm or Blood Brothers. None of us really wanted to dress up as animals so we decided to do Blood Brothers and just be human beings.

But Tim left the course at the end of the first year before the production of Blood Brothers. He came to see the show and was quite emotional. It turned out the course just wasn't for him. But after that we became super-close. We had a lot in common. We had the same hopes and ambitions.

As we came towards the end of that year, Phil called me into his office to have a chat. Unlike all my previous experiences of being called into authority figures' offices for a chat, this one was all good. He told me my grades were so good I didn't have to sit the second year if I didn't want to. In his opinion, I'd done well enough to warrant going forward and maybe going to university to do drama or theatre studies or whatever. And he would give me a letter of recommendation. He said I should think about it over the summer, and at the end of this chat, he said to me, 'I think you are very talented. You're twenty years old. You need to think about what you want to do next … '

I couldn't believe it. I'd found something I was good at and which I really enjoyed. Not only that, I had a kind of mentor who was helping me to get to the next step. He told me to think about it over the summer. But it didn't take me long to decide I'd take him up on his offer and get the recommendation from him and hopefully go to Bristol Uni to study drama.

After I talked it over with my mum and dad and told my friends, I called Phil, as he suggested, to tell him, yes, I did want to apply to Bristol University's drama course and yes, I did want a letter of recommendation from him please.

But I couldn't get hold of him. He wouldn't answer the phone. I kept calling him that summer, but to no avail. It was weird. It was as if he had suddenly disappeared. People at the college told me he was taking some time off. Then they said there might have been a death in his family. All kinds of rumours. But it was all very vague. One thing's for sure: I didn't hear from him that entire summer.

I spent most of that summer with my friend Tim. We borrowed a video camera from the audio-visual department, which was run by a lovely guy called Brett Owen. We started making silly films. The first ones were called Out And About, because Tim and I would go and hang out in places and do silly things. One character I played was called Barp Beep Barp, and I basically acted like I was severely disabled with motor neurone disease or something. I joined a party of elderly tourists in Bath and I walked behind them as if I was disabled, all the while saying, 'Barp beep barp.' We also visited the Wallace Store in Bath and I walked around this store going up to people and saying, 'Wwww … allace! Wwww … allace!' Completely random. No point to it.

And we had a Spartacus routine where we'd take it in turns to walk round shops saying, 'I'm Spartacus!' One of us would do the Spartacus routine while the other held the camera. We put all these filmed bits of random idiocy together on a tape and called it Out And About.

We sent Out And About to Hat Trick, a TV production company in London. We got the details from a contacts book. Unbelievably, we did get feedback. A guy called David Young even called me and told me what we did was shit. He told me it was nonsensical. He was right.

We then went to Channel 4 to show them our tape and we pretended to have an appointment with a commissioning editor called Seamus Cassidy. I told the receptionist we had this appointment and she looked through her list and told us she couldn't find any record of our names. I told her, 'Well, he just told us to turn up!'

She immediately rumbled us.

We asked if we could just leave him the tape and she said that was fine. We received a letter telling us our tape wasn't very good a few weeks later.

We tried to write a Spinal Tap-style spoof horror film called The Ram. But we never got further than a barely-thought-out script.

The more we worked on these projects together, the more Tim and I got to know Brett Owen from the college A/V department, because we were borrowing his equipment. He was an interesting character – very mild-mannered but he had a severe stress problem. He was on medication from stress. And he was suffering from male pattern baldness, which was a huge issue for him because he was only in his mid twenties. He was of a nervous disposition, a meek person, but we really liked him because he was essentially a lovely man.

He was just the kind of person I am drawn to. The kind of person I like becoming friends with. Unassuming. Sweet. Not showy-offy people. I hate show-offs and yet I know some people would regard me as one of those.

After a while, Brett told us he made his own homemade films, which were a series of sci-fi/fantasy adventures in a Doctor Who style featuring a character called Mr Smith. Brett played Mr Smith. Unfortunately Brett had a bit of a speech impediment which meant he couldn't say 'Smith' properly. He would say 'Smiff'. He could not pronounce his 't-h' sound properly.

He asked Tim and I to appear in one of his Mr Smith adventures, which we were happy to do. Then Tim and I decided to write our own Mr Smith adventure, which we called Mr Smith Goes Berserk. We shot in and around Bristol and Clevedon.

After that Tim and I decided to create our own short film, which was hugely influenced by Mike Leigh and specifically Nuts In May, which both Tim and I loved.

We called it Those Darn October Days. (You can clearly see the influence of Nuts In May on that title.) It wasn't a particularly good film. We shot it in Brean in my parents' caravan largely. We cast Brett as a man on the verge of a nervous breakdown. Basically he was playing himself, and the film traced his descent into a breakdown. We even called him Brett. In the film, his wife had left him, so his friends, played by Tim and me, decide to try to cheer him up by taking him away to Brean Sands. We were trying for a Ken Loach/Mike Leigh-style naturalism.

We sent this film to various people for feedback, including one of my tutors, who told me that the only person in the film who was any good was Brett. And she was right. He was real because he was basically playing himself.

Brett was a man of routine and structure. A place for everything and everything in its place. That type of philosophy.

One day we were in the A/V suite with Brett and I went too far with him.

Brett would bring in a packed lunch. I've always found the concept of a packed lunch funny. The whole idea of arranging the elements of lunch and packing them in a lunch box amuses me.

So Brett had his lunch box on his desk at work. He left the room. I opened the box and everything was neatly laid out. He had his sandwiches, a piece of fruit, a chocolate bar (maybe it was a Penguin), and in the corner there was a yoghurt. It might have been a Munch Bunch or a Petit Filou or even a Ski.

And I decided to remove the yoghurt and hide it from him as a little joke.

Brett came back into the room, opened his lunch box and he immediately noticed the yoghurt isn't there. He looked everywhere. He didn't think to ask us. Why would he? He's a nice, decent guy. He phoned home and asked his wife Helen if she remembered to pack his yoghurt.

At that point, Tim and I started laughing. I told him that I'd hidden his yoghurt for a joke.

But suddenly it became very clear that I had crossed a line and in a very formal tone he said to me, 'Pease don't touch anything in this office.'

Luckily we got over the hidden yoghurt incident and stayed good friends with Brett.

Autumn arrived and I went back for the second year of the course, full of excitement and anticipation and with the full intention of just starting it and then getting my tutor Phil's approval and help to leave for university to take my drama studies to the next level, as he had suggested.

But he'd gone. Phil Crane had officially gone. He'd left the college for good.

This is the story of my life! I'd found out what I was supposed to be doing, and I was getting incredible encouragement from someone I admired and respected, and then nothing happened – through no fault of my own this time.

It happened with the radio and Dave Barrett. I got on his show and he was starting to consider me to be a regular guest and then Fun On The Phones was axed. Now I had found a mentor who liked me, who told the class of twenty-one students that statistically only one of us would make it in showbusiness as some kind of performer, and he thought that I could be that one. Then he mysteriously left. The axe had fallen on my plans.

So I was back at college for the second year and there were all these new people there. But I had been given the option of not coming back ... and now here I was.

Of course there were problems that second year. The main problem was that the course was totally different to how it was in the first year when Phil taught it and we all liked Phil and the way he worked with us. The new tutors were much more rigid and traditional. And because we were quite resentful that Phil had gone, I suppose we ended up being a bit difficult.

We had one teacher who broke down in tears and blamed my glands!

The other major thing that happened to me during that second year at Filton was that I ended up with glandular fever. But I didn't realise I had it. In fact six weeks went by before it was eventually diagnosed. I had a lump on my neck the size of a golfball. I was feeling completely exhausted and lethargic. I felt like I was underwater. Yet I couldn't sleep either because I felt like shit. I would be awake all night and not fall asleep until morning. So of course I ended up being late for college.

All I could tell them was that I was having trouble sleeping. I didn't go to the doctor because I felt bad about wasting the doctor's time and anyway, I'd always had swollen glands on and off. So for about six weeks I was going in to college about an hour late every day and I would arrive explaining that I had swollen glands.

One of the teachers on the course was Suzie Ross and she found us, as a group, quite difficult to deal with. And we probably were quite difficult because we missed our old tutor.

One day Suzie had enough and exploded with anger. She started naming the names of those students she found difficult and most of the ones she named had been pretty horrible to her, I must admit.

But then she looked at me and said, 'Justin, as for you ... you're always talking about your glands ... every day it's "My glands! My glands!" I'm sick of hearing about your glands. Go to the doctor's!'

She had a complete outburst about me and my bloody glands. All I could say was, 'Yeah, but they are really swollen ... look! Feel them!'

She burst into tears.

But I have to say she was right. And I did think, yeah, it's about time I went to the doctor with my glands.

The doctor saw spots all over my tongue and felt my neck, which had the swollen gland, now the size of a tennis ball, so he took tests for glandular fever. And he told me I had it. He asked how long I'd had the symptoms and when I told him I'd had them for six weeks he was incredulous.

'Oh my god – you have to go home and have total rest and do nothing. Otherwise it can get really serious.'

So I went in to see Suzie and told her I had glandular fever. I felt I needed to tell her after her outburst about my glands. Then I went home and for about three months I did absolutely nothing. I stayed at home and slept as much as I could.

When I went back to college I realised that my fellow students had been working on their audition pieces and I had missed the entire process. So I had to find an audition piece and picked a speech from American writer Eric Bogosian's show Sitcom, which was about an American agent pitching an idea for a sitcom over the phone. I'd read it while I was ill and managed to learn the monologue off by heart.

So I waltzed into class where they were practising their audition pieces and I launched into my Eric Bogosian speech and I have to say it blew them away. They loved it. All the lecturers gave me a glowing report and Suzie 'Your glands! Your glands!' said it was a professional performance and that she would have been happy to see that in a proper theatre. Yet as soon as I finished my monologue I just went straight back home again to bed, because I was still a bit poorly.

Having taken so much time off, I had to have a meeting with Diane Morris who was in charge of the course. She asked me what I wanted to do, because I'd missed a lot of the course, and she gave me the option of sitting out the rest of the year and coming back the following year to retake the second year. I thought, 'Fuck that.' The other option was that I could take the work home and try to catch up there. So I decided to do the work from home and try to pass the course that way.

And in the end I did receive my BTEC diploma in performing arts. It's still the only meaningful qualification I've ever had in my entire life.

At the end of that part of the course, we were supposed to form a production company and create a play for ourselves to direct and perform to the public at the QEH Theatre in Bristol where Hugo Weaving went as a child.

But because of the problems we had in that second year after Phil left, when we were never really told what had happened to him, we realised we probably wouldn't have time to create a proper play of our own. Yet we somehow came up with the idea of doing a little original piece about the National Lottery. We spent ages coming up with a name for it and we came up with lots of terrible names along the way. The decision came down to either Chaos From Cash or Cash Chaos. We decided on Chaos From Cash. But after that we changed our minds and eventually decided to call it Lottery Fever.

My favourite thing about Lottery Fever was that a Welsh girl in our class called Kelly Hurst announced she'd written a song for the show. Tina the tutor thought this was great and said, 'Okay, let's all sit and hear Kelly's song.'

With some trepidation, we sat there in the class and Kelly got up to sing, a cappella.

This was how her song went: 'Lottery! Lottery fever ... Lottery! Lottery fever ... Lottery! Lottery fever ... '

That was Kelly's song. We all sat there watching her sing Lottery Fever. It was amazing.

After I received my only qualification ever, Diane Morris at the college did an incredible thing for me. She sorted out an unconditional offer for me to study drama at York University, where they had one unfilled place in their degree course.

But I decided not to go because I didn't want to be away from home for years. My mates were here in Bristol. My family was here. I didn't want to go away.

Luckily, Diane told me about another option: if I decided to stay in Bristol, I could do their one-day-a-week Higher National Certificate in performing arts back at Filton. That would be perfect for me. And I also started a sign-language course for no particular reason.

I was nearly twenty-one and I wanted to be out there doing it and performing for real and I thought doing a part-time course would give me the chance to carry on learning and also get out there and try to make it in the real world.

This was a huge thing in my life. It was a chance to carry on doing the thing I'd always wanted to do – act and perform. I'd done drama at school and then it had been cancelled. I ended up in retail and hated it. And was hated for being too happy and singing too much. And now I had a qualification in the subject I loved and I was being given the chance to learn more about acting and do it for real.

My parents had played a big part in all this. They had allowed me to give up full-time work and become a student and still live at home. My dad had never not worked in his entire life. To this day he's still working in his mid-seventies. But he and my mum had happily allowed me to become a student and learn about acting.

My dad has always supported me whenever I needed any help. So when he had a heart attack at the age of fifty-nine, it was as if my world was crashing around me.

I was upstairs in bed and it was quite early and suddenly I heard my mum on the phone, audibly in tears, telling someone something awful.

I shouted, 'Mum? What's wrong?'

She put the phone down and came up to tell me dad had had a heart attack and was in the hospital. I remember running from room to room and pacing about and crying and saying to myself, 'What am I going to do without my dad?'

It was awful.

The whole event terrified me. The thought of my dad not being there was awful. I didn't know what I would do without my dad.

Whenever I've been in trouble in my life, if I ever needed anything, my dad has always been there. He's been such a strong influence on my life.

The worst thing about it was not knowing what to do. I just never thought that would happen to my dad. He'd never been a big drinker. He would go out on Saturday nights with his friends but wouldn't drink very much. I can count on one hand the number of times I've seen my dad a bit drunk. He'd never smoked in his life. He was fit and slim and active. He's still working as a tradesman even now.

To make matters worse, my twenty-first birthday was approaching in the next few days and I'd arranged a party with catering and a disco at a venue in Frenchay, just down the road from the hospital where my dad was admitted,

But I told my dad I didn't want to have the party if he wasn't going to be there. He told me very firmly, 'You're *going*. Don't cancel your party.'

There was no way I wasn't going to do what my dad told me. But I didn't have much of a twenty-first. I was worrying about my dad.

Luckily he made a full recovery. A couple of years later he had a triple bypass and our doctor told him we had the worst family history of heart disease he'd ever seen.

But my dad's been fine since then. And as I say, he's still working. He's still the biggest influence on my life.

One other pretty significant thing happened that year.

I got together with Karen, my second real girlfriend. We met properly during Euro 96. Mike, Karen's brother, worked in the video shop with me and he had invited me round to his house to watch the first England game of the European championships.

I was thrilled. Not because I was so excited about watching the football, but because I liked Mike's sister Karen and wanted to get to know her better.

Karen was a girl I had admired and fancied for ages. She was special.

I remember driving along the road on the way back from the video shop and I noticed a girl walking along the right-hand side of me and I literally said to myself, 'Oh my goodness me ... that girl looks amazing.' And I turned my head to see her more clearly and that girl was Karen.

I'd been talking to my mate Tim about her for months. So I coveted her. And when I found out she was single ... I had to do something.

For ages she would come in the video shop, usually on a Sunday, and she would chat to me and ask me about what films were good and we'd have a nice talk for quite a long time. Then maybe an hour or an hour and a half later, she would leave without hiring a film. After that happened a few times, I realised she liked me. In that way.

She was friendly and sexy and very down-to-earth. She was gorgeous in fact. I'd been single for about three months by this time and Karen was single too.

So we watched the football together and got on quite well. Then we went to the cinema together on a proper date. We went to see Robert Redford and Michelle Pfeiffer in Up Close And Personal. He was a newsman, she was a weathergirl and Celine Dion sang the title track. It was pretty average to be honest.

But it was a perfect film for a first date. It was a Hollywood film, it was romantic and you didn't have to think too much, although it would be quite nice to be able to say our first date was some kind of cool film like Buffalo 66 or something. But it wasn't. It was Up Close And Personal.

I drove her home after the film. Handily her parents lived about five minutes away from mine, and in my car at her parents' driveway, I looked at her in this great, tight, leopard-skin top, which showed off her magnificent breasts. And we kissed.

I was nervous, even though I'd been seeing another girl and had sex and everything, but I was only tense because Karen was a girl who I knew I really liked. But the kiss was great.

I didn't feel very nervous any more after that. In fact, after we'd been seeing each other for about three weeks, we went to my parents' caravan in Brean one weekend and that was the first time we made sweet love.

A couple of months after that, we planned a holiday together. I remember her dad was a bit dubious about it because we didn't know each other that well and maybe they weren't sure about me. Fair enough. But we went ahead with our plan and decided to go to Gran Canaria and stay in unnamed accommodation. We went to a travel shop and booked a sixteen-night stay. A bold step considering we'd only known each other for a few months. The travel agent said, 'If you go unnamed it's ninety per cent certain your closest resort will be Puerto Rico.' Puerto Rico was the place I wanted to go because supposedly it wasn't full of 18–30 types.

But the only problem was, in the run-up to this holiday I'd been cast as Bottom in the Filton College class production of A Midsummer Night's Dream, and we'd started rehearsing every Thursday night. So the holiday interrupted the build-up to the big show.

I just had to go on holiday with Karen, though, so I took the script with me because it was a huge part and I was nowhere near being 'off book', as they say in theatrical circles. It means you haven't learned all your lines yet. I struggled with A Midsummer Night's Dream anyway, because it was by Shakespeare and I've always struggled with Shakespeare.

Here's why I struggle with Shakespeare – because I think Shakespeare is shit.

I just hate it. Did he actually exist? Was it Francis Bacon? Was it a collection of writers? I don't care. Obviously he was a very clever man but that doesn't mean I have to like his stuff. And it doesn't mean I have to like being in his plays. And I didn't want to be in any of his plays. If Shakespeare came back now and said, 'I wrote that play because I knew somebody like you would be in it. You're my Bottom,' I still wouldn't want to be in it and I still wouldn't care. I respect it. But I have absolutely no love for it. Nevertheless Chas our teacher had cast me as Bottom and he said, 'The beauty of Shakespeare is that you can interpret it in any way you see fit. There's no set way to perform it. You bring yourself to it and do what you will.' Which is great and I'm sure that's why all the great actors love it. But I didn't.

Then Chas told me to try to be funny as Bottom. So I started doing Bottom like Tommy Cooper and it started to work. Oddly I also had another part in the production – a small role in addition to Bottom. But Bottom was enough for me. It was ridiculous to even consider doing an additional role on top of Bottom. So I ducked out of that and stuck to Bottom. From then on rehearsals went well.

Chas had even told me that I could make it as a professional actor, when I took part in a piece he'd written called Sweat. I don't remember much about the play, other than it was called Sweat and it also starred a guy on the course called Dennis who looked like a fat Bobby Ball. Dennis played a tramp called Horsebottle in Sweat and he was useless. A few years later I saw Dennis one night on Noel's House Party with a chainsaw as some kind of weird variety act. I thought that didn't say much for the state of House Party that Dennis had been booked.

Anyway, knowing that I wasn't yet off book on A Midsummer Night's Dream, my plan was to go on this sixteen-day holiday with my new girlfriend Karen, and have long days on the beach learning my lines. Then when I was due to come back from the break – on Bonfire Night – I knew I'd have a whole week before the performance, during which I could make sure I knew the lines.

Well, Karen and I had a fantastic time on holiday. We were in Puerto Rico on Gran Canaria, it was laid-back, we got on really well and the sun shone every day. It's still one of the best holidays I've ever had. So good in fact, so nice to just lie there next to Karen and relax and chat and make her laugh and get romantic with her, that making sure I knew my Bottom lines wasn't really much of a priority.

So I have to admit that when the holiday finished I still didn't know all my lines, because not only had I not been in the slightest bit focused but they were also bloody difficult to remember because it was bloody Shakespeare.

I did think, 'Shit, I've got one more week to get off book, but it'll be all right … '

Now this is where there's a controversy about the order of events.

When I got back at 2pm for the Thursday rehearsal, I was told that there was to be a full dress rehearsal that very night in front of faculty, invited family members and such. It was supposed to be a full performance. But I didn't know anything about this dress rehearsal/unofficial performance thing. It had been decided in my absence.

Now you could say that I should have been off book by that time anyway, and I wouldn't necessarily argue about that. But I just wasn't ready for this performance because I hadn't been told about it.

As it turned out, not only was I not ready for that surprise first performance of A Midsummer Night's Dream, I also had a clash that night. I'd started doing some stand-up comedy stints, you see (I'll explain how that happened in a bit), and I was booked to do a stand-up show for Live! TV, this cable channel that was based in Canary Wharf.

So I had to get to Canary Wharf to do seven minutes on this TV show.

Chas the drama tutor was saying to me, 'Why haven't you learned your lines for this performance that we're doing at seven o'clock?'

To which I said, 'Never mind that. I have to leave early anyway to get to this gig at Live! TV in London at seven o'clock!'

Then the heavily pierced Ollie Boulter, who was the oldest person on the course by about ten years and used to do poetry slams (open-mic events where anyone could go and drop some rhymes), asked me, 'Where have you got to go?'

I said, 'Canary Wharf.'

He told me, 'Oh yeah, Isle of Dogs – it'll take you two hours.'

Now there's no way that the journey from Bristol to the Isle of Dogs could take two hours, even with a clear run, with no traffic on the streets and a high-performance vehicle. My dad had phoned Live! TV on my behalf and they'd told him to allow three hours for the journey.

It was about two o'clock and the Live! TV show started at seven. So I thought I'd have to leave at about 4pm at the latest, despite what Boulter the poetry slammer had to say.

Chas the tutor, who was a professionally trained actor and briefly made a living as a performer, took me aside outside the classroom and said, 'I think you should go. Go and do your gig. And tonight, I'll be Bottom. But' – and here was the big moment – 'what I'll have to do is put it to the class. I've cut you a lot of slack ... but I'll have to let the rest of the class decide whether you stay on the course or not.'

I immediately said, 'That's fair. You have cut me a lot of slack so I can just leave the class if you want ... '

He replied, 'No, I want this to be fair. I'll go back in there and put it to a vote.'

I thought that was fair of Chas. But there was still no way I was going to be able to take part in the performance because I hadn't known about it, and it clashed with my chance to perform on Live! TV.

There were twenty people on the course. Chas said to them, 'All those in favour of Justin being thrown off the course, show your hands.'

Nineteen of my classmates put their hands up.

Then Chas said, 'Okay, all those in favour of Justin staying on the course, show your hands ... '

One person put his hand up, and that one person, who – albeit reluctantly – supported me in that vote, was a friend of mine called Toby, my only real mate left on the course. But really, even Toby thought I was taking the piss. He just voted for me because he was my friend.

So I'd been voted off the course. More or less unanimously. And bearing in mind the only person who voted for me was a friend, effectively it was unanimous. I still maintain to this day that nobody told me about that dress rehearsal.

But I had been thrown off my drama course and no one ever did get to see my Bottom.

I wasn't bothered about that, of course, mainly because of my Shakespeare hatred. But the disappointing thing about how my stint at college ended was that Chas was another guy who saw something in me and wanted to help me, but he must have felt that I'd let him down. And let him down badly enough to put it to the vote to chuck me off the course. Really, it was absolutely right that I had to go. I probably wasn't committed enough. Even if I'd stayed that week and taken part in A Midsummer Night's Dream as Bottom, I still wouldn't have stayed on the course for a whole year. I just wasn't bothered about getting the certificate that I was supposed to earn at the end of it. Those qualifications made no difference to me whatsoever. And I already had my BTEC.

I was only there because it enabled me to perform and it meant I didn't have to leave Bristol, to leave my comfort zone. I didn't really care about the course.

So I was left with the video shop, Weatherglaze PLC and a course I was doing in sign language. I took the signing course because I'd always been interested in learning a new language. After I'd signed up to the course I was told it took about seven years to learn sign language fluently. I left that course after a couple of months because I found out there was an exam I'd have to take. I didn't want to do an exam at all.

You're probably sensing a pattern here.

CHAPTER 7

THE FRANK CARSON JOKE SCANDAL

'Why do you think you're funny? How are you funny? What have you got that's funny? Why do you think you deserve a slot in my club? Why do you think you've got what it takes?'

I didn't really know what to say to that.

It was my mate Tim's idea. He thought I'd be a good stand-up. It won't have escaped you attentive readers out there that I've already mentioned my Live! TV stand-up booking in the previous chapter. Yes I did. I'm just explaining now how it all came about. And it was all down to Tim. It wasn't something I'd ever really considered. The idea terrified me.

We were working in the video shop and one day Tim just gave me the number of Chris Jacobs, who was a big comedy promoter at the time. Chris was a guy who booked the open-mic slots, in which anyone could have a go at stand-up for five minutes without any pay, at various venues in Bath and Bristol.

I really wasn't sure. I didn't think I had an act. Well, I didn't have an act.

But I thought I might as well call him and see what he said ...

'Tell me how you're funny.' That's what he said.

He was grilling me like this over the phone, essentially interviewing me, to test whether I was good enough for a five-minute, unpaid slot. The way he was talking to me you'd think I was auditioning for Sunday Night At The London Palladium.

In the end he just gave me a five-minute slot in this venue called the Fez Club in Bath.

My mate Tim came to see me and I did a good five minutes of nonsense and silliness. I would say, 'I'm on fire! I'm on fire!' as if I had burst into flames when in fact I hadn't burst into flames. I would ask the lighting guy to dim the house lights and nothing would happen, which I made sure I previously arranged with the lighting guy. Nothing would happen and I'd say, 'Great – thanks!' and I'd carry on as if the lights had been dimmed. Just silly old-school comedy shit. Daft nonsense. Stupid, nonsensical, sub-Vic and Bob material. But I did manage to deliver this stuff well enough for five minutes for it to go down quite well. It was a bit of a stormer if I say so myself.

That night, the night of my first ever stint as a stand-up comedian in front of a proper audience, the compère was an experienced comedian called Noel Brittain and he told me to phone Chris Jacobs the next day and he said, 'Tell Chris that I said you were brilliant.'

So I called Chris Jacobs the next day and he asked me how it went. I told him Noel Brittain's quote about me being brilliant. He laughed but he did promise me another five-minute open-mic slot, this time in Bristol at a club called the Comedy Box which was above a pub called the Bristol Flyer on the Gloucester Road, and it seated about a hundred people. It's been turned into toilets now.

Anyway, I did five minutes there and that went well. So for the next six months I did about one gig every other week in Bristol or Bath and they all went quite well.

I did the Ashton Court Festival – the biggest free festival in Europe. Robert Plant played there one year.

They had a comedy tent and in the summer of '96 I was booked to play at the Comedy Tent, along with Marcus Brigstocke and another local comedian called James Dowdeswell.

My friend Tim who came to most of my gigs, along with my girlfriend Karen, was sitting in the audience and after the gig, which I thought went really well, he told me that he was sitting behind a guy who was laughing his ass off. And at one point this guy turned round to face Tim, with tears rolling down his cheeks, and said, 'The thing is, he just ain't fucking funny ... '

And actually, that kind of sums up me and my stand-up routine in a nutshell.

My material was shit, but there was something about me that was funny. So this guy was in hysterics, whilst brilliantly realising that he was laughing at a comedian with awful material.

In that first six months of my career as a stand-up I did about thirty gigs.

One of them was at the Comedy Café in Rivington Street in east London. They had a new act night and I sat there chatting to a London-based comic and he told me he'd done about 150 gigs in his first six months. That was the difference between London and Bristol. We only had three venues between Bristol and Bath. In London there are literally hundreds of venues.

My first ever London gig was in August '96 at the Cosmic Comedy Club on the Fulham Palace Road. But it was too soon. I should have waited.

It went well but I broke the golden rule: nicked another comedian's joke.

The comic was called Noel James, a very good Welsh comedian, and I would share the bill with him a lot in my local gigs. He was the first comedian that I saw live who really inspired me. He was very surreal, which I loved. He wasn't nonsensical, like me. He was a lovely guy and he was always very nice to me. A lot of the established comedians aren't very nice to the new, open-mic acts, because those new acts are often quite annoying. They're eager and enthusiastic and are after advice. Much to the experienced older comedians' chagrin. They often can't stand the new acts.

Anyway, this one night I was on the bill with him and he told this joke which I thought was genius. I won't tell you what the joke is because it's still his joke and I don't want to write it down here without his permission. I told all my friends this joke and they all loved it.

So a few days later I was in London at the Cosmic Comedy Club, along with Al Murray, the Pub Landlord, and the hosts of the night – a double act called Chris and John.

I did my act, which by then was about ten minutes long. It went well, but there was one minute when my flow got clogged up. Comedians have a set list in their head and as you tell a joke, the next one drops into place mentally and it's ready to go. In that process I had said one stupid line from my act and I was searching for the next stupid thing to say, but it didn't come. I had a mental blank. It must have happened because I was nervous of being on in London for the first time at this big club which had a proper stage. It was a big deal for me. And my girlfriend was in the audience. My mind went blank. I was searching for the next thing, the next 'joke' in my act, and what came out was Noel James's joke. And it brought the house down. It was obviously the best bit of material in my whole act.

After that I performed another few minutes or so and brought my stint to an end, with the audience laughter at Noel James's joke still ringing in my ears.

As I walked off Chris and John, the double act who hosted the night, both gave me a knowing smile. I thought they were smiling as if to say 'Well done, mate' but later on I realised they were smiling because they noticed I'd told Noel James's joke.

I walked off the stage and into Karen's arms and she congratulated me and said how well it went.

I said, 'Yes, it did go well, but did you realise I did Noel James's joke?'

Karen nodded. 'Yes you did.'

I just said, 'That was naughty.'

I knew the rules. Well, I knew THE rule. The one major rule of stand-up comedy: you do not steal other comedians' material.

But they do, of course. It happens all the time. Some comedians make a living out of stealing other comedians' jokes.

I had stolen a joke. I was only a young open-mic act who'd made a stupid mistake. But I still knew it was a big no-no.

A few days went by and I soon forgot about stealing Noel's joke.

Then I was out with Karen one night and when I got home my dad told me that I'd been left a phone message from a comedian called Noel James. I was excited because I liked him and admired him and was thrilled that a top comedian was calling me and I thought maybe he'd decided to book me or something.

Then it clicked. 'No,' I thought, 'he's called me because he's heard that I stole his fucking joke.'

Clearly someone at that gig realised that I had told his joke and they had then told him.

I called him immediately.

I said, 'Hi, Noel, how are you doing?'

He said, 'Hey, Justin. Did you do a gig at the Cosmic Comedy Club last week?' Straight in there. Of course I knew which way the conversation was going.

So I said, 'Yes, I did. And I'm so sorry, Noel. I did one of your jokes ... '

I don't think he was expecting me to come out with it like that. I didn't even give him the chance to accuse me, which I hoped would defuse his anger. And maybe it did. I think it threw him.

He said, 'Yeah, I know.' I felt awful. Then he explained, 'I know the compères Chris and John and they told me.'

I said, 'I feel really bad. I'm so sorry ... '

Then he told me how Chris and John had told him some open-mic comic from Bristol had stolen one of his best jokes. And he asked them, 'Was it the one about Frank Carson?'

Of course it *was* the one about Frank Carson.

But they said to him, 'Yes, that was one of them ... '

So, weirdly, they'd implied that I'd done some more of his material. But actually, what had happened was that I think I'd been so inspired by him, having seen his act a few times, that my delivery had become like his delivery. He had this fantastically laid-back approach. And obviously I had delivered my routine in his style. It was pretty much like a Noel James tribute act. But I had only actually stolen one of his jokes. And I knew it was wrong.

But when he told me he thought I had used his other jokes, we tried to work out which other jokes I might have stolen. We both had heart bypass jokes, for example. But in the end we realised I'd only actually stolen the Frank Carson joke. It wasn't difficult for him to work out that I would have stolen that joke because as soon as I saw him tell it, I told him afterwards how much I loved the Frank Carson joke.

And it *is* a great joke.

*

Generally at that point in my stand-up career, when I was twenty-one years old, I was enjoying it. I would only do five or ten minutes. Five or ten minutes of Noel James's act! I was getting a decent little reputation – getting written up nicely in Venue magazine, the local listings guide for Bristol and Bath. It was a good outlet for me. Even though I never wanted to be a stand-up comedian, it was a way for me to get noticed. That's the only reason I did it. Honestly, I was totally ambivalent about being a comedian. I had no ambition to be the next Billy Connolly. I loved Billy Connolly but when I watched him I had no desire to be him. Quite the opposite. I knew I couldn't ever be as good as him.

So when I became a regular on the stand-up circuit, I just hoped someone would come along to see me perform and maybe offer me a part in a sitcom or give me my own TV show. That's why I was doing it.

After about six months I had performed all the local venues and tried a few out in London.

The following year, I entered the BBC New Comedy Awards.

Chris Jacobs called me in early '97 and asked if I was going to enter the BBC New Comedy Awards this year. I told him I hadn't even thought about it and asked if I was eligible because it was only for non-professional comedians. So if I was being paid regularly to perform then I couldn't take part. As it was, I was just starting to get beer money for stand-up shows but in general I was still doing unpaid, open-mic slots.

Well, I'd been paid thirty quid beer money for one gig in Midsomer Norton I'd done in support of a comedian called Dave Thompson, who became Tinky Winky in Teletubbies. Until he got sacked. Dave later became a great friend of mine and was my first real friend on the comedy scene.

Anyway, Chris told me I was definitely eligible and he said I should enter. The regional final for the South West was at the Watershed and so I took Chris's advice and sent a tape to the organisers, which you had to do, then there was an initial gig for the judges, which was at the Bristol Flyer and they would decide if you were good enough to go on to the regional final.

I did my seven minutes in front of the judges and it seemed to go well and there was another local comedian, this really tall, lanky chap, who was also trying out for the regional BBC New Comedy Awards final, and he also did very well. I'd never seen him before on the local scene.

His name was Stephen Merchant. And he was really good.

After that gig I got through to the South West regional final and there were eight of us – including James Dowdeswell, who I think was in Extras, Mike Tombs, Stephen Merchant, and an Irish comedian called Gareth Hughes.

I was on last but one and I had a really good gig. I had a stormer. When all of us had performed I actually thought, 'I've won that.' In my mind I was the best.

Marcus Brigstocke, who had won the national award the previous year, performed a twenty-minute set while the judges made their deliberations. I stood next to Gareth Hughes waiting for a musical comedian called Richard Norton, who was the compère, to announce the verdict. But Chris Jacobs couldn't wait for the official announcement and he ran over to Gareth to tell him he'd won. He said, 'It's you!'

I thought, 'Really? Gareth's won?' I liked Gareth. He was a nice guy, but I was surprised. I thought maybe he'd got it wrong.

But seconds later, Richard Norton made the official announcement: 'So the winner of the South West regional BBC Comedy Award final, and going on to the national final in Edinburgh later this year is ... Gareth Hughes!'

So it was Gareth after all. He seemed quite taken aback himself. I thought I was robbed!

Later, Richard Norton took me aside and told me he thought I was going to win it. And one of the judges had possibly disagreed with the decision and told me there was a very strong chance I would go through to the final as an overall runner-up. After that I had a conversation with Stephen Merchant when we were commiserating with each other and he told me that one of the judges had told him there was a very good chance that he would go through to the final as an overall runner-up!

A couple of months later I got a call from one of the producers of the BBC New Comedy Awards telling me that I had got through as an overall runner-up to the final in Edinburgh.

So off I went to Edinburgh that August.

Among the finalists were Gareth Hughes, Neil Fitzmaurice (who was the other overall runner-up and played Ray Von in Phoenix Nights and was at that time known by his stage name Neil Anthony), Paul Foot, Deirdre O'Hare and Peter Kay.

The BBC put us up in two flats. Four of us in each flat. I stayed with Gareth, Deirdre and Peter Kay, who brought his girlfriend Susan.

I only spent one night in that flat, though, because my girlfriend Karen came up with three friends of ours and they booked a flat to stay in so I spent three nights staying there.

I met Peter Kay on the second day I was there. We were sitting in the kitchen and Peter walked in semi-naked. He was just wearing boxers, with his belly hanging out. He introduced himself to me and Gareth. It turned out Peter had entered Channel 4's competition called So You Think You're Funny and he'd performed at that the previous night. And he'd won it. There were three rival competitions for new young comedians: the BBC one, which I was in, the Channel 4 one, which Peter won the previous evening, and a Daily Telegraph one too.

Later that day we all had to meet to shoot the titles sequence for the show (because each year the BBC filmed the final and put it on TV).

As we gathered, Paul Foot got out of a black cab with his agent, who was also Peter Kay's agent, and Paul was carrying this big prop cheque. And that was his prize as the winner of the Daily Telegraph New Comedian Award.

Gareth and I were both thinking the same thing: what chance have we got against these guys who have got an agent and have already won the other two competitions?!

From that point on I assumed I wasn't in the running for the competition at all.

The final was held in the Pleasance Theatre and we had to go to a rehearsal in the afternoon. The host was Ardal O'Hanlon and the act who was going to perform while the judges deliberated was comedy magician Paul Zenon. When Paul was rehearsing his act, Peter Kay kept heckling him.

In fact, I don't think Peter Kay stopped talking that entire day.

But I did realise that Peter Kay had something. He was funny.

Zenon got annoyed and said, 'Bloody hell, I'm being heckled at rehearsal!' He was laughing, though, because it was funny. It was funny that he was being heckled during his rehearsal by some unknown young comic called Peter Kay.

When we got to the venue we were told that our names were drawn out of a hat to determine the running order. So this crucial event was apparently conducted behind our backs. Which was a bit odd. You see, for a stand-up comedian, the order in which you go on stage is crucial.

And I was told that my name had been drawn out of this hat first. I had to go on stage first. Which is, beyond all doubt, the worst position to be in.

The judges that night were Graham Norton, Barry Cryer, Rhona Cameron and Graham's agent Melanie Rockliffe.

Before the show started I went to go to the toilet and I could hear what sounded like retching coming from the cubicle. Turned out it was Gareth being sick. I asked him if he was all right and he told me, 'Yeah, I'm just having my usual pre-gig puke. I do it all the time.'

I later learnt that it's not unusual for performers to be sick before they go on. I've never been that bad. I get nervous but I've never had to vomit.

So I went on first and I didn't have a great gig. I started quite well but then I soon petered out. I immediately knew I wasn't in the running.

Peter Kay went on fourth, just before the interval, which is a good position to be on in the running order, because if you're good then the audience is talking about you in the interval and you've made a big impression. The other good position to have is the penultimate act because you make it difficult for the final act who has to close the show. So penultimate and last before the interval are the food slots. And Paul Foot had one of those slots and Peter Kay had the other.

I have to say they were both really good. Foot and Kay were great, but there was a general feeling that Peter Kay was the best by far out of the two. He tore the roof off the place. He went down a storm. He brought the house down. All those clichés.

When it came to the announcement of the winner, they named the runners-up first. The second runner-up was Neil Anthony.

Now even though I didn't think I had a very good gig, I did for some reason manage to convince myself that I stood an outside chance of getting one of the runners-up slots. I think the reason was because I knew that Gareth had won our regional heat by going on stage first and bearing that in mind he did really well. He had the added pressure of going on first and I think he got some credit for that, quite rightly. So I thought maybe the fact that I had to go on stage first might work in my favour.

Then they announced the first runner-up: Peter Kay.

We were stunned. Everyone was stunned.

And the winner was ... Paul Foot.

I looked at Paul in the wings and he was saying, 'Ooh, is it me? Is it really me?' in his funny, fey way, as if he was still doing his act.

Peter Kay looked at him and said, 'Yeah, it's you ... Get on, you fucking –' and he just stopped himself from saying anything else. He did seem rather aggrieved, did Peter. And no one could really have blamed him.

But Barry Cryer thought Paul Foot was a genius. Maybe that's why he won.

Of course the whole idea of comedians competing and being judged against each other is completely ridiculous. It's not right!

But in my opinion if you're going to have such a competition then you should judge it on how they go down with the audience. And Peter Kay clearly got the best reaction from the crowd. Paul Foot might have been the cleverest. If the award was the BBC New Clever Comedian Award then yes, maybe he should have won that night. But Peter Kay was the clear winner as far as the audience was concerned.

I wasn't even in the running.

Here's a postscript to that night, the final of the BBC New Comedy Awards.

My friend Richard Drew, who is a journalist, was one of the gang who came to see me that night in Edinburgh.

And Richard found a running order on a piece of paper on the floor. And on the running order, I was the fourth act, the last act before the interval. The best slot.

I don't know who compiled that running order but it went by the wayside and another running order was used.

So ask yourself, what might have happened?

We were told, remember, that our names were drawn out of a hat. So did they draw the names out of a hat, and then realise they'd made some kind of mistake and started again?

Now none of this really matters one bit, especially since the whole event had worked for me in the sense that it was being televised so there was a chance that someone would see me on TV being fairly funny, which was the whole point of putting myself through it in the first place.

But I don't even think there ever was a hat. That's what I think. I think this hat didn't ever exist. I don't think our names ever went into this mythical hat. I don't think that ever happened.

Don't get me wrong – it was a good experience for me, and I met Peter Kay who I thought was hilarious and deserved to win, but there was definitely something mysterious about that whole drawing-names-out-of-a-hat affair!

For me the best thing about the whole BBC New Comedy Awards experience was that it was shown on the BBC about a month later, because one day when I was staying at Karen's place my mum phoned me to tell me that I'd had a call from someone at MTV who'd seen me on that show and wanted to speak to me about doing an audition for one of their MTV shows.

Well, this was like a dream.

This was what I'd always wanted. I wanted to be recognised and to get something from all this stand-up nonsense that I'd been doing for eighteen months.

So I called MTV back and they wanted me to go to London and audition for this show called MTV Hot which they were in the process of revamping to give each show on each weeknight to a different presenter and they wanted the presenters to make the shows their own.

And they were interested in me becoming one of these presenters. They were asking me if I wanted to audition to get my own TV show.

I couldn't believe it.

But there was one problem. The day they wanted me to go down to London to audition clashed with some work I'd already committed to.

You see, I'd been doing work as an extra.

It all started about a couple of years earlier when I was still at Filton College and I started to buy The Stage every week, after I heard the more theatrical students talking about it. I also heard them mention this thing called The Contacts Book, 'the essential handbook for the entertainments industry'. I realised that some of the students were doing extras work, which seemed like an easy way to make money in my spare time. So I looked up local agencies in Bristol and surrounds. I called the Riviera Artistes based in Torquay, and the Edward Wyman agency based in Newport in Gwent. I spoke to Ed's wife Jean, who was lovely on the phone to me.

All I had to do was send a 10x8 photo of myself. Unfortunately the only photo I had showed me with a really spotty face. I had a sudden attack of acne when I was eighteen. I had to take ointments and everything. So the photo of me that this extras agency had on file showed me with a very spotty face.

I even got a call one day from the agency asking if I could do a newspaper photo casebook shoot about a guy with acne. They thought I was perfect for it! I was mortified. They wanted me to play a man whose acne was so bad he was almost suicidal. I said no quicker than any other job I've turned down before or since.

But the Ted Wyman agency got me my first ever extras work on Casualty. Jean phoned and asked if I was available for a couple of days to appear in a big football hooliganism story and she also asked if I could rustle up some other youngsters to take part. So I asked Tim and two other friends if they wanted to take part, and we all did this scene.

The basic rate at that time (1994) was about sixty-five quid a day for background artist work.

The only problem was that the money always took weeks and weeks to come through. It was difficult to work not knowing when you were going to get the money. But some people do earn a living out of it.

Over a three-year period I must have been on seventeen or eighteen episodes of Casualty. Because Casualty was the big BBC show and was filmed at their Bristol studio.

This latest Casualty gig was going to be my best yet because the episode was all about a huge car crash on a motorway. It was going to take three nights to film at this RAF base in Lyneham and because the filming would be taking place late at night, I was going to be paid a special unsocial hours rate. Which was significant for me because I needed the money.

It was a huge production. They had all these cars that had supposedly been in this big pile-up and I was one of the victims and I had a gash on my head. There were people out of their cars looking at this big smash and I was supposed to be one of the crash victims who had got out of his car and was running around in distress.

Now the thing about extras work – or background artist work – is that it is by and large intolerably dull and boring. You mainly just sit around and wait for hours on end – sometimes twelve or thirteen hours – talking nonsense with your fellow background artists. So of course I used to try to relieve the boredom by having a laugh. By doing something silly. By doing little things to amuse myself.

That night on Casualty I was told to run around like someone in terrible pain, while screaming in general.

So sure enough, I ran around, I screamed and I decided to yell, 'We're dying! We're dying! Help us!'

And then I added my own improvisation.

I started screaming, 'Mr Grimsdale! Mr Grimsdale!'

Just then I turned around and there's this chaotic, mad scene – there are all these cars on fire and all these people screaming and yelling and I can see all the people who have supposedly just got out of their cars and they're looking at us and just then I saw this one woman staring at me. I established eye contact with this one other actor, and I yelled at her.

At that moment for some reason I decided to yell, 'Help us … help us … we're Christians!'

No one was telling me to stop, by the way. No one from the crew seemed to notice.

Eventually they did cut, and as we stopped, I noticed the woman I'd yelled at was laughing quietly to herself.

Months later I watched that show go out on the Saturday night on BBC1 and part of me wondered whether, because there was so much going on, my little bit about Mr Grimsdale or being Christians might have made it through on the soundtrack. As it was, you could actually hear me yelling, 'We're dying, we're dying!'

But you couldn't hear me adding, 'Mr Grimsdale! Mr Grimsdale!' or 'Help us, we're Christians!'

Which was a shame.

In another Casualty episode I was just playing a random bloke who was in A&E. At this time I had really long hair which I wore in a ponytail. I'd been asked to stand next to the receptionist and pretend to be in conversation with her about my ailment, whatever it was supposed to be. So I decided to do something else just to make myself laugh, and I took a pencil which was on the desk in front of me and I placed it in the front of my hair. So I was standing there chatting to the receptionist and sticking out the front of my hair was this pencil.

And that shot was used. If you happened to be watching Casualty that night you could see this bloke in the background with a pencil sticking out the front of his hair.

But the biggest one I ever did was when I was in this episode about football riots and I played a football hooligan. I looked at someone from the opposing team, and I said, 'Oi you – the twat in the hat!'

And again, that went out. You could clearly hear me saying that.

I also took this role in a children's TV drama called Aquila, which was about two kids who'd found a crashed UFO. I was taking part in this scene as one of a big group of archaeologists on a dig, and I had to hold a trowel. I was in this scene with a mate of mine called Simon Lewis who I did a lot of this extras work with. In this scene something had been discovered on this dig. We were all surrounding this mysterious object, this relic, which had a cloth over it. And the climax of this scene is the cloth being removed from this relic and we were all supposed to stare at the object as the cloth is removed and be surprised and start nudging each other and everything.

Now none of us knew what the object would be. And when the cloth was removed, we all at the same time and for the first time saw that it was ... a boomerang.

A boomerang.

Upon seeing this boomerang, words tumbled out of my mouth and I found myself saying, in my own version of the Aussie accent: 'Fair dinkum tucker, mate. Put another couple of shrimps on the bloody bar-bie!'

There was a pause. The director, who was about twenty yards away, yells, 'Cut!' And then he says, in a rather posh accent, 'Erm ... whoever is talking about putting another shrimp on the barbecue, please stop, because we are picking that up ... '

That was the kind of thing I got up to as a background artist.

So I'd already filmed one night on my last ever Casualty in the big car crash scene when I was asked to do this MTV audition.

I called my extras casting agency and told them someone from MTV wanted to audition me for this MTV Hot show the following night but I had already been booked to be an extra on Casualty that very same night.

My extras casting agent was lovely, though. She told me not to worry, that she would find someone else to fill my place and sort it all out and that obviously I had to take this opportunity to audition for my own show.

That night after filming my first stint on the Casualty car crash scene, I drove down to London.

I had no agent. I was doing unpaid comedy gigs. I did the audition and it seemed to go well but I only thought it went well because I managed to make the crew laugh.

I'd been asked to prepare little bits of chat or comedy that would go in between the music videos. So I prepared five or six bits of nonsense. The crew laughed. I felt good about it. I drive back to Bristol from Camden thinking it had gone okay. I even started to think that maybe they would offer me the job.

But I didn't hear from them for ages. I had no agent to hurry them up or check with them. And I didn't want to do it myself because I thought it would be weird and unprofessional.

A good month went by and I didn't hear a thing. So I assumed that was it. I assumed it wasn't going to happen.

Then in November, out of the blue, I got a call from MTV. It was a lady called Christine and she told me she was the one who first saw me on the BBC broadcast of the New Comedy Awards. She told me they liked me and that they would like to offer me my own show – and that they would like me to host the Friday evening show. I thought that was great. To me, if there's a show on every weekday, then the Friday one is the best of them to get. The last one of the week. The one before the weekend.

Then she told me about the money.

'The thing is, Justin,' she said. 'The thing is, we can offer you £150 per show. And what could happen is that you go away and think that's not enough and then you come back and tell me you think £150 is not enough and then I tell you we can give you £200 per show. And that really is all we can afford to give you. So we can go through that procedure or we can just go straight to the part where I offer you £200 per show and you accept it. Because that's all we can pay you.'

That's what I call a good negotiator.

Now this is the time when I'm earning money from the video shop, the extras work and the in-store demonstrating. But between them I'm not earning anything near £200 per week.

So I was twenty-three years old and I was being offered £200 a week to have my own show on TV.

Of course I said yes.

(Once I'd been offered the show, and the money, I did realise that I needed an agent, so I asked my mate Dave Thompson from the Teletubbies if he could recommend anybody and he said I should try his agent Duncan, which I did. And luckily Duncan remembered me from the BBC New Comedy Awards show and agreed to represent me. The first thing he did for me was to raise my fee for my MTV show to £250. Duncan was my agent for the next eleven years. A few months after I signed with Duncan I was having a drink with him in Camden after my show and he told me he'd just signed two new artists. One of them was a guy I knew – Stephen Merchant, who I'd met at the regional final of the New Comedy Awards. He told me I wouldn't have heard of the other guy – he was a local radio DJ, who was quite old, thirty-seven years old, in fact. I thought, 'Why on earth has my agent signed a thirty-seven-year-old local radio DJ?' But Duncan said there was something special about this 37-year-old radio DJ. He was called Ricky Gervais. (It was true – I hadn't heard of him.)

I'd gone from doing my first open-mic show in March 1996 to getting my own TV show in November 1997.

I thought it was absolutely brilliant.

So my plan to get myself noticed had worked.

(I later found out that among the other people who auditioned that night for the same show was Sacha Baron Cohen. But he didn't get the gig.)

But it was too soon. I wasn't ready for it. I didn't know what I was doing.

I didn't think that at the time. At the time I thought it was exactly the right time.

CHAPTER 8

IN A SLEEPING BAG WITH KYLIE

I asked one of the crew guys to roll up his trousers and I crouched down and sang Rod Stewart's Hot Legs with my head peeking out between this guy's big hairy legs. That was my first link on MTV Hot.

My job on the show was to introduce new music videos. The other presenters who hosted the other nights were Richard Blackwood, Sara Cox, a stand-up called Ben Norris, and comedians Brendan Burns and Ed Byrne did their show together as a double act.

My first show went well.

I also put in some werewolf fangs and said 'I'm a werewolf!' after one video and then I ran around the set and threw myself into one of the walls of the set and fell to the floor.

I just did bits of nonsense and slapstick between the videos. In my own little way I was trying to turn it into my own sketch show.

After that first show I was sitting at home in the lounge at my mum and dad's in my dressing gown and I got a call from the bloke at MTV and he asked me what I was doing in the next week. I told him I wasn't doing anything, aside from the next show on the following Friday. He told me they would fly me out to LA the next morning to interview a new British band called Catch on the set of their new video for a special one-off show.

I was like, 'Fuck! This is brilliant!'

I'd been there a week. It was my first job on TV. And I was now being given the chance to go to LA to interview this band. So of course I said yes and the next thing I knew I was flown first class to Los Angeles and when we got to the airport in LA there was a limo for us. And this man called Anthony was our driver.

Just a year and a half previously I had performed my first stand-up gig.

Now I was being driven in a limo down Sunset Boulevard to the Argyll Hotel. There was a woman in the car with blonde fuzzy hair and she didn't speak to me the entire time we drove to the hotel. She was doing some kind of PR job for another music channel. I don't remember her name or who she was but she didn't even give me the time of day. She hated me.

But she couldn't ruin the moment.

I sat there thinking, 'This is amazing.'

I was in LA about to interview a band. A band I'd never heard of.

The interview took place on the set of the video for their single called Dive In.

It went: 'Still waters run deep ... so dive in, dive in ... '

Their first single was called Bingo. They were signed to Virgin and they'd spent a million pounds on them apparently. They were going to be the next big thing. They had a very thin, malnourished-looking lead singer and two other very thin-looking indie guys. There were only three of them; they didn't have a drummer. The song Bingo sounded like it was actually about bingo. 'And then I discovered bingo!' went the chorus. It was a minor hit in the chart.

There was a guy in the band called Ben who I spoke to off camera and he seemed embarrassed to be there. I asked him how old he was and he said, 'I'm twenty but keep it to yourself because as far as the band are concerned I'm eighteen.' I thought, 'Wow – twenty isn't young enough for this group – he has to pretend to be eighteen.'

After we shot my interview with Catch we had a couple more nights in the Argyll Hotel which was wonderful and then we came back after four days in LA. I loved it.

After my second show went out on MTV, my second episode of MTV Hot, I was told it was the second most popular show on MTV that week and it got about 30,000 viewers. Not many, I admit. But it was the second highest figure of any show that week.

I thought it was all going really well.

Then it went a bit quiet and I just got used to doing my weekly show every Friday.

But I thought I was doing well enough to give up my regular jobs. I went in to see Pete at the video shop and told him I was leaving after four years. I called Stefon the area rep of the double-glazing firm and told him I was leaving them too. And I gave up the extras work.

I was now a TV presenter.

The other thing I really wanted to give up was the stand-up comedy. But I couldn't yet because basically my week was now going to London on a Friday to do this MTV show then doing not much else for the rest of the week at home in Bristol with my parents, and then getting ready to go back up to London to do the show.

I was also starting to wonder why the people at MTV weren't asking me to do more things for them. When were they going to ask me to do more stuff? When was that going to happen?

But that didn't happen.

But they did tell me they wanted me to start interviewing people on my show. They were going to ask bands and singers on my show so I could chat to them between the music videos.

The first person they booked for me to chat to was Kylie Minogue. So the first celebrity interview I ever conducted was with Kylie. She came on my show in early '98 when she was promoting her indie Kylie album called Kylie Minogue (it was originally called Impossible Princess but they renamed it after the death of Princess Diana).

I was incredibly nervous for the whole week leading up to that Friday. Kylie was a huge star and I'd never interviewed any big star on TV before.

I decided I was going to try to conduct the interview in a sleeping bag. One of the silly things I did on the show every week was me pretending to be a contortionist. Every week I would contort my body into a tiny space. And then I'd freak out and say, 'Get me out! I'm claustrophobic!' (And I really am quite claustrophobic so there was a truth to the comedy!)

So I thought I'd get Kylie to do this silly bit with me where the two of us contort our bodies into a one-man sleeping bag.

I brought a sleeping bag from home on the train with me to London. I always brought my own props with me.

When I got her in the sleeping bag I said to her, 'Kylie, can I just take this opportunity to tell you I love you and I've always loved you.' And then we'd freak out and I'd yell, 'I'm claustrophobic!'

I also had an assistant I called Mr Greenslade – a mute sidekick in a Mung mask which made him look a bit like Freddy Krueger.

When I had Kylie on the floor with me, Mr Greenslade came on with a Jason Donovan album for her to sign. And Kylie went along with it and said, 'Mr Greenslade, what are you doing?'

I thought it went really well with Kylie. I loved her and she was incredibly nice to me. I asked her to sign my diary and she was hovering with her pen over the page and she was saying, 'Ooh, what shall I put?'

So I thought about the two of us in the sleeping bag and I suggested she should write, 'Thanks for a great time in the sack,' and so she wrote, 'Thanks for a great time in the sack, love Kylie.'

And I completely fell in love with her. She was adorable.

Here's the best thing about it, though.

About a week later I was introduced to this MTV bigwig called Dave and he told me that after I interviewed Kylie, he was at some kind of showbiz do and he met her there and she asked him, 'Who was that guy whose show I was on? He was absolutely brilliant.'

Fast forward to 2008 and Alan Carr and I are asked to present a Woman of the Year award to Kylie at the Glamour Awards.

I hadn't seen her since that first interview with her ten years previously. But after we handed over her award, I hugged her and I whispered in her ear, 'Do you remember getting in my sleeping bag years ago at MTV?'

She looked at me and thought about it for a second and she said, 'Yes!'

Now I don't know if she really did remember me from that first ever interview but I like to think she did. I'm saying she did. Let's say she remembered, despite the hundreds, thousands of interviews she must have done down the years. But how many of them have been conducted in a one-man sleeping bag?

The second celebrity interview I conducted the following week was with pop star Louise.

Then after that it went downhill.

The producers started to bring new indie bands on to the show. I had Symposium. Addict. Strangelove. All these bands with one-word names that were tipped to be the Next Big Thing came on my show. But they all pretty much went nowhere.

When Symposium came on I got one of them to hit me with a French stick for a comedy bit. I told them to show no mercy. This member of Symposium took me at my word and beat me mercilessly about the head with this French stick. Unfortunately it was quite stale and hard and the French stick had cut my eye open. I was bleeding profusely.

The poor bloke from Symposium was mortified and was apologising. But I told him, 'It's all right. Don't worry. It's not your fault. Everyone knows bread cuts are the worst.'

Shortly after that bread stick incident I stopped doing interviews on the show.

That July, after I'd recorded my latest Friday night show, one of the MTV executives called Diane came to see me for a chat. I was wearing a shower cap on my head. We'd used it on another silly bit we'd done. Diane from MTV asked me if we could go and have a private chat.

She took me aside, with me wearing this shower cap, and she was holding this bottle of vodka. She told me there was some good news and some bad news and asked which news I wanted to hear first.

I said, 'Well, tell me the good news. It's always best to hear good news first I think.'

She said, 'Well, the good news is that the show has got a new sponsor. We've replaced the old sponsor Wella Shockwaves with Smirnoff vodka. They're our new sponsor!' And she handed me the bottle of Smirnoff. Not that I really liked vodka very much.

I thought, 'Well, if this is the good news, that we've got a new sponsor, then the bad news isn't going to be that bad.'

She continued, 'So the bad news is … they don't want you to do the show.'

So I was sitting there with a bottle of vodka from the new sponsors who didn't want me to carry on hosting the show.

I think at that point she could see that maybe this good news/bad news tactic hadn't worked so well.

I wasn't looking too thrilled to have a bottle of vodka but no show.

So she explained quite nicely that the new sponsor was financing the show to such an extent that they needed to make sure they were going to get good ratings, and by that time the highest-rated night of the week of MTV Hot by far was the one hosted by Sara Cox. She was the only properly famous host among us.

Cox's shows got 30,000 viewers. My show got about 15,000 viewers and all the other shows got about 7000. But they decided to strip Sara Cox across the week, in a show co-hosted by Richard Blackwood.

So that was it. I did one more week and then I was gone. I'd been dumped by MTV after eight months.

It took me four years to get over it.

I did get another TV job soon after MTV ditched me, though. Two weeks later, in fact. It was a show called Pirate TV being made for the ITV network about extreme sports to be shown late at night. Sponsored by Wilkinson Sword. They wanted two Wayne's World type of characters. In fact they had names for these characters – Fab St Claire and Tony Entwhistle.

My agent called me up and told me that a production company was looking for a show to be hosted by two presenters who were friends in real life. They wanted two people who had a rapport already so there would be a chemistry on screen.

They already had one guy in mind, though, and so they asked me to audition with this guy they'd already shown an interest in.

I thought I might as well go for it.

So I met this guy called Rob the Gob. That wasn't his real name.

And we were supposed to try to convince the production people that we were mates.

There were three people in the room when we were auditioning. I had no great illusion about this audition. I was really just doing it as a favour to my agent, and to this guy Rob the Gob. So I was very relaxed about it. We sat down in front of a desk and on the other side were three producers or execs or whatever.

In the audition we pretended to review new equipment in a product-test style – snowboards and energy bars and stuff like that. A couple of times while we were doing these test reviews they asked Rob to calm down a little bit. He was clearly getting a bit nervous.

After the audition they took me aside on my own and told me they wanted me to be their Fab St Claire in the show, but they weren't going to go with Rob. I never saw him again.

A while later the executive producer told me they'd found the right Tony Entwhistle to host the show with me and I travelled to London to meet him. He was an Australian dancer called Roy who'd appeared in the Billie Piper video for Because We Want To. We couldn't have been more different. We had absolutely nothing in common. We didn't click. We never clicked. In fact we never really got on. Even though we did kind of like each other deep down. He was a nice guy really but I annoyed him. I know I annoyed him because one day he said to me, 'You know, mate, sometimes I just wanna punch you.'

So I figured, yes, he really does find me annoying. And to be fair I didn't try not to annoy him.

But there was something about him I took against. How can I describe it?

Let me put it this way: he was full of shit. We didn't get on. He was sensitive. The real shame of it was that we didn't get on better. We worked so closely together and it was an opportunity to make an enduring friendship.

We weren't treated very well by the producers either. We made thirteen half-hours and we were treated diabolically, probably because it was such a low-budget show. And the main producer himself was out of his depth. We worked from August to December '98.

My agent warned me not to take the job because he told me it was a terrible contract. There were fifteen points on the contract and my agent got them to change something like fourteen of those fifteen points. I mean, originally they weren't even going to pay our travel expenses.

But it was either take this job and have a TV show to make for the next thirteen weeks or say no to it and end up having to do stand-up, which I just didn't enjoy doing. I only did about eight gigs around that time. And I only did one show during the time I made Pirate TV and I was shit.

After I met Roy, who was very styled – wearing a white T-shirt which was a size too small and jeans around his arse and big sunglasses with big, spiky hair, I knew we weren't going to work well together. But the part of Tony Entwhistle, which he was supposed to be playing, was a geeky character who was going to end up trying all these extreme sports. The idea of the show was that when it came down to it, Tony could do all these extreme sports which my character of Fab was trying to get him to do. He told them that he could do all these sports.

But in week two when we made a surfing show in Cornwall it soon became very clear that he could not surf. Then we did a show in Shropshire about downhill mountain biking. Which he did. Very slowly. And he was terrified.

So he got rumbled. He wasn't an extreme sports dude at all.

During the filming of Pirate TV on location in the States, I went out drinking one night with Steve, one of the Australian crew members. I wasn't getting on with Roy, obviously, or anyone else really.

So I was desperate to try to fit in with the crew and make a friend and Steve seemed the one who I could get on with. He was a big drinker. He could drink pint after pint. In an effort to impress Steve I tried to keep up with him, but I was so rubbish at drinking that when I thought he wasn't looking, I tipped my pint on the floor. What an idiot. I wasn't sixteen. I was twenty-four. But I succumbed to peer pressure because the job was a nightmare and I was desperate to make friends. He caught me tipping my pint away and he was disgusted. He didn't say anything. He just had a look of utter disgust on his face. It was the worst thing. It was like I'd just pissed in his eyes.

It was dishonest and humiliating. I was trying to fit in. Pathetic.

If you're going to tip your pint away, don't get caught.

I could offer no defence.

It must be what it's like to be caught masturbating by your mum.

It was never mentioned.

So Pirate TV was not a happy experience, to say the least, but at least the year came to an end with an interesting evening.

I was asked to do the warm-up for the Radio 4 Christmas panto, which was the only warm-up I've ever done in my life. Ruthie Henshall was in it with Robbie Coltrane, Arthur Smith and John Gordon Sinclair.

When the Radio 4 Christmas panto recording was over, I ended up at Les Dennis and Amanda Holden's Christmas party. My agent invited me, not Les or Amanda.

I wore quite an outfit that night: my best Hawaiian shirt with the surfboards on it. I'd really got into the Hawaiian shirt look when I was filming Pirate TV. I was supposed to look like a surfer dude, I suppose, and I loved the shirts. So that became my default look. That night, then, I was wearing a Hawaiian shirt, plus a pair of Michael Caine-style glasses with yellow lenses, which basically looked like sunglasses. It was Christmas time. I looked like a freak.

As I stood there in Les and Amanda's house, I watched a group of people chatting and it included Bob Monkhouse, Ronnie Barker and Jeremy Beadle. Monkhouse, Barker and Beadle. And they were all engrossed in conversation.

I had no one to talk to. I felt completely out of place. Les had an amazing CD player which had a motion-sensor operation and I thought it was so brilliant I went up to it and waved my hand around near it to test the motion sensor.

I caught Les Dennis's eye. He must have wondered if I was going to steal it. He must have thought that there was some freak who'd somehow got into his party and who was eyeing up his lovely CD player.

I felt deeply uncomfortable. I had no business being there and I have never been to a celebrity party since then. I've had to suffer awards dos and TV launches and after-show parties when I rarely stay till the end. And I never feel comfortable at any of them. I feel the same way I did that night at Les and Amanda's, even if I *do* know people there.

As we left his house, my agent finally introduced me to Les, who was clearly thinking, 'Who is this guy?'

I said, 'I love your CD player.'

'Oh yeah, it is a good one ... ' he replied.

But the evening didn't end there for me. Oh no.

My agent, who lived in London, went home.

At which point I realised I was completely drunk. I was so drunk that I effectively blacked out because I ended up at Paddington station and I was the only one there. Just me and a couple of cleaners. I must have got a cab there but I have no memory of that. I looked up at the boards and the last train was a few hours earlier. I put two and two together and realised that there was no way I was going to get home that night on a train.

At that time I didn't have the money to stay overnight at a hotel. And anyway, I just wanted to go home to my girlfriend.

So I walked out of the station to the taxis. I flagged down a taxi and said, 'Bristol, please.'

I explained I was really drunk and needed to get home. He told me it would cost £175. I told him that was too much.

I flagged another cab and asked how much it would cost to go to Bristol. He said £150. So I took the cab. It obviously would have been cheaper to stay in a hotel for the night.

Anyway, this kind cabbie took me to Bristol. But it took *hours*. Mainly because he had to keep stopping on the hard shoulder while I got out of the cab to vomit. This happened five or six times. I would fall asleep, then jolt up in the knowledge that I had to puke. I'd shout, 'Pull over – I've got to be sick!'

In the end, when we got to Bristol, at Filton, my old college, which is miles from where I live, he woke me up and asked me where he should go. He was a London cabbie, remember. He had no idea where to go in Bristol. And I was still almost asleep. So he started to get angry. He'd had a gutsful. He was asking me where to go and I was in no state to give him directions. Luckily, I just about realised that we were in Filton, so I decided to just get out there.

'Just let me out here … ' I told him. He dropped me off at a bus stop outside Filton Technical College. It was 4am. I was at least five miles from home. So I called my girlfriend Karen, who was ill with a cold at the time. I was pissed and I asked her to please come and pick me up.

My poor girlfriend had to get out of bed and drive to Filton College to pick up her boyfriend who was sitting at a bus stop, barely conscious. It was one of many many times in my life when Karen came to the rescue and saved me.

CHAPTER 9

THE WORST YEAR

1999 was a bad year. The worst year of my life.

I had one job in 1999.

I hosted a pilot for a BBC3 show that was called Girls And Boys. It was a game show in which teams of girls played teams of boys in various challenges which involved a lot of running around. In fact the joke on set was, 'Don't mention Runaround,' the old kids' game show hosted by Mike Reid in the '70s. It was also very similar to a show called Boys And Girls, hosted by Vernon Kay, which later aired on Channel 4. But BBC3 didn't pick up our show.

So that was it for TV work.

For the first half of the year I just lived off the money I made the previous year. I was living at home with my mum and dad so I didn't need a huge amount of money. I managed to do nothing for most of the year.

I did drive myself slowly mad. I mooched about with my mate Tim, who similarly wasn't doing much at the time.

We'd go to shopping centres in Bath and Bristol. It was soul-destroying.

Tim was working at TGI Fridays and Warner Village cinemas. The two of us were thoroughly miserable. He was in a job he didn't want to do. He wanted to be an actor or in a band. But he was working in Warner Village cinemas. I wasn't working at all.

I would sleep half the day. Then I'd get in my car and drive to Cribbs Causeway and meet Tim when he was on a break from the cinema.

He was miserable because nothing had happened to him yet, as far as his desire to be a performer was concerned. I was miserable because I'd had some success but then it disappeared and now I had nothing.

We never rowed or argued at all. But there was one moment of high tension.

We met at this bar where you had to be over twenty-one to get in. I waited for him at the bar, then I saw Tim having a few words with the man on the door, who seemed to be challenging Tim about his right to enter the bar. Tim came in and sat down with me and the first words out of his mouth were a tirade. He lost it. He was ranting about the doorman and his shitty job and this shitty place. I was already down and I was suddenly being hit by Tim's outpouring of negativity. We were both in a dark place. And we were kind of shouting and being aggressive, even though we weren't actually arguing with each other. We were letting out a lot of frustration I guess.

My mum and dad were very kind to me at this low point in my life. It must have been quite difficult for them because I was still living at home and I'd had a year when things seemed to be starting to happen. Then there was nothing. But I never felt any pressure from my mum and dad. There was never a moment when either of them said, 'Well, you can't live here all your life.'

But by that point, what I'd already done by being on MTV and ITV late at night was so out of the ordinary and different that my parents, like me, thought the phone would eventually ring. They'd seen me achieve that much and so they felt, well, I could and would achieve more.

Most days I'd get home after a day of mooching around with Tim, and in those days I didn't have a mobile phone, so the first thing I did when I got in was to ask my mum if anyone had called, if my agent had called, and my mum would say, 'No, my lovely. Sorry, Justin. No one called.'

If my mum wasn't there I'd check the answering machine and if there was a light flashing I'd be very excited. Every day I'd be excited when I got home.

And every day at some point my lovely mum would say to me, 'I've got a good feeling today. I think the phone's gonna ring today.' She'd tell me she'd read my stars and that they said luck will call at six, or whatever. She didn't believe in the stars. She was just trying to be positive for me. For my sake.

Bad times.

Eventually in May I did my first stand-up show of the year. The only reason I resorted to doing gigs was because my money was running out. I was faced with the dilemma of doing gigs or getting a proper job. I couldn't face another, pointless job doing something random that I didn't want to do that wouldn't go anywhere.

So I did some gigs.

As I've already mentioned, I didn't enjoy doing stand-up at all and I didn't have much of an act, but I knew I had it in me to entertain and amuse an audience, at least for a few minutes. Often I did manage to make people laugh, and while I was standing there on stage and the crowd was laughing, I enjoyed it. But I hated the build-up to each show and I almost dreaded getting each booking. But they were my only source of income. I didn't have much choice really.

It was stand-up or retail. Or just aimlessly hanging out with my mate Tim.

While plenty of my shows went off without incident, there were also some absolute disasters.

The one I did in front of Bristol students might have been the worst.

I performed at a Bristol Student Union gig and no one at all was listening. I just couldn't get anyone's attention. There was a bar at the back of the room and people just kept on going to the bar and trying to buy drinks really loudly. I just stood there trying to do my act (and I'd been booked to do thirty minutes, which was a ridiculously long set for me at the time). I thought, 'This is ridiculous.'

So I put my mic down on the floor and walked off.

The Student Union guy tried to convince me to go back on stage.

I said, 'But they don't want me to go back on. They don't want me on there at all. It'll be far better for everyone concerned if I don't go back on. They don't need entertaining. They're quite clearly having a nice social time drinking and talking without me interrupting them.'

So I suggested he just give me half the money because I'd done half the gig. He did and I went on my merry way.

Then there was the one at the notoriously tough Up The Creek club in Greenwich, south London. That might be even worse.

I did an open-mic slot at Up The Creek, which was hosted by the legendary Malcolm Hardee. (Who covered my petrol money so I could drive from Bristol to London and back. Which was really nice of him.)

Sunday night was the slot for new acts and it was notorious for being the toughest night on the circuit in London with the toughest crowd.

The host that night was a comedian called Lee Hurst, who was quite famous at the time for being one of the regulars on They Think It's All Over, the sports-based comedy panel game on TV.

I took my girlfriend Karen with me.

I did five minutes of my act and the response was total silence. The audience just stared at me. It was awful.

I walked off stage and Karen consoled me by saying, 'Don't worry, babe, I still love you.'

I also noticed the actor and comedian John Thomson in the audience. I caught his eye and he looked at me and gave me a wink and a smile as if to say, 'Don't worry, mate, we've all been there.' I thought that was really nice of him and I really appreciated it.

Lee Hurst, on the other hand, sidled up to me, shook his head and said, 'Gotta work on it.'

He just said, 'Gotta work on it.'

Now at that moment as a stand-up comedian, when you've died, you're quite aware that you're shit and that you've died and that it's awful and that you have to work on it. No one needs to tell you how shit you are.

But Lee Hurst did feel the need to tell me I had to work on it.

I thought, 'I know! I'm aware of that! I know it was shit!'

That was the last stint I did at Up The Creek as a stand-up, but I did do many gigs years later as a compère.

The best gig I never did was also at Up The Creek.

My agent had booked me a show there but I didn't know about it so obviously I didn't show up. The next morning I had a call from my mate Dave Thompson, the Teletubby, to ask why I hadn't showed up. I told him that I didn't know anything about it. He told me it was probably for the best that I didn't know about it because somebody in the audience pulled out a gun.

Luckily, no one was shot.

But that's how scary that venue could be. That's why it gave me sleepless nights.

I did another quite notable gig at Up The Creek when I was compèring. I always picked people out of the audience to speak to and this one night there was a guy who was very good-looking, very beefy, with very long, luscious hair. He looked like a Chippendale. In fact he said he was a stripper. It ended up with me inviting him on stage and him stripping off down to his pants. His name was Chico.

Years later I saw him on The X Factor.

Impressive, I'm sure you'll agree.

The funny thing that happened that night with Chico was that a great comedian called Phil Kay was on the bill and he was on after I'd done this bit with Chico on stage.

Now some comedians might get annoyed that an unknown guy strips off and gets the crowd all worked up, because the poor comedian has to try to follow that. Not Phil.

He came on stage, dropped his trousers, turned round and revealed that he'd got 'Chico' written in shaving foam across his arse-cheeks.

Wait, there was one show which was totally awful. This one might take the prize for sheer embarrassment.

I did quite a few gigs in the South West for a guy called Pete Bentley. He was a fisherman who put on comedy nights in places like Lyme Regis (where they filmed The French Lieutenant's Woman, with Jeremy Irons).

I did one show in a British Legion Club in Cornwall. It was full of pensioners, many of whom were presumably war veterans. Pete hosted the show, and I had to go on straight after two lady snake-charmers.

The snake-charmers went down a storm. I died on my arse.

People started to walk out during my act. I noticed one table of elderly gentlemen dispersing and as they walked out I started singing the theme tune from Dad's Army.

At the end of that gig, there was an irate woman who was the wife of the bloke who ran the British Legion club. She came up to me and told me I was offensive. She read me the riot act for swearing and being offensive. I wouldn't normally be bothered but the weird thing was that the other acts were quite rude too, including Pete the host. She told me that the difference between me and Pete is that he could get away with it because he's funny. 'He's funny and you're not,' she told me.

I stood there thinking, 'I've just had to follow snake-charmers. I've died on my arse and now I'm being berated. For goodness' sake!'

Thinking about it, I did another show for Pete Bentley which was even more of a nightmare ... in this caravan park in Newquay as part of the Volkswagen Beetle Run To The Sun Festival. There were three or four comedians booked that night, including Stu Who, Ian Cognito (who was considered by Malcolm Hardee to be one of the very best stand-ups of that time) and a Mancunian comic called Brendan Riley.

I was first on the bill and I wore my swimming cap with flowers on it, which I used to wear on my MTV show, and the audience absolutely hated me. I can still see to this day the face of one particular young man in the audience who was screaming at me: 'FUCK OFF! YOU ARE SHIT!'

His face was contorted with rage.

'YOU'RE NOT FUNNY! FUCK OFF! JUST GO!'

I literally stopped and just stared at this bloke while he was abusing me. That wasn't heckling. It was quite terrifying abuse.

I was worried that if I carried on with my act this guy might start a riot. So I went off after less than five minutes.

After the show I was talking to Ian Cognito and he said, 'Don't worry, mate ... they never gave you a chance.'

Then there's a weird one which in many ways was one of my best gigs. But that's what made it simultaneously one of the most annoying, because I was performing to seven people, including the bar staff.

The gig was at a club in Tonbridge Wells. I was friendly with a jester called Jonathan. He dressed as a jester and he juggled and balanced himself on a large rubber ball. Anyway, Jonathan the Jester lived in Salisbury and he had this venue in Tonbridge called the Forum. It was a total shit-hole. But in its own grubby way it was quite a cool place, too. It had a really high stage and at the back of the stage was a grubby old dressing room and the walls were covered in signatures of acts that had performed there in the past.

I'd performed a few times there before, I did one open-mic stint there in late '99 and I drove there with my mate Tim and there was no one around. It was a Sunday night and it was like a ghost town. Quite bizarrely there was a funfair on that week. So Tim and I decided to check out the funfair before the gig and we were literally the only ones there. It was like something out of The Twilight Zone.

When I started the gig – which I was being paid fifty quid for to do half an hour, by the way, and half an hour was almost unheard of for me – it didn't go very well. I was doing my usual rubbish old jokes and nonsensical material. But because my mate Tim was in the audience, rather than just allowing myself to die as I had done many times before, halfway through this set I dropped the act. And I started to talk about the funfair. I said, 'What the fuck is a funfair doing in Tonbridge Wells in late October?' And they started to laugh. I was just making observations about this funfair off the top of my head. And it worked. The second half of my act, once I ditched the act and started being real and talking about the funfair on their doorstep, was a revelation.

That was a turning point for me as a stand-up comedian.

I realised that I could just be honest with the audience and that it could then go well. Quite simply, honesty is the key to connecting with an audience.

But this is the story of when I went back to the Forum in Tonbridge. I turned up and there was just Jonathan and me on the bill. Jonathan did some juggling and stuff and I took part in a James Bond-style sketch that he wrote. Bu there were only seven people there and four of them were bar staff. They all sat in a row in front of the stage. I thought it was ridiculous to stand up there on the stage so I jumped down and stood right in front of those seven people to perform a twenty-minute set. And I absolutely stormed it. I stunned those seven people. I improvised the whole thing and they loved it.

When I finished my act, one of the members of staff, one of the seven people, looked at me and said, 'Oh mate ... *fuck* Eddie Izzard!'

That was one of the best gigs of my life. But it was only to seven people.

In fact, maybe there is one show that was even worse than all those, certainly in terms of audience reaction, when I performed a show in Prague with Ross Noble and Marcus Brigstocke.

There's a big ex-pat community in Prague and this guy from Bath decided to set up a UK comedy gig in a club in Prague.

We were supposed to do three gigs but we only ended up doing one.

I compèred the gig and initially it went well. But halfway through the show, after I'd introduced the first act and before Ross Noble was supposed to come on, the audience turned on me. I'd lost them. And they started throwing things at me. Hair bands and serviettes and scrunchies. Not lethal scary things like glass bottles. I wasn't being bottled. But nevertheless they were throwing stuff at me. They registered their disapproval of me by throwing soft objects. I stood there looking down at the floor filled with serviettes and hair scrunchies. But I had no idea why they hated me. What had I done? What had I said?

I found out afterwards when we went for a drink at a local bar that the reason they turned was that in my spiel I had started to refer to the Czech Republic as Czechoslovakia, which apparently is not the thing any more. Slovakia has gone. It's just the Czech Republic now. They thought I was deliberately disrespecting their country but of course it wasn't that at all. It was just ignorance.

Needless to say we only did the one show and not the three that were planned.

So we had a couple of days to ourselves which was wonderful. I wasn't bothered that the two other gigs didn't happen. In fact, I was relieved.

In fact, I've just thought of my real worst gig ever.

In 2001, I was booked to do two slots at the Frog and Bucket in Manchester – which was a well-established gig – in the run-up to Christmas. I'd done a couple of shows in Manchester before and they'd gone quite well, and I got this booking on the recommendation of one of the local promoters.

I drove all the way from Bristol to Manchester and I didn't have anywhere to stay, even though I was booked to do two nights. I got to the venue and it was packed full of people in party hats and drunken festive revellers.

I got on stage and for the first five minutes it went quite well. But after that I totally lost the crowd. There was a big group in front of me – they looked like they were all from the same office.

It was a difficult night anyway, because half the audience was drunk already. So there was already a bit of a combative atmosphere. It was all running away from me. I had hold of the reins but they were very slack and I was losing them.

So I caught the eye of one guy in this crowd, who seemed to be particularly enjoying himself. He had a big smile and a paper hat and he was wearing a big heavy jerkin, a big colourful festive knitted jumper. He seemed like a fun kind of guy so I invited him up on stage and made a big deal of him, asking the crowd to give him a round of applause, as you do. Often I would invite an audience member up to try to get things back when you've started losing the crowd. It often worked to get them involved when I didn't have their attention.

But as soon as he was up there standing next to me, I immediately realised that something wasn't quite right with him.

He was, as my mum would say, 'a bit touched'.

He was, not to put too fine a point on it, a bit below par.

I thought, 'Oh shit. I have to get this guy off the stage. And he's only just got up here.'

To the rest of the audience it looked like I was picking on a guy who was clearly impaired. But I couldn't just get rid of him. I only caught his eye in the first place because he was smiling and seemed happy to be there.

As it turned out he was happy to be anywhere.

I think I asked him what he did. But I don't think he did much. He didn't do an awful lot. He just kind of shrugged.

He was still smiling. He was the only one in the room who was. For the rest of us it was an awful experience.

After a few minutes of him smiling and not saying very much, I eventually helped him down from the stage and desperately tried to regain the audience. But it was over. I'd totally lost them.

So I stopped my act early after a few more minutes and left the scene.

I went to see the promoter during the interval and he just didn't know what to say. Finally he looked at me and said, 'Justin, I'm really sorry but I can't have you back tomorrow.'

My reaction was one of huge and complete relief.

Most professional comedians would have enough pride and determination to come back and get over this one bad gig. But I really didn't care that much, because stand-up wasn't by any means the be all and end all of my career. It was the only element of my career that was paying me any money but I still didn't enjoy it.

I was hugely thankful that I didn't have to put myself through that experience again the following night and I gladly drove straight back home.

Okay, now I really come to think about it, the definite worst gig experience of my life was the one when my dad came to see me ...

I did a ten-minute set in Jester's comedy club in Bristol and it went really well. So well that the promoter asked me to do another gig the following week and he said he would book me if I could add another ten minutes of material that were as good as the show he'd just seen.

But I didn't have ten minutes' more material.

In that week I tried to come up with ten minutes of stuff. I came up with five minutes of new stuff and to fill out the time I padded it with a load of old jokes that my dad told me. There was an old Ken Dodd joke about milking the bull. Now it might sound bad that I would do these really old jokes, but it wasn't like stealing material from fellow current comics. It was acceptable to do really old jokes – classics if you will. Jokes from the time before Alternative Comedy had ever been invented.

Having said that, at Jesters when I finished my twenty minutes filled out with old jokes my dad told me, the promoter did look at me and say, 'Justin, some of those jokes ... were so old! So old!'

I thought, 'Yes they were. You're absolutely right.'

Nevertheless that same promoter kindly called me many months later and offered me a slot back at Jesters.

But the day before the show, he called me to tell me he'd actually double-booked the slot. He apologised and gave me the option of not doing the gig and he would still pay me, which was very nice of him. Looking back, I should have taken that money. But I didn't. I took the second option he offered me of doing a shorter, ten-minute gig for less money. The only reason I decided to take that option was because I wanted to make a good impression.

Now that gig was the one and only time in my entire part-time career as a stand-up comic that I allowed my dad to come and watch.

I died on my arse spectacularly. To this day it was the worst gig I've ever done. And it was in front of my dad and my Uncle Martin.

My dad had wanted to see me perform for ages. My mum never did. She always got nervous about that kind of thing. My mum can't watch me on TV. She has to leave the room or go upstairs. She doesn't like bad language and rudeness of any kind. Even now, when I'm about to do a TV programme of some kind, she'll say, 'Please don't swear. You don't have to swear.'

But my dad has to watch everything I do. He often watches me on TV, records it and lets my mum know it was fine and then my mum might watch it at her leisure, safe in the knowledge that it didn't all go horribly wrong for her son. She certainly never had any desire whatsoever to see me perform a live show.

My mum would often ask me to tell my dad to come to a gig for ages before I ever did. She would tell me that he was hurt that I'd not invited him. He's a very sensitive man, my dad. So this one night at Jesters, against my better judgement, I allowed my dad to come along with his brother-in-law Martin. Noel James and Noel Brittain were also there – two of the guys who'd been instrumental in getting me that far in the stand-up comedy business.

Now Jesters wasn't the most classy of venues. They've moved it now to a much nicer, bigger club. But few comedians enjoyed playing the club in those days. It could be quite raucous. And it was L-shaped.

Most of the audience was in front of you but then there was another section off to your right as you were performing. Very odd. And not ideal from the performer's point of view.

That night, as soon as I was on stage I could sense that there was a nasty atmosphere in the place. I could see a bunch of blokes in that bit of the audience off to the right. There were about twelve of them on a stag night and they contributed to this tense, rather unpleasant, volatile atmosphere. I was nervous. I was shitting myself and my dad and uncle were sitting there in the middle of the room.

These stag-night blokes were horrible. They wouldn't let me tell any of my bad jokes or do any of my material. It was like a battle. I tried to take them on. I tried to deal with them. I asked them which guy was getting married. A very pissed man stood up and walked towards the stage and then he climbed on the stage. So I wasn't only being heckled but I had the stag up on stage with me, uninvited. I had asked which of them was the stag. But I hadn't invited him on stage. I was completely out of my depth.

The only thing I could think to do, because I'd lost control completely, was to push him away. So I did. I pushed this guy off the stage. Not violently. Quite gently in fact. But that's all I could do.

I'd pushed the stag off the stage and his mates were getting louder and angrier with me. The only option I had was to bring the whole horrible show to an end and I said, 'Well, that's it. Thanks, my name is Justin Lee Collins.'

As I walked off the stage, Noel James looked at me and gave me a smile that said, 'Don't worry, mate.'

But Noel Brittain couldn't even look me in the eye. He wasn't being horrible. It's just such an awful, humiliating situation for everyone.

And the thing is, it happens to every comedian. Young and old. Famous and unknown. They all die at some point or other. It's the worst thing that can happen. And when you're there witnessing it, it's difficult to know how to deal with it. Sometimes you give your condolences, sometimes you say nothing. In this instance, I was so bad that Noel Brittain just said nothing.

I wanted the whole room to swallow me up. And to make it worse, two of my mentors were there. And my dad and my uncle. My dad's reaction was that if this guy who ruined everything hadn't been a stag, then he would have confronted him. There would definitely have been words if the stag hadn't been with all his mates.

I told my dad that night that I didn't want him to see me doing any more gigs. I just couldn't take the added pressure of people I love being there while I'm being rude and being heckled and swearing. It would just throw me off.

Those were the bad stand-up comedy times, during which I was only doing it to earn money because if I didn't then I would have to get a proper job. I say a proper job – obviously I wasn't going to do anything arduous.

I was twenty-five years old. My parents were very good to me but I did need *some* money to get by.

This is how much I hated the stand-up: I went round all the local video shops to ask if they had any vacancies and I applied to Choices Video and their new store on Whiteladies Road. They were holding interviews at the Marriott Hotel and I went along, met the guy who was going to be the new manager of this new store and I applied to be the assistant manager. They were looking at my CV and it had 'Stand-Up Comedian and MTV Presenter' on it. But I was so reluctant to make stand-up comedy my main career choice that I preferred the idea of being the assistant manager of a video shop. Choices Video sent me some forms to fill in but I didn't bother.

A friend of mine called Kevin who worked at M&S said to me, 'Look, mate, why don't you do part-time work at Marks's just to earn yourself some money?'

I said, 'I can't. I can't go back there because that would be like admitting defeat. If I did, that would probably be it. I would probably give up on all this ... '

Of course I never even considered going back to M&S but I did often have dreams that I had gone back to work there, especially when things weren't going well. I had these anxiety dreams about being back at M&S. I would dream that I was back working in Menswear temporarily, putting out stock. It was quite controversial that I was back there. Members of staff would ask me what I was doing there and I'd tell them that I was just temporary seasonal.

And I'd wake up in a cold sweat.

I went into another local video shop called Gerry's Video because they had a sign in the window saying they had a vacancy. The lady in the shop gave me a form to fill in but she did warn me that they only paid minimum wage.

At that point I thought, 'What am I doing?'

I could have taken that part-time job in a video shop and waited for the phone to ring but I would need to work a ten-hour shift at this video shop to earn thirty quid, whereas even if I got a really shitty gig above a pub, I could earn that in twenty minutes.

I also knew that I could get comfortable working in the video shop and that I could end up doing that for the rest of my life.

I decided not to work in a video shop.

Instead, I picked up the phone, called my agent and told him I really needed to start earning money. I told him to get me any paid gigs he could. Anything. Anything at all.

I also called people myself. I called anyone who I'd met in my time as a stand-up. One of the people I spoke to was a promoter called Jeff Whiting who I first met at the gig I did for Live! TV which got me thrown off the drama course. He had put a lot of work my way, and he almost immediately gave me about twenty gigs.

I was back as a proper stand-up comedian and I really tried to commit to it. My one rule was that I would only do gigs where they were prepared to pay me. They could pay me anything, I would do it. And it started to go well ...

The main reason it started to go well was that I'd found a new niche which suited me. I started to specialise in being the compère.

Here's the difference between being a comic and a compère. When you're the compère, you're not expected to have an act as such. The audience isn't necessarily expecting you to make them laugh with your amazing jokes and observations. They just want you to keep them entertained between the acts and introduce the acts. In fact, the worst compères are the ones that just do their material. The best ones are those who get up there and engage with the crowd. So that's what I did. I had no material whatsoever but I could go on and improvise and talk to the audience.

For example, I often compèred at the Up The Creek club, which as you know was a notoriously difficult place. It was a tough crowd. But I always had a good gig there, just by interacting with the audience.

Having said that, I still didn't love doing those gigs. I still wanted to be on TV. That was my dream. But I knew that at least by being out there and visible that maybe TV people would see me or maybe people that knew TV people would see me.

So I did stand-up gigs from late 1999 to May 2002. And that was my main source of income. But I never enjoyed it. I endured it. And all the while I was telling myself that any day the phone would ring and it would be my agent telling me someone from the BBC or Channel 4 had seen me and wanted to give me my own show. Or some casting director wanted to give me a role in a new sitcom. Or a producer was interested in me taking a part in their stage play. Something. Anything. But no, there was nothing. I was Justin Lee Collins – stand-up comedian. Something I never, ever wanted to be. And I wasn't sure how much longer I could carry on doing it without it making me feel too miserable and stressed out and having dreams about being back at M&S.

One other thing I must mention is that, as I'm sure you've heard before, being a stand-up comedian is, for many performers, a surefire way of getting in with the opposite sex. I always used to hear from other stand-ups that this was true. People would tell me it's a great way of getting girls. Now for someone like me, who was, growing up and throughout my life, absolutely useless in front of women and fearful of the opposite sex, this was quite intriguing. I would ask why and they'd tell me that women in the audience would see you up there being funny and that they would often find that attractive.

Well, this was certainly never the case for me.

Of course while I was doing my stand-up I was never single, so I wasn't in the market, even if there was any opportunity. But there wasn't even any opportunity.

Except maybe once.

This was at a gig in Stoke on Trent that I was compèring and during the interval I went to the bar to get a Coke (I never drank at gigs) and there was a young woman standing next to me at the bar. I fumbled around in my pocket for some money and dropped a few coins on the floor and while I was bending down to pick up these coins, this woman stood next to me said, 'Ooh, what are you doing down there?'

I just laughed and paid for my drink. But it was clear to me that she was being flirtatious. She turned and walked away with her drink but then she suddenly stopped and looked at me and said, 'I just want you to know I think you're absolutely gorgeous.'

I said, 'Wow. Thank you very much.'

And that was the one and only time in my entire time as a stand-up comedian that any woman ever showed any interest in me in any way whatsoever. I'm not complaining about it. It's just a fact.

CHAPTER 10

A GIANT TWIGLET

I stood there pretending to get myself psyched up to dive into a small polystyrene cup.

I was wearing my floral swimming cap that I used to wear during my MTV show and I'd placed the cup on the floor, stood on a chair and attempted to dive into the cup. That was my big idea for this audition, which was for a show called Hey DJ for a channel which doesn't exist any more called UK Play. They were looking for comedians to play a DJ who lived at home with his mum where he played his records.

So in front of two executives from the production company, I was about to pretend that I was going to dive into this cup. Clearly there was no way I was going to be able to dive into a cup. That was obvious to everyone. But I did a big build-up to the dive: Three. Two. One ... and then I just let out this ridiculous noise like this: 'Eurrrrrrrrrrrrrrrghhhhhh!' and I acted as if I was having some kind of episode, some kind of seizure, and very slowly I kind of fell to the floor and lay there writhing around on top of the cup.

The looks on the faces of the two TV executives basically said, 'What the fuck is he doing? What is he doing? Who the fuck is this?'

Needless to say I didn't get the job. This was one of many auditions and meetings around that time that did not go well for me.

At no point had I thought about what these people were looking for or what would be appropriate for the show for which I was auditioning. That was typical of me in those days. I was always hiding behind something.

It was fear. That's what it was all about. I wasn't assured or confident enough to just talk to them and explain how I could do the job they wanted. Instead I pretended to dive into a cup and have a seizure.

Years later ... I was asked to be a judge on the regional final of the BBC New Comedy Awards and one of my fellow judges was the producer who had auditioned me for Hey DJ. She took me to one side and said, 'I'm sorry, Justin, but I have to ask you something ... do you remember that day of the Hey DJ audition?'

Of course I did ...

'What were you on? What were you on that day?' she asked. 'You must have been on something!'

But no, I told her, I wasn't on anything. That was just what I was like.

In fact, this is a bit of a theme down the years. People have frequently asked me what substance or drug I was on at various times after seeing various of my performances. They sincerely thought I was on something. But the simple fact is I have never ever been on anything like that in my life.

One time I went to a members' club in London with my mate Dave Thompson, the Teletubby.

I was always nervous around other performers, probably because somehow I didn't ever think I deserved to be there with them. I never felt comfortable in those situations. But I would make up for my nerves by talking ten to the dozen and being overly chatty and animated.

Dave and I were at this members' club at a table of other comics and I found myself constantly having to go to the toilet. We couldn't have been there longer than two hours but I must have gone to the toilet four or five times.

When we left, Dave told me that the other comedians at the table thought I was going to the toilet to do cocaine and they were getting disgruntled because I wasn't sharing it with them.

But I've never taken cocaine in my life and had no idea about drug-taking etiquette in showbiz circles. I was just really nervous which was why I was talking too fast and I was drinking and I've never been able to hold my drink very well so that's why I kept going to the toilet.

So there was a time when people assumed that because of my enthusiastic, overly friendly behaviour that I must have been on something. Especially people I would meet in London. But back home in Bristol I wasn't the only one who was that enthusiastic and friendly. I knew lots of people like that. Very very friendly people. Complete strangers will give you the thumbs-up or ask how you're doing. It was different in trendy London with those trendy types, where it's so full of bullshit and bollocks and people are all very guarded. But I've always been very open. And so everyone assumed I was on something.

Apart from various other awful auditions, I did get one more little TV job in 2001. But it was one of the worst things I've ever done.

It was for a series called Show Me The Funny which was on E4 and hosted by Mark Dolan in which he would introduce comedians doing silly things. It was a showcase for new comedy talent. It was the first place I ever saw Leigh Francis do his character Avid Merrion, for example.

They asked me to do a slot called I Told You I'd Do That, a hidden camera bit where I had to find members of the public out and about and do something outrageous or ridiculous with them. So for example I'd go into a pub and ask for a pint of milk and then say 'I told you I'd do that ... ' or I would walk up to a rubbish bin, take something out of the bin and eat it and say, 'I told you I'd do that.'

Then one time we filmed a scene and I was nearly physically attacked.

We filmed it in a bowling alley in London and the idea was that I would interrupt some guys bowling and disrupt their game by bowling a ball into their lane.

So I picked a group of blokes and did it. And they weren't happy. They were extremely unhappy. They looked like they were about to attack me. So the producer told me to leave the area because it would just be better if I wasn't there, and in the end they gave these guys forty quid to placate them.

The forty quid did stop them from attacking us.

But I couldn't help wondering if it was all worth it.

For the same show we filmed an item in Trafalgar Square in which I walked up to a woman feeding the pigeons and I was interrupted by a homeless guy and it turned out the pigeon-feeder was the homeless guy's girlfriend. He threatened to take the camera.

That definitely wasn't worth it.

Finally, in early January 2001, we filmed a bit in Soho Square in London and it was really cold. The idea was that I had a device hidden in my jogging bottoms which, when I pressed a button, made it look like I had wet myself. So I would go up to people, engage them in conversation and ask if they knew where a toilet was, and then I'd effectively wet myself.

On this freezing cold day I went up to one guy, who was in his work gear of a fluorescent jacket and he had his packed lunch, and I interrupted him, but before I could really get any words out, he just looked at me and said, 'I'm just trying to eat my lunch.'

I said, 'I'm so sorry … ' and I left him alone. I thought, 'Exactly … you're bothering this poor guy on his lunch break – and for what?!'

I felt terrible.

But they used my material in which I peed myself in the actual show called Show Me The Funny. It went out after Avid Merrion, who was really funny. And I thought my bit was absolutely terrible.

I was ashamed.

That Show Me The Funny period was also a terrible time for me because my grandmother was really ill, and I just didn't want to be in London filming a show in which I was basically just bothering people.

I was skint and I was ready to do more or less anything for money. I was doing my stand-up but not really making much money out of it. I probably earned a few hundred quid a month from the stand-up shows at best. I was still living with my parents.

Thank god I had my girlfriend Karen to support me. In every way. She had a proper, regular job as a secretary. And she always believed in me.

There was one moment in that lean period when she raised the question – what if it doesn't happen?

We were in the car and all of a sudden she said that maybe I had to consider the possibility that it might not work out, because we knew we wanted to buy a house and get married one day.

It never led to any argument.

I just said, 'It will happen. Because it has to. This is all I want to do, so it has to happen. And it will happen.'

And that was pretty much the end of that.

I was slightly miffed that she'd brought it up. It was her only slight note of doubt. That threw me a little bit, because it was the first and only time she'd ever put even the slightest little pressure on me. But, really, I couldn't blame her. And she never said anything like that ever again. Even when things got even worse for me, much later on.

But there was one other way I could earn some proper, decent cash there and then, while also using my desire to perform: ads.

To be specific, Twiglet ads. Now I don't remember ever telling my agent to go out there and find me some well-paid TV adverts I could star in, because I don't think it would even have occurred to me. Luckily, I think this was simply a time when the phone did ring, out of the blue. And it was a call from the Twiglets people.

They were launching new flavours of Twiglets, including tangy ones and curry ones.

Now my agent told me that for this Twiglet ad they were only auditioning stand-up comics who knew how to improvise. This basically meant there was no script. There might have been a slogan and a concept for the campaign, but not much else beyond that.

I went to this audition, which was being held on a street in Soho in London outside a newsagent.

What I had to do was stop people on the street and convince them to go into the shop to buy some Twiglets. They were shooting the action from an upstairs window above a shop on the other side of the street. Essentially I had to bother people.

So I did.

I jumped on one chap's back and rode him around. I judged it well, though. He seemed to enjoy it and went with it. I rode him into the shop.

But a policeman saw me doing this and assumed I was causing some kind of disturbance. The cop came over and asked me what I was doing. So I explained it all to him, but I did it in a comedic way knowing that this was all being filmed for my audition. I asked the policeman if I could jump on his back and ride him into the shop to sell him some Twiglets.

He looked at me and told me to calm it down. 'Just calm it down, sir.'

But I kept going with my shtick because I thought it was funny and he got to the point of making it clear he would slap the cuffs on me and arrest me if I took it much further. At that point a runner from the production team came over to intervene and let the copper know I wasn't a proper trouble-maker.

I got the job after that audition but I was later told that most of the ad agency creatives, as they're called, weren't sure about me and that they thought I was too wild, too over the top. It was the director, a lovely guy called Mark, who thought I'd be perfect for Twiglets.

Originally this campaign was just screened in cinemas and I was paid £4500.

For that fee I had to wear a ten-foot-long Twiglet costume.

Now to me at the time this was a fortune. It could have paid for my entire life for a year. So I was jumping for joy. I was going to be earning some money by performing. Admittedly I would be performing in a Twiglet costume but nevertheless it was performing.

But what I didn't take into account was my claustrophobia.

The first thing I had to do was go to a costume fitting in a big shed in Elstree where I had to try on this huge, ten-foot-long brown foam-rubber tube, which looked more like a giant piece of shit.

They were still putting the giant Twiglet/shit together at this point, so there was solvent all over the costume. But there wasn't a hole where the eyes would be.

They asked me if I would mind trying on the costume so they could work out where the holes for the eyes and the arms should be. And of course I had to agree – that's why I was there.

So I put my arms up above my head and crouched down with my arms still up while about three of them had to handle this giant brown tube and slide it down over my head.

There I was – inside a foam-rubber tube in total darkness while I'm inhaling noxious adhesive fumes which reeked. And I'm badly claustrophobic.

They got the costume down to around my waist before I started to freak out.

I shouted, 'Get me out of here! Get me out now!'

My eyes were running and my head throbbed. I had been subjected to adhesive abuse.

They just looked at me, and must have been thinking, 'We've made a mistake. They've hired a claustrophobe.' And you can't have a claustrophobic Twiglet.

I was thinking, 'Have I just screamed myself out of four and a half grand?'

In the end I just had to control myself, calm down, get my breath back and let them put it over me again. They promised me they would only take ten seconds. I did it because I had to.

The actually filming took three days and the days were long.

The first day I was working in a newsagent's behind the counter and the idea was that whoever came into the shop would be confronted by me, improvising a way to get them to buy Twiglets.

Then the next day I would be dressed as a Twiglet running around a shopping centre trying to get customers to buy Twiglets.

The last day we filmed on Brighton beach and I would be running around the beach in my giant Twiglet costume again. I ran into the sea yelling, 'I'm on fire! I'm burning up!' I did it but I was worried that if I went down in the sea I would need to be helped up immediately, otherwise I'd drown.

I ate so many Twiglets that first day that my mouth ended up riddled with mouth ulcers. I'm not saying Twiglets give you mouth ulcers. Certainly not. But I am saying that having to eat forty or fifty bags of the things did give me mouth ulcers. A lot of them.

But I have to say, despite the claustrophobic incident in the costume and the ulcerated mouth, that experience of filming TV ads for Twiglets was one of the most satisfying creative experiences of my life, even though I was dressed as a Twiglet and some people might find that humiliating, but I didn't mind, to be honest. I was allowed free rein for three days and I improvised for the whole shoot and I loved it.

In those days I loved nothing more than going to the cinema and I would often go three or four times a week. So I found myself sitting there many times in a darkened cinema watching myself on the big screen in a giant Twiglet costume.

That job led directly to me starring in the National Lottery campaign because the director from Twiglets was working on the ads. This campaign was for a specific twenty-million-pound jackpot and I starred in radio spot and TV ads.

For the radio campaign I conducted a series of prank phone calls in which I pretended to have twenty million quid that I'd just won in the Lottery. So for example I called a football club chairman and asked if he would sell the club for twenty million.

The TV ads were built around me carrying a huge long purple foam sign which spelt out '£20 Million' while wearing a purple corduroy Paul Smith suit.

After they measured me up for the suit, they made two of them so there would be a spare if anything happened to the suit.

When we finished filming, and they'd given me the suit to keep, I was then called in to film some re-shoots and I was asked to bring the suit with me. That surprised me because I thought I could just wear the spare suit. I went back and filmed the re-shoots. But I asked the wardrobe guy what happened to the other suit. He told me he kept it himself. But the weird thing was, this guy was a long, tall, thin Australian. I was a short, stocky man. So somewhere there's a man walking around looking like Herman Munster in my purple corduroy suit.

I kept the corduroy jacket from the Paul Smith purple suit for years and wore it many times. I loved it.

Before we filmed the ads, I was called in to the production company office in Soho to check that I could carry this huge foam sign around. They needed to check that I could work with it.

At one point while I was standing in the street carrying this purple foam '£20 Million' sign, I noticed Ricky Gervais and Steve Merchant, who'd recently signed up with my agent, walking down the street. By that time I'd met Ricky a couple of times and I knew Steve from the Bristol stand-up scene, but they hadn't noticed me yet. So as soon as they came into view on the other side of the street I decided to call out to them. 'All right guys – how are you doing?'

They look back at me and of course I'm carrying a huge purple '£20 Million' foam sign and they look at me and just laugh and say hello back.

Shortly after that chance encounter I saw Ricky and Steve again and Ricky said that I was the only person he knew who would not be embarrassed to run into people they knew in that situation. He thought most people would be embarrassed to be seen carrying a huge purple foam '£20 Million' sign in the middle of the street and would do everything they could to avoid being seen by anyone they know. Whereas I not only wasn't embarrassed at all but I actually went out of my way to draw attention to myself and say hello and smile and wave at them. Of course he was totally right. I didn't care. I wasn't embarrassed.

Anyway, in the ad campaign itself, I had to walk round with this big sign and bother people in the street, asking them if they could help put my twenty million quid into the bank. So again, there wasn't really a script and the ads were built around me improvising.

The great thing about the National Lottery ads was that I earned enough money from them to enable me to put down a deposit on a house. So if it wasn't for the purple foam-based National Lottery ad campaign I wouldn't have been able to buy my first house – a cottage in Hannam, Bristol – with Karen. We would never have had the money if it hadn't been for those ads. Though my dad also gave me some money towards the deposit.

I also starred in a French advert.

I was auditioned in London for a French company called Riqules to star in an ad for their new energy soft drink type of affair. Weirdly, they were looking for British performers to take over to Paris to take part in an ad for the French market for a French product. I still don't know why they did this. Why didn't they just choose French performers? you're probably asking yourselves. And I have absolutely no idea.

I was one of three cast members and together we played the members of a rock band. We filmed the ad on the same day that France won the final of the 2000 European Football Championships.

A French guy called Jean Luc was our runner and driver and he gave us a midnight tour of Paris in his car. I'd never been to Paris before and I thought it was amazing and beautiful.

One of the other performers was this guy called Ben and he was obsessed with going to a club that night. He kept saying, 'I want some drum and bass. Drum and bass.' He kept saying it from the back seat of the car. Jean Luc was giving us this wonderful tour. We went to the Louvre. I got out and ran round the glass pyramid. We stood beneath the Eiffel Tower at about three in the morning. And this dickhead Ben kept going on about a drum and bass club.

In the end Riqules didn't even use the ad and I didn't get paid for about nine months. That's advertising for you.

The best thing about doing those ads, including the fact that the Twiglet one was actually one of the most satisfying creative experiences I'd ever had, was that I had been earning some decent money for a change. I thought it was about time to put the money to some good use and settle down properly with my lovely Karen. We'd been seeing each other for five years, and I knew we were perfect together.

My relationship with Karen felt right from the very beginning. As well as being very attractive she was also just lovely. My mum said she was perfect for me. She chilled me out when I was tense. She calmed me down when I was over-excited and stressed out and anxious. She was clearly just a properly nice person. I've always been attracted to people who are fundamentally decent, unassuming, good-natured. She brought balance to me. I didn't have to perform with her. I just had to be myself (though, thankfully, I did make her laugh, right from those early days when she came into the video shop). The silences were never uncomfortable. She was – and still is – the most laid-back person I have ever met. She chilled me out.

From quite early on it was almost a given that we were going to get married and have kids. It felt right. It was completely natural. We just knew.

So when I decided to ask Karen to marry me it wasn't so that we could be engaged for three or five years, it was to get married.

It was, however, possibly the gayest marriage proposal ever.

It was Christmas Eve, 2001. It was pissing down with rain. I took

Larry and me in California. Look how proud I am to meet him!

Live long and prosper, Leonard Nimoy, you lovely man!

Forced to capture the signature look of Fame - sorry crew!

The Hoff and
I re-enact
Baywatch.
I really must
get to the gym.

Moyles and I have become proper mates,
despite us forcing him to do this shit.

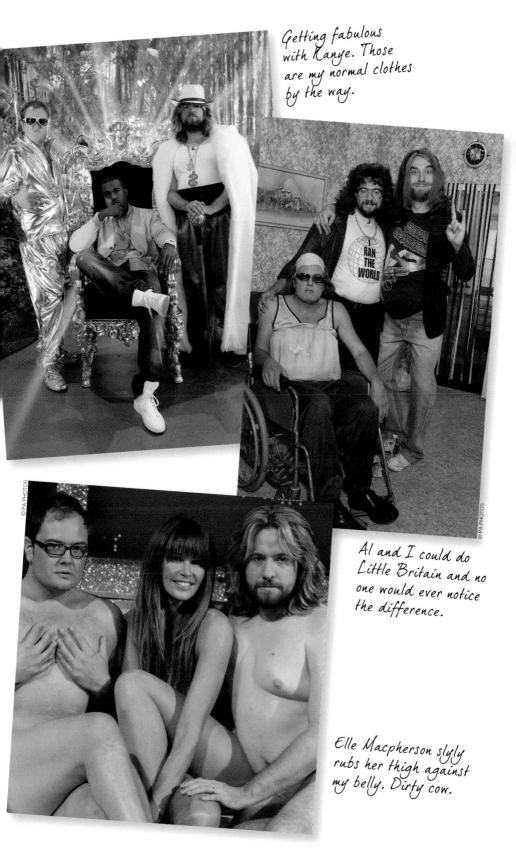

Getting fabulous
with Kanye. Those
are my normal clothes
by the way.

Al and I could do
Little Britain and no
one would ever notice
the difference.

Elle Macpherson slyly
rubs her thigh against
my belly. Dirty cow.

© PA PHOTOS

Just your regular shopping trip with Kim Cattrall.

Al and I in the worst Tellytubby costumes ever. So we decided to hump.

'They tried to make me go to the gym and I said No No No!'

For Convention Crashers I became Justin Illusion with my trusty assistant Panache. Now that's magic!

I've always dreamt of being hurt by a Mexican transvestite wrestler called Cassandro.

I've velcroed my beard to Karen's hair. But she's still happy!

Behold! Four generations of manhood
– Archie meets my dad and grandad.

Archie and me.
This will soon be
available from all
good poster shops.

Archie's just like
me as a kid.
Except much more
fashionable...

Karen for a really nice lunch at San Carlos Italian restaurant and then I took her to the Bristol Old Vic to see a stage production of The Wizard Of Oz.

We came out and I took her to Queen's Square – reputedly the largest Georgian square in Europe. That was where I had decided beforehand to propose, because it was such a nice location. But it was in the other direction to where I had parked my car so I practically had to drag poor Karen through the streets of Bristol in the rain, much to her bewilderment. We were getting drenched. And it was raining so hard that I couldn't go down on one knee. Luckily she still said yes.

We decided to wait till 2003 to get married so we could save enough money to do it properly and get our first home sorted out. I also planned a surprise exotic honeymoon, using the money I'd earned from doing ads – because another one came along which looked like it might turn into a long-term money-spinner for me.

I was asked to star in an ad for Ski yoghurt.

Again, these ads were being made by Mark, the same director who'd hired me for the Twiglet and National Lottery campaigns. They were re-launching Ski yoghurts because they'd just been acquired by Nestlé. Remember, this was the age of Müller crunch corners and fruit corners and choco balls. So simple Ski yoghurt pots had maybe gone out of fashion. Yoghurts had come on since the glory days of Ski.

The idea of the campaign was to relaunch the brand via a series of Friends-style commercials featuring a group of trendy young flatmates in a trendy apartment looking cool while eating Ski yoghurt. I was going to play one of the flatmates and there was going to be another guy and a girl. We were told right from the beginning that if the ads went well this could be a long-running campaign featuring the same characters. We could become like the Oxo family. Except with yoghurt and not gravy. They asked me to pencil in another set of Ski ad filming in the summer and even inquired as to my availability for the autumn of that year and the beginning of the following year!

Obviously I was thrilled at the prospect of earning that kind of money.

After I got the role of the first flatmate and they found an actor called Tony to be the other (he's now a regular on Holby City I believe), they decided to audition actresses for the other part and they asked me to help them audition by reading along with the actresses. One of the actresses I worked with in the audition ended up as Bill Nighy's secretary in Auf Wiedersehen Pet when they brought it back. But she didn't get the Ski ad.

They gave the role to a very pretty young girl. But I've never seen her in anything since.

We shot the first ad in a studio over two days on this huge apartment set which consisted of a bedroom and a kitchen with a Smeg freezer and loads of trendy furniture. I'm sure it would have been cheaper to film in a real flat.

Now unlike the Twiglet and National Lottery ads, these Ski ones had a proper script. And learning lines and sticking to an actual script has never been my strong point.

The script entailed me talking to my flatmate who was called John and the idea was that at the end of every sentence we would add 'ski' to the last word. So I bounded in and said, 'Hello, John-ski,' and he said, 'All right, mate-ski.' 'How are you-ski?' You get the idea. Hilarious.

Then I improvised a line after my character noticed he's eating a yoghurt. I said something like, 'Ooh, what have got there, John-ski?' He said, not surprisingly, 'Yoghurt … ' and then I leapt over the sofa and shouted, 'I love yoghurt!'

But when I shouted 'yoghurt', I pronounced it very deliberately in a super-heavy Bristolian accent and said 'Yog-*art*' with the emphasis on the 'art', not 'Yoe-gurt' as most people pronounce it. I just found that pronunciation funny. The wrong pronunciation.

The director was very particular. We did take after take after take. After take. I felt like Shelley Duvall in The Shining. Although it was actually fairly easy for me because all I had to do was jump over the sofa and say, 'I love yog-art!' But poor Tony had to eat the yog-art as we were filming. He had to eat about fifty of them in one day.

At the end of the day of filming in which we did about fifty takes of me saying 'I love yog-art!', the director asked me to do one take: 'Just for safety, just in case the client wonders why you're not saying yoghurt properly, can you just say it properly?' So I did one take in which I said 'yoghurt' normally. But incredibly they ended up using my weird pronunciation version.

When we were packing up for the day, one of the cameramen sidled over to me and leaned over and whispered in my ear, 'Hey, mate – how do you normally say it? Yoghurt? How do you usually pronounce it?'

Clearly I had intrigued him with my curious way of saying 'yog-art'.

I looked him straight in the eye and just replied, 'Yog-*art!*'

The highlight of the two days' filming for me was a short scene we filmed with me and the girl in which we're sitting there on a sofa watching telly and eating our Ski yog-arts and being all lovey-dovey and at one point she smears a bit of yog-art on my nose and we're laughing and flirting about it, and then she licks it off and we both laugh again, and then I improvised a response: I threw the entire contents of my yog-art pot in her face, then I grab her head and start licking the yog-art off her face like a rabid dog.

That scene was never used. I was told later on by someone who worked on the campaign that the company was quite nervous about this re-launch of the Ski brand and they thought that scene was a bit too risky. I thought it was hilarious. I really wish you could have seen it.

Not only was my favourite yog-art over-the-head scene never used but we never went on to film any more ads. We didn't become the Oxo family of the yog-art world.

But I still had enough to pay for the huge, brilliant honeymoon I'd already planned in my head for after I'd married my beautiful Karen.

CHAPTER 11

MASTUR-BATING WITH STINGING NETTLES

I was so excited. I went to Maximum FX, my favourite hairdresser's in Bristol, that morning and Shaun did my hair specially for the interview, and I wore my favourite Hawaiian shirt which had surfboards all over it (I was still living in Hawaiian shirts all the time, week in, week out).

But it was the first job I didn't have to audition for. Which was great for me because I had clearly become terrible at auditions. They actually came to see me and offered me the job. I would be hosting fifteen shows and each show would have a different theme: Ten Things You Didn't Know About Transport ... Ten Things You Didn't Know About Life and Death ... Ten Things You Didn't Know About Sex. Each show would be based round me exploring these ten unusual facts about each topic.

I'd be presenting an entire series for Bravo called, as you may have realised, Ten Things You Didn't Know About.

I was amazed. It seemed like quite a big gig to offer me. But I would have been quite cheap at the time and I presumed they'd offered it to lots of other people first. In fact, the producer told me their first choice was Ross Noble, but he didn't want to do it and would have been too expensive anyway.

We filmed the series from April to July that year which meant I was away five days a week filming here, there and everywhere, and I really enjoyed it. It was hard work and we had a very low budget with a very small crew. Only three of us would go on the road filming – me, the presenter, a researcher, and my friend Giles the director who was also the cameraman and he would also do the sound (most normal TV shows have a soundman). Needless to say we had a lot of problems with sound and various scenes had to be re-shot. And some items had to be re-shot a third time.

The first item we did was filmed in a busy bar in Birmingham and was something to do with stacking coins. We had to re-shoot it because it was too noisy and then we had to shoot it again.

Among the highlights was a trip to Tennessee to do an item on the famous Tennessee fainting goats. They would seize up and literally tip over when you frightened them. Sure enough I scared some of them by sitting on the farmer's quad bike to chase after his goats and some of them did freeze up and keel over. I've no idea why these particular goats in Tennessee were so susceptible to fainting but nevertheless they certainly didn't let us down. They fainted. En masse. We did have issues with it. We wondered whether it was entirely appropriate to go goat bothering and whether it was a bit cruel, but they were all fine afterwards we were assured. They just faint, keel over and eventually get back up again. I asked the guy who ran the farm, 'Is this all right? Is this healthy for the animals?' And told me, 'Oh, it's fine. They love it!'

But I suppose most of the stand-out experiences came during the filming of the Ten Things You Didn't Know About Sex episode.

First, we travelled to San Diego where we filmed an item on the oldest working heterosexual male porn star in the world. Now I'm not sure if there was any independent verification that he was the oldest working heterosexual male porn star in the world but he claimed he was. He was sixty-three. His name was Dave Cummings. I think he did a film called Cummings To America. I don't think Cummings was his real name. In a way I didn't think sixty-three was that old. I imagine there are much older homosexual porn stars. I bet there's an eighty-three-year-old gay guy still banging away somewhere. There must be. But Dave Cummings was very clear that he was the oldest hetero porn star.

We went to his condominium to film this man work. I was supposed to interview him first and then film him actually taking part in a scene from one of his pornos. So we turned up and we met this quite nice, white-haired older guy who was a Vietnam veteran – he had photos of himself in uniform on the wall – and he told us a story which was quite sad. He told us he was with his wife for about forty years then she left him after she had an affair and so he thought, 'Well, what am I going to do now? I've never been unfaithful to her and now I'm an old guy on my own. Right, that's it – I'm gonna become a porn star.' And that's what he did.

On the particular day we were there, he had arranged for a young woman to join him for this scene which we had permission to film. She was a nice young girl and she worked in the local supermarket as a checkout girl. She turned up still wearing her supermarket overalls from her day job. She had just turned twenty-two but she was still pretending to be twenty-one because that was a better age for Dave's film.

Dave made it clear that this wasn't going to be a full-on sex scene; it was just going to be oral. She was going to give Dave a blow-job. That was the scene.

I had a bit of a dilemma about this item because I wasn't exactly enamoured with the idea of appearing on screen in the background of this blow-job porno scene while I'm just standing there observing. It seemed a bit weird. I thought, 'Do I want to be in this? Do I need to be in this?' To be fair, Giles the director said to me, 'You don't need to be in this scene. If you don't want to be in the room I understand. You don't have to be.' But then again, I thought that maybe it would be best for the programme if I was in the scene, so you could see my reactions. And really – there was nothing wrong with it. These were two consenting adults going about their business.

Also, to be totally honest, I did find the whole idea quite titillating. It was quite arousing. But that felt weird too – to be aroused by something we were filming for work. It was all very confusing.

All kinds of thoughts swam around my mind: 'Do I want to be seen on TV watching this scene? What will my mum think? Do I want my mum's friends from the church to see this?'

The other thing I should mention is that we needed to use a big boom mic on a stick to record the sound of this porno scene and because we didn't have a soundman and because our director did all the sound himself, but would be rather busy holding the camera, he decided we needed to use a boom. There was no way he was going to be able to attach little remote radio microphones to two naked people while they performed all manner of oral activities on each other in all manner of positions. So Giles the director had to ask our researcher Sonia if she could stand in there and hold the boom mic. She shrugged and agreed because she had to.

I thought, 'Well, if Sonia has to be in there then I should be too really.'

As soon as the filming started, Dave had to stop because he realised he had photos of his grandchildren on display there in the bedroom so he insisted on removing them before he could carry on with the scene.

So there we were: watching this sixty-three-year-old Vietnam vet getting a blow-job from a twenty-two-year-old (pretending to be twenty-one) supermarket girl who'd just come from her checkout. I wasn't in any state of arousal at all. In fact, I suddenly had a new-found respect for adult performers because they have to do these really intimate things in front of a group of strangers watching them.

Giles was filming it, Sonia was holding the boom but she was looking the other way because she couldn't bring herself to watch it. And I was hovering about awkwardly in the background.

At one point the woman straddled Dave's face. At another point they adopted the 69 position. The scene drew towards its climax with the two of them on the floor directly in front of me – the lady on her knees attempting to bring Dave to a climax. At this very moment, while I was thinking, 'Bloody hell, I really shouldn't be here ... ', Dave Cummings looked round the room, clocked what everyone was doing – Giles holding the camera, Sonia holding the boom mic, and Dave had his own camera filming the scene for his own film, Cummings To America 2 or whatever – and he suddenly realised he had no one to take still photographs of this scene. So he looked up at me while he was having his cock sucked and asked me if I could take his stills for him if he gave me his camera.

What could I say?

I didn't want to take his bloody photos for him but of course I said, okay, I would.

He reached out, gave me his still camera and so I had to crouch down in front of them clicking away and taking photographs of the oldest living heterosexual porn star being fellated by a twnty-two-year-old checkout girl. I had become the stills photographer on this porn shoot. There will be a porn film out there somewhere with this scene in it and I should have the credit for taking the stills. I hope I've been given credit for the stills.

Obviously one of the very important scenes in any porn film is the pop shot. And what with me taking these photos and our crew filming it, there was a certain amount of chatter going on in the room. But suddenly Dave asked for some quiet in the room. He had to be focused to deliver the money shot. He had to concentrate so he could produce the money.

A deeply uncomfortable silence fell over the room as we all watched Dave intently trying to reach his climax.

Eventually he did produce his money over this woman and they went off and cleaned themselves up. The shoot was over, so to speak.

I was thinking, 'Good god. That was really uncomfortable.' While Dave had treated the young woman from the supermarket very well and while he was very nice and friendly and hospitable to all of us, what I found quite uncomfortable was something Dave told me after he paid her the money and after she had left. (And after he had kindly invited her to some weird naked fun run that was happening later that night in the nearby woods, where, from the sound of it, there would be loads of people running around naked, stopping to fuck each other, and then carry on running around.)

I was chatting to Dave on his balcony and I asked him if he thought the checkout girl would make it in the business.

He immediately shook his head. 'No,' he said. 'She won't make it. She'll just do the rounds ... '

And he just left that thought hanging.

I also asked him what the girl had been paid and he told me: 150 dollars.

That was the most uncomfortable experience of the whole Ten Things You Didn't Know About series. By far.

It stayed with me for the rest of the trip, and it bothered me even once we went back home, so I asked to be cut out of that scene completely. As it turned out, the producer told me that it was clear I was uncomfortable and that I didn't want to be there. Which was true.

We also did a show called Ten Things You Didn't Know About Life And Death and I interviewed a doctor about people who had been buried alive even though they had been pronounced dead. It used to happen quite often apparently. In the nineteenth century at least. We didn't use the item because it was a tad dull and I tried to make the interview more interesting by being quite silly and by conducting it with me attached to an ECG unit in the back of an ambulance. I said to this expert, 'Doctor, let me ask you this: that machine is telling you I am dead. I am telling you I am very much alive. Who do you believe?'

He said, 'That's just a ridiculous question.'

He made it clear the interview was over.

I did another piece about lice and this lice expert told me there were lice pretty much everywhere and that he could find lice anywhere. I slightly misjudged the tone of the lice man, though, when I asked him, 'Have you ever found lice in your penis?'

He pulled his mic off and said, 'That's the end of the interview.'

Quite right too.

We didn't use that piece either.

Another item for the Life And Death show involved us visiting the LA coroner's office and filming an autopsy.

The autopsy was going to be conducted on the body of a middle-aged guy who'd died on a boat and might have had a heart attack.

The pathologist who was going to conduct the autopsy looked like Kenny Rogers and he was a lovely man. He took us into this waiting room where we all had to suit up in biohazard-proof bodysuits and face-masks. The waiting room was like something out of Silence Of The Lambs. There were pictures on the walls of dead bodies and murder victims. It was macabre. I looked at this one display cabinet which had a photo of a naked dead woman in it – a crime scene photo of her naked body with a plastic bag tied over the poor woman's head and next to her head was a piece of lead piping. Next to this photo was a plastic bag with the lead piping in it. The actual murder weapon, I presumed. It was a bit unnerving.

Kenny Rogers came back into the room and handed us these disclaimer forms to fill in. One of the items on the form which you had to sign for was to tick a box saying you wouldn't sue the coroner's office if you were to become HIV positive after attending the autopsy. I looked at Kenny Rogers and asked him, 'What are the chances of getting HIV as a result of being in this autopsy?'

He said, 'Remote. The chances are remote. Because the one thing we know about the HIV virus is that it can't survive once it's airborne. But we have to get you to sign this waiver because there could be some infected blood in the system and an incision could be made, blood could spurt out and it could come into contact with you and there's always a remote chance you could catch something from that blood ... '

Nice.

I suddenly realised I was too squeamish for this autopsy business.

I didn't really want to watch this poor man being carved up and spraying blood everywhere.

I asked Giles, 'Mate, do I really need to be in there?'

He said, 'Well, it would help if you were.' I just don't think he wanted to be in there on his own.

I said, 'Mate, I'm sorry, I'm gonna have to say no to this one. I don't want to risk getting Aids from something I really don't want to see.'

And I didn't go in to watch the autopsy.

That was my line. The line I couldn't cross. I did go into the room to watch the world's oldest hetero porn star getting a blow job from a twenty-two-year-old. But I wouldn't watch the autopsy.

Poor Giles was in there filming it for about ninety minutes and later told me he was trying not to vomit for most of those ninety minutes. At one point he felt a wash of some liquid hitting him. He was in a state of shock. Was it blood? No. When he turned back round he realised it was just a spray of embalming fluid that hit him.

Giles's face when he emerged from the autopsy was ashen. And may god forgive me but I was struggling not to laugh. He said, 'Dude, listen, you did the right thing. You don't want to be in there.' He was deadly serious. 'There are some things in life we're just not supposed to see.'

But I didn't have a problem at all with the next incredible item we filmed for that show. That turned out to be the funniest thing I had ever seen in my life.

Mel Brooks has a great quote where he says, 'A man cuts his finger on a bit of paper – that's tragedy. A man dies falling into an open sewer – that's comedy.'

And for me, watching the girl perform a sex act on a sixty-three-year-old isn't comic, but what happened next in Ten Things You Didn't Know About Sex *was* comic.

The most incredible item of all was the man masturbating with stinging nettles.

Back in England, we went to Manchester to film a piece on men who get sexual enjoyment out of masturbating with stinging nettles.

The plan was that I was going to interview a man about this fetish and what it is they get out of it and then we were going to film another guy who would actually demonstrate.

The bloke who was actually going to be doing the masturbating was some kind of specialist performer who appeared in fetish videos and such, and he had apparently done this particular activity before.

The location for the interview was a gay sex shop. Downstairs in this sex shop was a sauna. We thought of doing the interview in the sauna but the steam prevented us. So we just set up in a corner of the shop.

At this point we discovered that the bloke who was going to let us film him masturbating with the stinging nettles had pulled out. A blow.

As for the man I was going to interview, he didn't want his identity revealed so we had to film him in silhouette. His name was John. And he worked in IT. He seemed a bit uncomfortable that we were in a gay sex shop. I assumed the reason we were conducting the interview in the gay sex shop was because he was gay. We could have conducted the interview anywhere – a park, say, in front of some stinging nettles. I thought maybe he'd suggested that gay sex shop location. So I said to him, 'Do you shop here often, John?' And he replied, 'Oh no – fucking hell, I'm not gay.'

I thought it was quite funny that he was so defensive about being gay. But he had no issue with masturbating with stinging nettles. In fact, he actually volunteered to step in for the guy who had pulled out of letting us film him doing it, although he'd never done it before himself. Turned out he was also married with kids, which was clearly why he didn't want his identity revealed.

So John, who didn't want us to film his face and who definitely wasn't gay, was quite happy to allow himself to be filmed masturbating with stinging nettles.

Now I didn't even know why this man was such an authority on masturbating with stinging nettles. Our researcher had found him from somewhere. That's all I knew. Was there some kind of secret stinging nettle grapevine?

It was insane.

We had a young runner with us that day called Emma and she had to get in the car, drive to someone's garden and pick up a bunch of stinging nettles while we were doing this interview, in preparation for the later filming of the actual masturbation scene. Luckily she had gloves.

At the end of the interview, Emma returned, stinging nettles in hand. John, meanwhile, decided it was time to go through the gimp masks in the shop to work out which one he would wear for the big scene.

The guy who owned the shop had sorted out a location for us to film the action. It was on an industrial estate and he told us it was a very famous building because it was where New Order used to rehearse. It had then been turned into a location for gay porn shoots.

We walked in and saw some Roman pillars. They must have been filming a Roman gay porn special of some kind.

Emma the runner put the freshly cut stinging nettles on one of the Roman columns. Giles sets up the tripod and camera about five yards in front of the column.

John, who had brilliantly volunteered to do the demonstration after the other guy had pulled out and let us all down, goes in the back room to change.

Five minutes later he emerged, gimped up in his mask, dressed only in a burgundy terry-towelling bath robe and white sport socks pulled up to shins.

He was trying to talk to me but the space in the gimp mask for his mouth wasn't letting him talk properly. It was as if he had a speech impediment. Eventually he sorted out the excess latex in his mouth and we could hear what he was saying, and he was just asking if he should keep his socks on.

Absolutely, I told him. Definitely keep the socks on. You have to keep the socks on.

At that point there was a knock on the door. There was a curtain around the door when you walked in and a guy poked his head round the curtain, looked at John in his gimp mask and white sport socks, and calmly said, 'I'm sorry, mate – you're gonna have to move your car.'

John, through his gimp mask, replied, 'Oh fuckin' hell … '

He had to go in to the back room, get out of the gimp gear and get dressed to move his car.

By this time Giles and I were crying tears of laughter.

When he came back from moving his car, John got back into the gimp costume and was ready to be filmed. He was ready to perform. I asked him if he could kind of commentate and talk us through it and let us know what he's feeling while he's doing it. He nodded yes and disrobed.

There I was confronted by the sight of a very tall man who worked in IT who was naked, apart from a gimp mask and white socks, and who, I must add, had a rather large penis.

He stood in front of the pillar and he pulled out some surgical gloves. He was clearly worried about stinging his hands. Not so worried about stinging his cock, mind.

Giles filmed this while crying with laughter. Tears were spilling down into his mouth.

John grabbed a handful of nettles and proceeded, indeed, to use the nettles on himself and to masturbate with them. He rubbed them into his groin.

Mindful of the fact that I had asked him to tell us what he's doing, John started commentating.

He said, 'Ooh yeah, I can feel that. It's starting to sting. It's starting to hurt. It's a bit unpleasant.'

John was looking directly into my eyes while he was doing this. I could see his eyes staring at me through the gimp mask. At this point I started to get unnerved by this experience and I hid behind the curtain by the door.

While I was behind the curtain, all I could hear were these words coming out of John's mouth: 'Oh dear – that is really quite excruciating.'

I thought, 'Well, I have to see this.'

So I came out from behind the curtain and carried on watching him and after a good five minutes of masturbating with the stinging nettles, with John at a state of semi-arousal, he had to stop. He announced, 'I'm sorry, you boys, but that is burning. I have to stop.'

He was apologising to us for not being able to work himself up to a full erection with stinging nettles. I couldn't help but look at his penis at that point and I have to say it was red raw and full of welts. He had a bright red Johnson.

We quite happily let him stop. Giles thought he'd shot enough. John then proceeded to take his gimp mask off, delve into his bag and produce a can of Wasp-eze. With one hand he elongated his penis and with the other he sprayed Wasp-eze onto it. But the spray ran out. He sighed, 'Oh, I've run out of Wasp-eze. Fucking hell.'

At this point his mobile phone rang with a singularly inappropriate children's TV theme tune ringtone. It was a wrong number, believe it or not.

We packed up for the day and we paid John his fee for masturbating with stinging nettles for the first time in his life on camera.

His fee was fifty quid.

Giles and I went back to Manchester Piccadilly train station together in the car and we didn't say a word to each other. The day's events were slowly sinking in – what we had done that day, what we had witnessed, where we were going with our lives.

Finally we arrived at the station and Giles and I walked up the escalator towards the platforms together and we still hadn't said anything to each other. He was standing one step ahead of me.

Eventually, he turned to look at me and said the immortal words, 'My dad's a *headmaster*.'

CHAPTER 12

BOBBING FOR PIGS' TESTICLES

I thought Ten Things You Didn't Know About was the best thing I'd ever done and I sincerely hoped that it would lead to something more.

While I was filming it, I decided never to go back to stand-up. I was enjoying the filming so much and I was so determined to carry on in TV, I resolved there and then that if that show didn't lead to any more TV work then that would be it for me. That would be the end of it. (I was going to write, 'That would be the end for me in this business.' But I hate the phrase 'this business'. It's so wanky. If you ever see or hear me use that phrase, feel free to shoot me in the face.)

So when I finished filming that series, I called my agent to ask if he'd booked me in for any gigs coming up. Sure enough, I was booked to host Up The Creek the following weekend. Now even though I always did well there, that venue still gave me sleepless nights. I would lie awake at night for the entire week prior to the gig in question. That was why I had to stop doing the stand-up. I told my agent to pull me out of those gigs because I was leaving stand-up for good. He thought it was a very bad idea and he was probably right. But I told him that stand-up was making me miserable and stressed out. It was affecting my health. It had to stop.

So that was the moment I gave up stand-up. I never did any more stand-up comedy shows.

Of course my agent would carry on asking me to do the odd gig every now and then. But I never did.

My last ever gig was in Bedford. It was okay.

I felt a huge sense of relief. It was brilliant not to have to worry about standing up in front of hundreds of people and trying to make them laugh and keep them happy and amused. I just wanted to keep Karen happy and amused. Luckily, I'd always managed to make her laugh, right from the first time we met when she came in the video store.

Now we'd found ourselves a lovely little cottage in Hannam, not too far from our families, and I'd also earned enough money so that I could be patient and wait for something to come along that I really wanted to do. I didn't have to do any old shit.

But, actually, I did. The reality was that if I was going to be offered a TV job that wasn't good, that was basically just something to do instead of staying at home bothering my fiancée, I thought I might as well take it. I suppose I still wasn't in a position to turn TV work down. That would have felt indulgent. I'd already told everyone I'd never do any stand-up and I did want to be a TV presenter, so when TV presenting gigs came along, who was I to snub them?

So I ended up doing a show I didn't really want to do that much. It was called Britain Versus The World. It was also for Bravo.

The idea for the show was that a team Great Britain, captained by me, took part in a series of stupid sporting events and weird challenges against teams from around the world.

For example Team GB would take on Team Sweden in the world sauna-sitting championship.

I was asked by the production company if I had a couple of mates who I wanted to have in my team for the show. Now you can take that in two ways – either it's a nice chance to get your friends involved in the show, or else, it's a bit weird that the production company is asking if you want to supply members of the team from your group of mates. It maybe signified that the whole project was a bit cockamamie.

I said no to the show at least twice. I'd just done a series that I really liked and I thought I would rather wait for the right thing to come along. In my continuing naivety I thought something else would come along that I would wholeheartedly want to do. But it didn't. In the end I agreed to do it because it was either that or sit on my arse until Christmas and beyond.

The team-mates ended up being friends of the director.

We filmed the series for five weeks and again I faced a lot of challenges that I really didn't want to do.

Bog snorkelling was one of them. It was November. It was freezing cold. They had St John's Ambulance nearby. And we had to snorkel in a bog. One of our team needed oxygen after he snorkelled in the bog. When he finished the weather got so bad that they had to put an end to the snorkelling. I thought, 'Thank Christ!'

Unbelievably we also took part in the world stinging-nettle-eating championship. Not masturbating with them, just eating them.

The technique was to roll up the nettle in your fingers very quickly, which would take the sting out of them. You might end up with stung fingers but that was preferable to a stung mouth. Then it was just a case of shoving them in your mouth as quickly as possible. Easy. So I actually took part in that.

We competed in the Redneck Games which were held in this Wild West town just outside of London. We took on three Americans and one of the events was bobbing for pigs' testicles. Similar to bobbing for apples except you bob for pigs' testicles.

The night before that event I had a phone call from the production manager asking me if I could store the pigs' testicles in my fridge. No I couldn't! I wasn't going to have pigs' testicles in my fridge next to my crunch corners.

The actual event itself was really unpleasant. I just had to try to get the testicles in my mouth without heaving. After the event, after I had bobbed, I spoke to the producer and commented that it didn't seem right that they did this in America – bobbed for pigs' testicles. He told me that in fact I was right. They bobbed for pigs' trotters in the real Redneck Games in the US. But the producers thought it would be better and funnier, I guess, if we were bobbing for testicles. So we did. But it wasn't right.

That was Britain Versus The World. It wasn't a great show.

But if that show was bad, if that series was just a job I took because it seemed silly and pointless to turn it down, then the other work I got that year was the real destroyer of my soul. The next job was the one that tested the limits of my desire to be a television presenter. In fact it tested all kinds of limits for me.

I became the operator of a rude cat puppet.

MTV UK wanted their own equivalent of Triumph the Insult Dog, which was a dog puppet (and his operator obviously) in the States which interviewed all the stars and was quite rude to them. Famously, Eminem got really annoyed by it and nearly attacked the poor puppet.

One of the executives who liked me in my first stint at MTV asked me if I wanted to do the same thing as Triumph the Insult Dog, except with a cat.

I was asked to do a pilot show featuring me operating a cat puppet and I wasn't very keen but my agent thought it was a good idea so in the end I agreed to do it.

In this pilot, we covered Michael Jackson's visit to the UK when he had some kind of dispute with his record company and there was a big demonstration in support of him.

I was with all the Jacko fans outside the Sony office in London while this open-top tour bus drove by with Michael Jackson on the top deck. It was like a convention of Jacko fans.

I was there with this cat puppet. They hadn't come up with a name for the puppet so I decided to call it Chet, after the bully older brother in Weird Science. And I, or rather Chet, interviewed some of these Michael Jackson fans and basically asked them a series of annoying and/or stupid questions. I bumped into Louis Theroux at one point, who was making his own documentary about Jacko, and we had a little chat about the programmes we were making. He didn't give me any good material in response to the cat puppet, but I can't say I blamed him. He was just being a normal, decent, nice guy.

I absolutely hated doing it. I hated having the puppet. It was a rubbish puppet (though it was deliberately rubbish). I didn't want to ever do it again.

But a strange thing happened. Once they'd edited and finished the pilot show, they sent a tape of it to me and my agent and my agent loved it. Then I showed it to my friend Tim and he thought it was hilarious. He told me I had to do it. He told me it gave me an opportunity to say whatever the hell I wanted, because I was holding this cat puppet in front of my face and it would be the cat saying those things. MTV loved it too, and what they wanted me to do was cover big premieres and awards ceremonies and stuff, with the cat puppet asking quests to the celebrities at those kinds of events. And it was a foot back in the door at MTV.

So I agreed to do it.

My biggest gripe was that I would be quite happy to be back on MTV as a presenter but instead I was going to be back on MTV but not really because you wouldn't see me, because I was operating this fucking cat puppet!

I found the whole idea soul-destroying.

Nevertheless everyone around me thought it was a good idea so I took the job.

The first show I did was the premiere of Lord Of The Rings. At the Lord Of The Rings premiere my cat stopped Cate Blanchett and I made some bad joke about the possibility of letting the cat hide up her dress – with the cat puppet asking, 'Is there room for another pussy up your dress?' No, it wasn't funny but she said, 'Yes, if you like.' She was lovely.

I tried to stop Griff Rhys Jones but he just said, 'Oh god ... ' and moved on. I thought, 'Yes you're right.' That's what I would have done in his position – ignore the annoying cat puppet bloke.

Tina from S Club 7 was there and I called her Liv because she looked a bit like Liv Tyler and she just kept saying, 'I'm not Liv!'

I stopped Bob Geldof and said to him, 'Bob, could you just go and get me a sandwich? I'm absolutely starving.' And Bob responded to that quite well. He started to hit the cat. In a comedic way.

In the press pack at this premiere everyone was jostling for position to get access to the stars and I ended up significantly winding up everyone around me because I had to be deliberately obnoxious as the cat to try to get the stars to stop. That's what the cat had to do. And I hated it. At one point I could hear one of the cameramen standing next to me saying, 'If that fucking bloke doesn't shut up ... ' And I couldn't blame him. I would have been annoyed by me too.

But as bad and horrible and annoying as those premieres were, they paled next to my experience at the MTV Europe Music Awards in Barcelona. That was my lowest ebb.

When they asked me to fly out to Barcelona, where I'd never been before, to stand on the red carpet with the cat puppet at this big, glamorous event, it sounded like a good gig. Even though I hated doing the cat puppet.

But it wasn't a good gig. Not by any stretch of the imagination.

I had to fly out on my own. There wasn't going to be any producer or researcher or chaperone flying with me. But before I flew, I was asked to travel across London to a studio to pick up the new Chet the Cat puppet. Someone at MTV had taken the decision to upgrade the puppet. Even though part of the joke was that the puppet was a shitty sock thing. It was supposed to look shit. But someone had decided they needed a bigger, better cat puppet. And I was supposed to bring the puppet out to Barcelona with me on my flight.

I didn't mind. I thought, 'Well, I'm flying out on my own ... I could do with the company.'

But I got a shock when I saw the new puppet for the first time. It was three times bigger than the old one, and it now had a big pole attached to it so you could make it blink. It was the kind of puppet that, if you were a professional puppeteer, you would have loved working with. You could move its eyelids and everything. But I wasn't a professional puppeteer. And now I had a proper puppet that I had to control. Not only that, but I had been put in charge of taking this bloody thing through customs and into Barcelona with me.

I went to the airport, where I met Boyd Hilton from heat magazine for the first time (we later worked together on Xfm and Flipside and became best friends) and Boydo introduced me to one of his colleagues called Paul who had just become a news presenter on MTV.

It turned out I was going to be working right next to Paul at the awards in Barcelona.

As soon as I arrived in Barcelona I went to the hotel and met the MTV news producer who told me what I was supposed to be doing and then I was taken to the Olympic Stadium where the MTV Europe Music Awards were taking place.

It was a shambles. It was difficult enough to get in to the right area on the red carpet and I wasn't even give an Access All Areas pass. I only had access to certain areas.

The really depressing element of it all for me was that I met all these new MTV presenters like Paul and Tim Kash and Alex Zane, and I kept thinking that only five years previously I had been a new MTV presenter. And now I was just some guy with a puppet in front of his face. I wanted to be one of the normal MTV presenters!

What made it even worse was that everywhere I went that night, people from MTV would stop me or say hello to me and they would invariably say, 'Oh, you're the puppet guy' … 'He's the puppet guy' … 'You must be the puppet guy.' I didn't want to be the fucking puppet guy! I was better than that.

Eventually I was taken to the red carpet and I was standing with Paul and he's the new face of MTV News so out of the two of us, he's the most important. So once he got his stuff for the news, then I would have to try to get my stuff filmed. But we only had one camera between us. We had to share our space and our camera. Not only that, but the poor celebrities were supposed to be interviewed by Paul, then we'd have to stop and then I was supposed to do my stupid interview with them afterwards. It was never going to work. It was a shambles. I hardly managed to say anything to any of them, let alone say or ask anything funny.

At one point I saw Marilyn Manson down the line and I shouted a question at him about whether it was true that he starred in The Wonder Years, which was a popualr urban myth at the time. He completely ignored me.

The Sugababes went by and I asked whether there was room for another pussy in the band. Awful stuff. But Mutya yelled back, 'Yes!'

When I finished filming, I ended up right at the back of the auditorium. I wasn't in any exclusive backstage area because I didn't have an Access All Areas pass. And because I didn't have a team of people with me, I just ended up strolling around on my own in this huge auditorium. Just me and the puppet.

At one point I ended up with a group of people from MTV Sweden and I got talking to this stunning blonde woman. She was asking me questions about the puppet and I kept going on about how much I hated it and how it was ruining my life. I must have sounded a bit like Anthony Hopkins as the deranged ventriloquist who hated his puppet in the film Magic. This beautiful MTV Sweden woman found my anger with the puppet quite funny. My misery was making her laugh.

In the end I threw Chet the Cat puppet to the ground and we both started kicking it. It was a huge release for me. I loved being able to kick the shit out of that fucking puppet, which I'd grown to despise.

And that was the last I ever saw of that quite expensive cat puppet. I left it in a heap on the floor of the Olympic Stadium at the MTV Europe Music Awards in 2002.

And good riddance, might I add.

Anyway, after I killed Chet, and said goodbye to the lovely Swedish MTV lady, I was on my own.

There was no one there from MTV UK to look after me. No one to help me find a cab or a car. No one at all to help me get the fuck out of there and find my way home in a city I'd never been to before in my life. I don't want to sound like I was whining or anything but I was lost!

I briefly ended up with a group from MTV UK, including one of their new presenters, so I thought I'd have a quick chat with him. I asked him how his night had gone, and he looked at me and said, 'It's going all right, but I want to be careful because – no offence, I wouldn't want to be back here in five years' time with my hand up a cat's arse.'

I just looked at him and I thought, 'Yeah. There you go.'

He'd essentially pissed in my eyes. But of course he was right. I didn't want to be there with my hand up a cat's arse either.

That was it for me. I couldn't stand there any longer feeling sorry for myself. And no one else from MTV UK seemed interested in me, the puppet guy. Even though I didn't have the puppet any more. So I ended up just following the throng and left the stadium and I ended up walking the streets on my own for hours. I didn't even have Chet for company!

I had no idea where I was going and I walked the streets of Barcelona till about 4am before I finally found a cab queue which was ridiculously long and climbed into a cab which took me back to my hotel.

When I got home I thought, 'I'm never ever ever doing that again.'

In fact I covered the Jackass The Movie premiere with Chet the Cat.

We had to go back to the original crappy puppet.

Before the premiere I had to go to the MTV offices in London to meet one of the producers and I was moaning about the nightmare in Barcelona and this producer asked me if I knew what had happened to the cat puppet. 'No, I don't,' I told her. 'The last time I saw that puppet was when I left it on the floor of the MTV Europe Music Awards after I'd given it a good kicking!' What a bloody cheek to even ask me.

But I did cover the premiere of Jackass The Movie, because I was too weak to turn it down, and at that event one of its stars, Chris Pontius, known as Partyboy, showed up dressed only in a thong. My cat puppet asked him a question, and he leapt on me. He jumped on me. A wrestling match ensued. I had that cat puppet on the end of my arm and this almost naked American Partyboy was wrestling me to the floor. That clip made it onto the showbiz news the next morning.

That really was the end of my time with Chet the Cat. I told them I would never do it again no matter what.

Although about two years later, though, a call came through asking me whether I could do the cat puppet again for MTV.

No I fucking couldn't.

CHAPTER 13

NO MONEY FOR PIZZA

It was all happening, and yet in many ways, nothing was happening. I was about to turn thirty, I was about to marry the love of my life, I was planning the honeymoon of my dreams (and, I hoped, Karen's too), but I had no work. And no money.

I'd earned a pretty decent amount from my ads and from those TV jobs that I didn't really enjoy doing, and, forever the optimist, I totally assumed that more offers would come along. More ads, more TV shows. The phone would ring and keep ringing. So, with our wedding planned for June, I spent the preceding weeks, perhaps even months, not doing very much at all apart from planning our honeymoon. After all, I had all that fucking free time.

I totally planned the honeymoon without Karen knowing. I told her to leave it to me. (And believe me, Karen was used to planning everything that went on in our lives. She still does. She organises everything. It's just something she's brilliant at, and she enjoys it. She loves sorting shit out.)

There were loads of places we could have gone – the Maldives, Mauritius, Thailand – all the usual honeymoon destinations. (I've still resisted going to Thailand simply because people bang on about it so much.)

But Karen had never been to America and I'd always wanted to go to Hawaii – it felt exotic but it was also still in America. So I sorted out a trip to two Hawaiian islands and Las Vegas and San Francisco along the way. It was a honeymoon so I didn't want it to be a slog. I didn't want some kind of big trail. I didn't want to walk up a lot of steps or climb to the top of something. We could do that another time – try to find some Incas, or whatever. This was our honeymoon so I wanted it to be nice and relaxing and of course romantic. I just wanted us to relax and enjoy ourselves and be together.

I booked the whole lot – limos, hotels, flights. I worried and fretted about it. I wanted everything to be just right.

I knew what I wanted – to fly first class with Virgin, because everyone likes Virgin. I went into Trailfinders and the guy there kept telling me, 'United. Fly United,' but I wanted Virgin. And he wasn't listening. So I thought, 'I'm going to Lunn Poly!'

And I did. There was a young girl behind the desk and I told her exactly where I wanted to go and that I wanted to fly Virgin. She sorted it all out. It was a no-expense-spared situation and it completely wiped me out financially. But I didn't care. Something else would come along ...

Our wedding was on a beautiful June day at Kendleshire golf club. I booked a traditional jazz band, and they were great. We loved every minute of it, Karen and I.

But there was one disappointment about my wedding day,

I booked the best hotel room I'd ever seen in my life for our wedding night. It was at the Hotel Du Vin in Bristol – their fabulous honeymoon suite which had twin cast-iron tubs side by side with a little table in the middle on which to put your bottle of champagne and your flutes. I'd even taken my mum along to see this room, and she agreed it was perfect. I had this vision of Karen and I sitting in our tubs after a long, exhausting day, and we'd be sipping our champagne and having a wonderful, relaxing end to our wedding.

My plan was for Karen and me to leave the wedding a little bit early, after a really hectic day, and retire to this magnificent suite at the hotel in Bristol and fly off early the next morning to the first leg of our honeymoon in San Francisco. We were due to check in at stupid o'clock.

As it turned out, Karen didn't want to leave the wedding early. She wanted to stay to the bitter end. So in the end I realised we would only have a couple of hours at best in this glorious hotel room. So I cancelled the room in the end.

But to this day that slightly miffs me.

I think we would have had a lovely few hours in those twin baths.

But I totally understand why Karen wanted her wedding celebrations to last as long as possible.

As for the honeymoon – it could not have gone better. The trick for honeymooners is to tell anyone with ears that you are on a honeymoon, and have a smile on your face, and if you do that I promise you'll get upgrades all the way.

For example, on the Hawaiian island of Maui, we checked in to this beautiful open-air check-in and I'd booked a standard garden-view room which itself was ridiculously expensive. But they upgraded us to Ocean Front, which was absurdly expensive.

Just by being nice, polite and playing dumb a bit – and going on about our honeymoon, we got a triple upgrade.

We did the same thing at the Mirage in Las Vegas, on the way back from Hawaii. We got upgraded to a room with a view of the mouth of the volcano which erupts every thirty minutes. It's not a real volcano, by the way.

But when we got back off our honeymoon I was broke. And I had no work on the horizon. I had no money at all. I'd spent all my savings on the wedding and honeymoon. I'm not exaggerating. I didn't have a penny in the bank.

So Karen was working full-time and was paying for everything. She paid all the bills and paid for the upkeep of the house. I contributed nothing. I was a kept man.

This is how bad it got: one morning I said to Karen, before she went off to work to keep a roof over our heads, 'I'm going to go shopping for BOGOFs at Somerfield in Kingswood.'

I had nothing to do that day, like most days, so I went to the local supermarket looking for Buy One Get One Free deals on food.

I had no cash at all. I didn't have a penny in my pocket. I couldn't get any money out of the bank because I didn't have any money in the bank. I didn't have any money in the bank but I had got an overdraft. So I was going to rely on using my credit card or my debit card.

I filled up a trolley with BOGOFs and reached the till. I handed over my credit card. It was denied. Turned out I was behind in paying the minimum monthly payment. So I handed over my debit card. Turned out I was over my overdraft limit too. Neither of my cards was accepted. I literally had no money at all. Nothing in the world. And there I was with a trolley full of Buy One Get One Free foodstuffs. The disgruntled Somerfield employee was looking at me like I was a piece of shit. All I was trying to do was buy four Chicago Town Deep Dish Pizzas for the price of two (and some other BOGOF items like orange juice). I loved those pizzas – the small ones that were designed as a meal for one, especially the ham and pineapple, and the cheese and the pepperoni ones, I loved them all – honestly, ask my mum and she will tell you I've always loved the Chicago Town Deep Dish Pizzas, and they were always on offer to Buy One Get One Free.

So what could I do? I couldn't pay for them, so I asked the disgruntled checkout lady if I could just leave the trolley with all my bagged-up pizzas with her for five minutes so I could run to the bank and then come back and pay for it all later.

Of course I knew I didn't *have* any money in the bank. So I just left and never came back.

It was humiliating.

Now I'm not expecting the violins to start playing in the background. I'm just telling you how it was: I was a grown man, a married man, with a mortgage, I was twenty-nine years of age, and I did not have a penny in the world. Not a penny to my name. So I had to go back home without any BOGOFs, without my Chicago Town pizzas. And I had to call my wife and tell her I couldn't pay for the shopping because I had nothing.

I kept thinking about 1999, the worst year of my life since my career in performing took off in any meaningful sense. I knew I never wanted to get into that position again where I just had nothing to do and was earning no money at all. That year, I resolved that if I did ever get into that position where basically I was just sitting there waiting for the phone to ring, I would call it a day. And get a proper job.

But here I was in 2003 in exactly that position. And this time I was a grown-up, twenty-nine-year-old man with a wife and a house.

So I was thinking, 'This might be it. It might be all over.' I'd given up stand-up, I wasn't offered any more ads. No more TV. There was nothing on the horizon.

I had so little to do that I decided to spend time growing a beard.

Yes, I was twenty-nine when this thing you see on my face on the front cover first emerged. Until then I was clean-shaven. In fact, like everything in my life, I was a late developer when it came to facial hair.

I couldn't shave for years. I was seventeen, working at M&S, when a few of the supervisors told me I was getting bum-fluff and that I should shave. But my dad always told me to wait as long as possible because once I started shaving then it would never let up and my face fuzz would grow like there was no tomorrow and I'd have to shave all the bloody time. The first few times I shaved, my dad did it for me with a wet razor. Then he bought me a Philips Coolskin which had gel you could squeeze out on to the heads. It was great.

But the real reason I started growing my beard when I was nearly thirty was that I was sick of my chin.

I've always struggled to be comfortable with my look, although at the same time I have always been fascinated by it! I've always had this big, jutting-out chin, for example. Some people say a strong chin is a sign of masculinity or whatever. I just saw a fucking great big chin in the mirror and I didn't want it. I've also always hated shaving, as soon as I started back when my dad helped me. So I decided to hide the chin under a beard. It may be a cliché, but it's true: the beard is a mask.

I had a beard to stroke and I needed it. Because I was seriously worrying about whether the phone was going to ring ever again with an offer of work, and somehow it's quite comforting to have a bit of facial hair to play with.

Just as I was beginning to seriously doubt if I could continue down my chosen path, following my dreams from those very earliest days when I watched movies and wanted to be in them, there was a slight glimmer of a whisper of a possibility of work.

But it was nothing to do with appearing on screen. It was a possibility of a radio show. And it was all down to Ricky Gervais and Steve Merchant and that time I bumped into them in Soho in London.

I was in London for a meeting with my agent about possible auditions that would almost certainly lead to nowhere, when I saw Ricky and Steve. It was the first time I'd seen them since they'd caught sight of me carrying the foam '£20 Million' Lottery sign, and I bumped into them again in the same Soho street.

I was always very nervous in those days and I would talk ten to the dozen. So I proceeded to chatter nervously about how I didn't have any work and so on to Ricky and Steve, who were both being very nice to me and listening to whatever I was wittering on about. In the middle of the conversation, Ricky asked me something but I didn't quite hear what he said, but because I was nervous I said yes anyway. It was all a bit confusing. And he said, 'Okay, I'll have a word with Karl.' When I heard that I did ask him to repeat what he meant. What was he going to ask Karl? Who was this Karl?

He explained that Karl Pilkington, his producer at the London indie music radio station Xfm, had told him they were looking for new talent, new DJs to take over a couple of slots. And Ricky was asking me if I would be interested in doing something for Xfm. Of course I said yes.

Steve joked: 'Hold on a minute, we can't have everyone from Bristol on Xfm!' I gave my number to Ricky and wondered if anything would come of it.

A few days later when I was back home in Bristol, I got a phone call from this Karl Pilkington asking me if I would be interested in doing something. I told him I loved radio and would definitely be interested. He asked me what kind of music I liked because Xfm was mainly an indie-rock type of station. Karl was very laid-back and relaxed and made it clear he was just sounding me out. He told me not to say anything to my agent, and said that I should have a think about it and maybe have a think about the kind of show I could do. It was a nice casual chat really. I didn't think anything would necessarily come of it.

And nothing did come of it, until many months later.

Eventually Xfm approached my agent directly to ask about the possibility of going into their studios in London and doing a pilot for a show which would be celebrity-based and would be co-hosted by Boyd Hilton from heat magazine (who I'd previously met purely by coincidence at the airport when I was on my way with the cat puppet to that fateful MTV awards farrago in Barcelona).

It was all down to Ricky Gervais, really. Ricky was the one who mentioned the idea of me hosting a show to Karl. And Ricky had also had the idea of getting Boyd involved, having been interviewed by Boyd a few times for heat. Ricky brought me and Boyd together, thinking that we'd be good foils for each other, me with my ridiculous enthusiasm and Boydo with his knowledge of TV and films and celebrities and all that. So I had a meeting with Boyd at my agent's office and instantly we got on really well and agreed to do a pilot for Xfm. Like all the people who ever appeal to me, Boydo was very laid-back and relaxed, and let me go on about whatever I wanted to go on about. He also loved films and TV like I did. And I've been great friends with Boydo ever since.

As it turned out, I recorded the pilot with Boydo but in the end Xfm wanted me to do a show on my own because they had two specific slots in mind for me.

I could go in and work with Jimmy Carr on his show on Sunday morning, but I immediately knew that wouldn't work (and why would Jimmy want to have me thrust upon him?). Or they had the graveyard slot from 1 to 4am on a Saturday night/Sunday morning. I immediately said yes to the graveyard slot. I thought I could make it my own and I actually love late nights. I'm always up late anyway. Since the days when I was watching Red Triangle films on Channel 4.

They gave me that show. And even though the pay was diabolical, at least it was something.

A few months earlier I couldn't afford to buy Chicago Town pizzas.

A few months earlier all I had to do was grow a beard.

You could say I was more than a little relieved that I had something to do. And I did love listening to a good radio show, going right back to Fun On The Phones. I thought this was my chance to have some Fun On The Phones.

Before my first show they decided I should learn how to work the desk in the studio – how to select the songs and do all the technical side of things because I'd never presented my own radio show before. It was all new to me, apart from my days as a hospital radio assistant, of course.

So they asked me to come in for a couple of Thursdays and shadow one of their experienced DJs – the lovely Claire Sturgess. I thought it was a good idea.

But I had a grotesquely embarrassing start with Claire.

The first Thursday I was due to shadow Claire, I arrived in London a few hours early so I decided to kill some time by going to Soho and buying some porno videos.

I bought some porno vids that I liked, put them in my bag and arrived in good time to shadow Claire on her show. I got to reception at Xfm's building in Leicester Square and told the bloke behind the security desk that I was Justin Lee Collins, the new DJ at Xfm and that I was due to see Claire Sturgess that night. The guy on the reception desk looked at me and said, 'Yeah, I just need to search your bag.'

My heart sank. I coughed a bit and said, 'Are you sure? Are you serious?'

He said, 'Yes, we need to search your bag – when you go in and out … '

I said, 'Oh, for goodness' sake. I'm about to start working here and coming in every week … do you really need to search *my* bag?'

He said, 'Well, you could refuse the bag search but if you do refuse the bag search I have to make a note that you refused the bag search.'

I thought, 'Fucking hell – this is my first week at Xfm. I haven't even done my first show yet. I've just turned up for the first time – I do not want it entered into the book that I've refused a bag search. I'd get a reputation as a trouble-maker.'

There was no option. I had to hand over my bag.

He opened it and pulled out my copy of Bend Over Spunk Junkies.

He gave me a wry smile and sent me on my way.

I didn't tell Claire Sturgess what happened.

But the following week I did wonder whether she knew about my porno shame.

They taught me how to run the desk in the studio but they also gave me an experienced producer to help me out. So every week I'd drive to London from home, arrive at about 10.30pm, potter about for a couple of hours thinking about stuff to do on the show, and then go on air at 1am for three hours.

I really enjoyed it. And after I'd done about eight shows in two months, the new station head offered me a new slot – Saturday afternoons following Ricky Gervais and Steve Merchant's show.

I was thrilled.

I made a bit of a concerted effort to be edgy and irreverent and one day I listened to Ricky and Steve's show while I was preparing for mine, and they were having a conversation about Neanderthal man, and Ricky said something about how the reason why men are attracted to the buttocks is because they remind them of breasts. In response, their legendary producer Karl Pilkington said, 'If that's true, how come gays don't like a bit of tit?'

That was at lunchtime on live radio.

Now I was thinking of doing quite a risqué bit on my show so when they finished their show, I checked with Ricky and Steve whether they thought it would be okay for me to do my risqué bit. Ricky said, 'Did you hear what Karl said?!'

I told them I did.

'Well,' said Ricky, 'anything goes ... '

With that in mind, I did test the boundaries I think.

We taste-tested flavoured condoms on the show one Saturday afternoon.

I used to get facts deliberately wrong, I said celebrities had sadly passed away when they clearly hadn't. I'd get the names of bands wrong or mixed up. I'd come up with utterly ridiculous non-facts. For example, every time we played a song by The Magic Numbers I would talk about the drummer being a serial killer and how he was wanted in twenty-nine states. I would say I know for a fact he's a serial killer.

I said that Starsailor were responsible for Phil Spector shooting his girlfriend in the face. I said they were so miserable that they inspired their producer into that kind of behaviour.

I said things that were so ridiculous that I knew no one would take me seriously. Although I did get a lot of complaining text messages and emails accusing me of being a complete idiot. They thought I was just stupid. They heard me saying this stuff with my country bumpkin accent and they'd think I was a complete moron. But I was just deliberately coming out with daft nonsense.

I enjoyed doing my radio show but not as much as I enjoyed hosting TV shows. There's no audience there in front of you responding to what you do. There's no crew. There's just you speaking into a mic, imagining people listening. Just you and the sound of your own voice. It is nicely intimate but I don't find that as rewarding. I hesitate to use the word 'buzz' because it's a wanky word, but I have to say I don't get as big a buzz working on the radio as I do working on TV. There, I've used the word buzz. Sorry.

The other thing about working for Xfm was that, just like my stand-up years, I hoped and deep down assumed that having my own show on the radio might just lead to me getting my own show on TV. Or at least more TV work if anyone out there from the world of TV was listening. I thought someone must be.

And it did lead to some TV work. Some of it fleeting and trivial, some of it very very important to me.

On the fleeting front, I was asked to go on Liquid News on BBC3 hosted by Claudia Winkleman and Paddy Considine – sorry, Paddy O'Connell – one night. It was a very late booking. On the day of the show. Clearly someone had pulled out at the last minute.

But I loved the show. It's long gone now, but at the time it was a great, irreverent look at the day's celebrity and entertainment news.

I got the train to London and while I was en route, a researcher talked me through the topics that we'd be covering on that evening's show. She told me I was going to be in the studio, on the sofa – actually it was more of a banquette – with Emily Eavis, daughter of Michael, the man who invented the Glastonbury Festival.

Then she told me that one of the stories that would be covered was the fiftieth anniversary of Playboy magazine. Immediately I wondered if they would ask me if I had ever read Playboy or regularly read magazines like that when I was a kid. I anticipated that kind of question might come up.

When I got to the show and the recording began, I soon caused a bit of trouble by interrupting Claudia and Paddy's live chat via satellite to their correspondent in LA. I just interrupted it with nonsense. But if I was hosting a show like that and someone crashed the LA satellite link, I would be annoyed. It's essentially an unhelpful and annoying thing to do, because there's always a delay on a satellite conversation so it's difficult enough anyway. Luckily Claudia and Paddy coped with me very well and didn't seem to mind my interruptions too much.

Then we got on to the subject of the fiftieth anniversary of Playboy magazine.

Sure enough, Claudia asked me, 'Were you a fan of men's magazines when you were growing up?'

I replied, 'Yes – do you want me to tell you about them, Claudia?'

She went along with it and said, 'Yes, please tell us ... '

I said, 'Okay, well, I was a big fan of Lazy-Eyed Over-50s.'

Then I paused. And I added, 'Actually still now at home under my mattress I've got a copy of Asian Amputees.'

Well, this caused a shockwave to reverberate through the studio.

Paddy shouted, 'No!', and then he said to Claudia, 'Why did you ask him that?!'

When I got to the Green Room after the show, it was like I'd killed someone. There were producers and researchers in the room and nobody talked to me. Eventually one of them said to me, 'That was a bit of a car crash ... '

But I thought I'd been quite funny. Now I was completely deflated. Clearly they all hated me. I felt weird about it because I realised that in their eyes I'd gone too far, but I thought it was funny.

When Claudia arrived in the room she turned to me and said, 'You. Were. Brilliant. You were hilarious.'

I was so grateful to her. Because everyone else seemed to think I was a disaster.

Nevertheless despite Claudia saying that to me, I still spent that night and most of the next day thinking I'd gone too far and that I'd done something terribly wrong. I was racking my brain to work out what had offended them about what I'd said. Was it that I'd said the word 'Asian' and then the word 'Amputee'? I wasn't making a joke about Asian people. And I wasn't making a joke about amputees. I was making a joke about what the most outrageous and funny and absurd thing was that I could get off on. I hadn't been racist or amputee-ist surely, and so it really bothered me what their problem was with my comment. I couldn't work out why they were so upset about it. Maybe that's just me.

Then a lovely thing happened.

I got a call from my agent and he told me he had someone on the phone who wanted to speak to me. It was Ricky Gervais.

And Ricky said to me, 'I just wanted to say I've had a really bad day today and I've just watched you on Liquid News and you really cheered me up. You were really funny and you've got nothing to worry about.'

CHAPTER 14

THE JOB THAT CHANGED MY LIFE

I'll never forget getting a phone call at home from my agent's assistant Lisa Toogood, and before she'd even told me what it was she had to tell me, she was laughing. I could hear her giggling. Eventually she said, 'You're not going to believe this, wait for it ... you're going to love this. Are you sitting down?'

So I was like, 'What? What is it?'

Lisa said, 'We've had a phone call from the BBC. They are bringing back Come Dancing. They're making a celebrity version of it, and they want you to host the support show for it. Strictly Come Dancing on BBC3.'

I immediately burst out laughing, and after I'd laughed my ass off, I told Lisa that whoever thought of that idea deserved a medal.

Then I found out that the reason I was asked outright to host this unbelievable new show was because the head of BBC3 was Stuart Murphy and his wife Polly had been watching me on this show that no one at all was watching. It was on an ultra-obscure cable TV station Nation 277 and it was a live television review programme called Flipside and Stuart's wife Polly happened to have been watching it, along with about forty-seven other people, mostly drunk students.

Now the way I got to host Flipside was this: Richard Bacon was involved with the creation of it, and he was looking for people to appear on it. He was an Xfm DJ at the time and he asked Karl Pilkington, Ricky Gervais and Steve Merchant's radio producer, if he could recommend anyone. So Karl knew me, because at that time I was doing a show on Xfm, and Karl recommended me to Richard.

So I went to Wapping, where the show was based, and because the Flipside people didn't have a clue who I was, I met journalist Michael Holden who was involved and Dave Evans who was a producer on the show, and basically I was auditioned by these two people. They asked me what kind of TV I liked, and they asked what I liked about TV and what I didn't like, and this was just to be a guest on the show! Not to host it or anything. I would have thought the fact that I had my own show on Xfm might be enough, but clearly it wasn't for them, and so I had this audition/interview.

As a courtesy I called my agent Duncan to tell him. 'Look, there's this show called Flipside which Richard Bacon is involved in and they want me to be a guest and I think I might do it. What do you think?'

And Duncan's attitude was: 'I don't know what it is, I've never heard of it, it sounds a bit rubbish, but if you want to do it, then go ahead.'

Now all I was doing in those days was one Xfm show, which paid me £150 a week. I had my first house, a mortgage, a wife, and I was literally earning £150 a week. That was my sole income. My wife, who was working as a legal secretary, was earning considerably more at the time, so she was supporting me.

Now Flipside was going to pay me £150 to appear on the show. So I wasn't about to turn it down.

When I first appeared on Flipside, on October 5 2003, and Richard Bacon was hosting, I would just try to find funny stuff on TV and be funny about it. After that first show, Bacon took me aside and said to me, 'You were brilliant. You completely took it, and ran with it, and turned it into something it was never meant to be.' Bacon used to say,

'We watch TV, so you don't have to.' So it was meant to be a relatively serious live television review show. But it wasn't meant to be a comedy show. But after I did it, Bacon wanted me back, and then in the run-up to Christmas 2003, I was asked to host it. And by the beginning of 2004 I was hosting it about three times a week, alternating with Bacon and Colin Murray and Iain Lee. They moved the channel from 277 to 218 on the Sky platform. And it was becoming a nice little earner for me. My main income, in fact, because I would get 400 quid each time I hosted the show.

It was the most bizarre of TV formats really, but at its best it was a fabulous show for me. And the best part of it was that I got to know and work with Boydo Hilton again. He ended up being a guest on most of the shows I hosted because everyone could see we worked really well together.

But as I've indicated, the really significant thing about Flipside was that it led directly to me being asked to work on Strictly Come Dancing.

So Lisa Toogood told me that Stuart Murphy, encouraged by his wife, had been watching me on Flipside for about a month, and now he wanted me to host the BBC3 Strictly Come Dancing show. Now I don't think Lisa or Stuart or even my agent knew that I had this thing for ballroom dancing. And apart from loving Come Dancing as a kid, as you know if you were paying attention at the beginning of this book, I would also search out ballroom dancing coverage on German channels like RTL or Eurosport on satellite TV. I loved it.

So in early 2004 I found myself at the BBC for the first time ever. It's quite an intimidating place. It's a horrible building really. It looks like somewhere that was destroyed in the Second World War and was hastily rebuilt in the 1950s. But there I was having this meeting – me, my agent Duncan and Stuart Murphy, head of BBC3 – about my dream job. Hosting a show about ballroom dancing. Stuart told me there and then that he wanted me to do the job.

I was ecstatic. The initial idea was that I would have a co-host on the show. And as it turned out I did it on my own and hosted shows Monday to Friday for thirty minutes live and then a live show on Saturday after the BBC1 main show, and on Sunday morning I would do the voiceover for a highlights show. So I'd be working seven days a week.

So I left the BBC thinking, 'That was a good meeting.'

I was more nervous than I'd ever been in my life about the first Strictly Come Dancing show. So nervous. And I'd been made more nervous by the fact that I had to interview Bruce Forsyth on that first show. Bear in mind that I'd grown up watching and loving Bruce, that my parents watched him and loved him, and that he'd been brilliant on shows like Hollywood Or Bust, Play Your Cards Right, The Generation Game, You Bet – I loved him on all those shows. I loved him.

Now the first time I'd met Bruce was during the pilot for my first Strictly show and during that interview he wasn't particularly nice. He wasn't very nice to me.

Remember also that this was for me the biggest opportunity of my life. I'd never really done live television before. Flipside was live. But there's live and there's live, and Strictly was a proper, complicated, live show. It seemed like a monumental task. I was super-nervous. Now I'm sure everyone was nervous. I'm sure Tess Daly was nervous. I'm sure Bruce was nervous. So to be fair, when we were doing the first full pilot, I'm sure everyone was trying to get their head round it, and that Bruce Forsyth was nervous too, because even for him this was a big show, a big gamble. But even so, I got to the moment in my first pilot when I had to interview Bruce, and I'd been running around and was sweating, and now I had to interview this living legend of TV. And he was clearly not happy. So this is how the interview went.

I had a list of the standard questions, like: 'Which couple did you like the most tonight?' 'Who do you think is going to win?' 'Did you think that couple deserved to be voted off?' The kind of questions that he himself asks on the show now to other guests. So I said, 'I'm here with the legend that is Bruce Forsyth, everybody ... Good times!' Lots of applause. Then I said, 'What a great start to the series, Bruce ... ' and he replied, 'Yes, yes, it's been a good night.'

Then I said, 'So I know it's early days but who do you think stands a chance of winning this thing?'

Brucie looked at me.

'Well, you're asking me that question,' he started. 'But it's a bit of a silly question really. This is the first week. How am I supposed to know who's going to win?'

He was being a bit unpleasant. And I was looking at him, and I was sweating profusely, and I was thinking, 'Please help me out, mate ... please just answer the question and be nice! Just help me out.'

But he wasn't being helpful at all. Clearly he wasn't thinking, 'I'm with a young presenter who's fifty years younger than me, and he's clearly nervous and I'll cut the kid some slack and I'll help him out.' Instead he was presumably thinking, 'This is a ball-ache. Why at my age have I agreed to do this? And who is this idiot?' I don't know if that's what he was thinking. I'm just guessing.

During the entire five-minute interview with me, the first time I've ever met him, he'd been nothing but awkward and short with me. So I was still super-nervous and the interview with Bruce wasn't going well, to say the least, so I thought of something that my mother used to say.

She would say, 'Kill them with kindness.'

So the idea is, if someone is being arsey with you, be nice back. And if someone gets even arsier with you, be even nicer back. So with my mum's words 'kill them with kindness' ringing in my ears, I was now upset and disappointed, because there was one of my TV heroes and he hadn't been very nice to me, and I could also feel my disappointment turning into anger. So then I became angry. Anyway, the interview ended and I introduced the next item, and I looked at Bruce, and, thinking 'kill him with kindness', I said to him, 'Thank you so much.' Even though I had absolutely nothing to thank the man for because he'd given me nothing. Then I added, 'I'd been so looking forward to meeting you ... '

And his parting shot was: 'Well, you've met me now.'

Then he walked off.

So that was the end of the pilot, and I walked off the podium, took off my earpiece and I looked at the producer and I shook my head and I said, 'That was a fucking ball-ache.' She looked at me and said, 'Don't worry, he won't be like that next week. He's a pro. This is a pilot. When it comes to doing the show for real, he'll be on and he'll be fine.'

So the next week came round and we were live and doing the show for real, and I was really nervous again, and he was exactly the same.

The killing with kindness thing didn't work.

The pilot was such a nightmare and so nerve-wracking what with Bruce not being particularly giving or gracious, so afterwards I sat there on the train from London to Bristol thinking, 'I might not be up to this. This might be beyond me and I'm not sure if I can do this.' I'd never done anything like it before – I'd just done a very small studio show for MTV years before, and all my other TV work was filmed and edited documentary stuff. Nothing prepared me for Strictly Come Dancing on BBC3.

But the shining light on the pilot was Brucie's co-host Tess Daly, who was lovely.

Then came the first show, and my very first link in the very first show proper was me doing a pre-titles bit of chat in which I would be saying, 'So this couple's just been voted off ... we'll get the reaction from them plus the reaction from the judges ... stay tuned for Strictly Come Dancing on BBC3.' I was supposed to do this pre-titles link to camera, look at the autocue above the camera and read the lines. And I'm good at reading. So it should have been fine. But because I was nervous and I'd never done this before, for some reason I got it into my head that the autocue above the lens was just a guide in case I forgot what I was supposed to say. The producer kept saying in my ear, 'You know this link ... you know this, you'll be fine,' which I took to mean, wrongly, that I should know this link in my head and be able to say it straight down the lens and do it to camera. Sure enough, when the time arrived for my first ever live TV link, instead of reading the autocue, which is what I was supposed to do, I decided to look straight into the camera lens, ignore the autocue above the lens and try to deliver the lines. But I got completely confused, and when I did look up to the autocue, it was completely out of time with my words.

I ended up doing a link which was literally me making random noises.

I managed to say, 'We've just seen ... ' then I forgot the name of the couple that had lost, and I was just spouting gobbledegook. Like *Mah nah mah nahhh mahhh mahh ... .* Honestly, anyone watching that moment on BBC3 would have seen this big hairy Bristolian they'd never seen before spouting total nonsense that wasn't even the English language. And Bruce was still ungracious. He still refused to say who he thought was going to win. That first live show on the Saturday night wasn't great.

Luckily, when it came to the daily shows on BBC3, which were more like magazine shows with lots of features, I felt much more at home. They were great. And at the end of the second live Saturday show, which went so much better, I walked into the BBC bar and the production team all gave me a round of applause.

In the end I absolutely loved it. I loved doing it. The best compliment I got was in one of the dance trade papers, I think it was called Dance World News, and they wrote that the best thing about Strictly is Justin Lee Collins's BBC3 show. They said I presented the show as if it was the most important thing since England winning the World Cup in 1966. And that summed it up for me, because for me it *was* huge. It *was* the World Cup. That's what I was trying to do – to make it feel as massive as that.

I loved the whole thing. I loved the dancers. My favourite was Paul 'Killer' Killick. I came up with nicknames for all of them, and Paul was a maverick dancer. He broke the rules. Killick would come out with Verona Joseph horizontal across his shoulders, with his shirt off, and he lifts her up and rolls her down his body and onto his knees. Like the Verona Roll – though that's not what it's officially called. I loved Killer Killick. But Verona pulled out after about three weeks.

I also loved Anton Du Beke, whose real name is Tony Beak. His partner was Lesley Garrett, who has an OBE, so I would introduce them as Lesley Garrett OBE and Anton Du Beke Not OBE. And I also decided that Anton was the star of the show when it came to the dancers, so I prefixed his name with 'The Legend That Is', so he became The Legend That Is Anton Du Beke Not OBE. I called Brendan Cole 'Coley' because I couldn't think of anything better. Claire Sweeney was The Sweeney and we played the theme tune to The Sweeney whenever she came on. Arlene Phillips was Miss Hot Gossip. I referred to Craig Revel Horwood as Revels, and I wanted to say,

'That's the trouble with Revels, you never know which one you're going to get,' but I was told I couldn't use it too often because I would be advertising the chocolates called Revels.

The winners of that first series were Brendan 'Coley' Cole and Natasha Kaplinsky. And she was lovely. She introduced me to her dad one time, and I said, 'Really pleased to meet you, Mr Kaplinsky. I think your daughter is great ... ' and her dad looked at me and said, 'She's full of shit.' Then Natasha introduced me to her mum and said, 'Mum, can you tell Dad not to say to Justin that I'm full of shit?' And her dad said, 'Don't worry, he doesn't mind – Justin's full of shit too.' And I thought, 'What a great guy!'

Of course it was all over the papers on a daily basis that Natasha and Brendan were maybe getting close, but we were told under no circumstances were we allowed to mention it. The other big story was Christopher Parker from out of EastEnders, who was a terrible dancer. Diabolical. But such is the power of the viewer vote that he got to the final, even though his paso doble was terrible. And that was a big controversy, way before the whole John Sergeant scandal.

Not everything that happened on Strictly went well. I interviewed Lesley Garrett and she ended up complaining about me.

My producer had prepared a list of questions for me to ask Lesley Garrett, who was partnered on the show with Anton Du Beke, as I've said, and a couple of those questions pertained to her breasts. Now bear in mind that Garrett had been marketed to some extent as a particularly sexy, buxom soprano. And she is, by any measure, a woman with an impressive physique. So to be fair to us, having some questions on the list about that physique wasn't completely off the wall. She's also got this reputation of being a very down-to-earth, working-class anti-elitist opera singer. So I had this question on my list which was something like, 'How does Anton feel about your breasts?'

To be fair to the producer he did tell me to judge it, so that if the interview was going well then I should drop it in, but if it wasn't going so well then I didn't have to ask it. It was just a silly, cheeky little question.

To be honest, if I was in the same situation now, I wouldn't ask it. But this was five years ago.

So I asked her the question, 'How does Anton feel about your breasts?'

She took umbrage. She pointed her finger at me, took her mic off and said, 'Right, I think we've finished now ... '

As she was leaving, we all kept saying, 'Thank you, Lesley, thanks for your time, thanks, Lesley ... '

She just looked at me and said, 'I'm not happy. I shall be having words.'

And sure enough, she registered a complaint. The interview was never used.

Then there was the David 'The Duke' Dickinson moment. David was dancing with Camilla Dallerup. They only lasted a few weeks and he was known for his jazz hands. He wasn't very good and it didn't seem like he was having a good time on the show. The other big problem we had about getting the celebrities to come on our show was that often they must have been reluctant to do it in the first place, but it was a contractual obligation for them. They had to agree to come on our show once a week. And of course they had to work really hard all week on their routines and on learning how to dance properly so they probably saw coming on our show as something of an inconvenience. It was hard for us to get the celebrities to be interviewed by me on my show, especially the live Saturday night one after they'd all danced their arses off. So this one Saturday night, my poor producer had to try to get Dickinson to hang around after the big live show on Saturday night to be interviewed by me. His reaction was this: 'What's all this shit? What's this BBC3 shit? I'll fuck off!'

The producer just said, 'Can I get you a drink of water, David?'

And that seemed to placate him. He did come on the show. But he wasn't happy.

But I loved every minute of it.

It was the only job I'd done since my very first TV job with MTV in 1997 where I learned anything. The main lesson was a brilliant piece of advice my Strictly producer gave me early on. She told me, 'Remember – it's not about you.' My job was to ask the questions then sit back, listen and shut the fuck up. If there was a clear window of comedic opportunity then I would take it, but if not, then I would just listen and wait to ask a follow-up question.

I am eternally grateful to the people who gave me that opportunity.

Amidst my total unbridled joy and excitement at being able to host Strictly on BBC3, something awful happened which was entirely my fault. Something I'll regret to the day I die.

I get upset thinking about it.

I never invited my mum to see Strictly Come Dancing. That was the show that changed everything for me. It was the job that changed my life. And Come Dancing was the show I loved watching with my mum when I was a little boy. And I never made a point of asking my mum or dad to come and see me working on that show. I never made a point of saying to them, 'I want you there. I would love you to come along.' And I will regret it for evermore.

I just didn't think of asking them. I didn't think they would be that bothered. But that's because my mum is so unshowy and undemonstrative and she gets embarrassed. Remember, she never wanted to see me doing my stand-up.

Partly based on that knowledge, I never appreciated how much my mum would have liked to come along and see me at Strictly Come Dancing and watch a show go out live.

To make things worse, I did invite my wife Karen and our friends Dan and Sarah. That was after Dan told me outright that they wanted to come to a show. I'd wanted to invite Karen but I'd been worried about her coming on her own and who would look after her at the BBC while I was working. Then when my friends told me they wanted to come, I thought that was great because they could go with Karen and they could all look after each other.

A few days after making this arrangement, I was in the kitchen in my parents' house. My mum walked in and she told me she heard from Karen that she was coming to see a Strictly Come Dancing show with our friends. And she was in tears.

It broke my mum's heart.

When I saw her in this state, heartbroken that I hadn't thought to invite her to the show, I tried to explain myself. I said, 'But, Mum, I'd love you to come. You can come any time. I'll arrange it. I'll arrange the whole thing.'

But that wasn't the point. I hadn't gone to my mum first. I didn't have the sense to go to my mum first and tell her I would have loved her to come and see me working on the new version of the show that we had watched together when I was a little boy, cuddled up next to her.

More than that, my mum then proceeded to show me the autograph book she'd bought specially in the hope of going to one of the shows and meeting all the stars. Amidst the heartbreak, she was showing me how much she was looking forward to seeing the show. I knew she wasn't a big, showy person. She's never shown any interest in getting anyone's autograph before. She's a shy, unassuming woman and I love that about her. Because of all that, because of what my mum is like, I hadn't realised that she needed to be asked first. Before my friends. And I should have realised that.

I can't remember ever seeing my lovely mum that upset.

I will always regret that.

The only reason I hadn't asked my mum to come and see me on Strictly first was because I knew she never wanted to see my stand-up and that she was uncomfortable watching me on TV, because she would be worried on my behalf. Worried and embarrassed. But I should have realised Strictly was another matter. It was special. For me and my mum.

Later on, though, in the run of the series, I did arrange for my mum and dad to come to a show.

I arranged with a girl on the production team to put two seats by for them, and I booked them into a hotel in London, but in the end my mum decided not to come. I don't think she took that decision because she was still bitter at not being asked in the first place. I think maybe she realised it might have been an uncomfortable experience in the end.

Strictly Come Dancing became a huge hit, one of the BBC's biggest light entertainment hits for ten years. And it was recommissioned very quickly, but I wasn't asked back to host the support show. The decision was made to move that show from BBC3 to BBC2 and it was given to Claudia Winkleman, who is brilliant and who I love. And she still does Strictly now on BBC2 and she does it brilliantly. But for some reason they didn't want me to do it, and I have to say at the time that was a huge kick in the nuts.

The show was moved from BBC3 to BBC2 and I was told that the show was wrong for BBC3 because it was for older people and not the kids who are supposed to be watching BBC3, and I was told that I wasn't very BBC2. Which at the time made some kind of sense. There might have been another factor as I've often suspected that the then Entertainment Controller didn't like me. It was weird because I'd filmed a lot of taped items for the BBC3 Strictly show and in the end they were never shown. Perhaps this same executive at the BBC wanted as little of me as possible on the screen. Maybe she thought, 'Who is this overweight hairy Bristolian? Why is he doing my show?' But I didn't think about this till later. My colleagues kept up their support.

A few weeks after Strictly finished, by which time I knew I wouldn't be coming back as the host of the support show, which was moving to BBC2, there was a dinner held at The Ivy restaurant in London for the talent on the show – the celebrities and presenters and dancers and producers. That was the first time I had ever been to The Ivy. But I was the only one of the whole team that wasn't coming back for the next series. I was the only one who'd been axed! Maybe I shouldn't have gone to that dinner but I couldn't resist it. I must admit I was a little bitter that they hadn't asked me to come back to host the next series, but I still wanted to see the team.

At that dinner I sat next to Bruce Forsyth.

I have to say after his initial, slightly unpleasant exchange with me on my show, Bruce had always been very civil to me whenever I bumped into him at the BBC. And at that dinner, after we'd finished eating, one of the big BBC executives came up to me afterwards to tell me that Bruce had been talking to him about me, and Bruce had said to him that he wasn't sure about me at first, but after seeing how hard I worked he thought I'd done a really good job.

I was pleased that maybe I'd won Bruce over by the end. That was something.

At the official wrap party, all the presenters were invited on stage in front of the entire crew and after Bruce and Tess Daly went up there and got a nice round of applause each, I was asked to go up there to join them and got a really lovely cheer. Bruce said, 'There must be a lot of the BBC3 crowd in tonight.'

It took me six months to get over not being asked back to work on Strictly. In fact, if they had put a contract in front of me saying we want you to host Strictly Come Dancing on BBC3 for the next ten years I would have signed it without a second thought. I loved the show that much.

Strictly is still my favourite show on television. I wish they'd bring back Come Dancing, the original one, and I'd gladly host it.

In fact, as I write this, I'm getting nervous because tomorrow I fly off to Orange County, California to take part in a proper ballroom dancing championship for a show I'm doing for Sky 1. I've been in training for weeks, and it's bloody difficult, let me tell you. But it's been one of the most exciting challenges of my life.

You see, in many ways when I think about the high points in my life, they've mostly been about ballroom dancing.

CHAPTER 15

BRING BACK!

I felt like a proper television presenter. That was now my job. I had a lovely wife at home who could tell anyone who asked that her husband works as a TV presenter, not that she'd ever boast about such a thing. More importantly, after the days where she kept me going and never ever doubted that I could and would make a living from being on TV, I could now provide a beautiful place for her to live and give her lovely things and know that we could start a family whenever we felt like it.

First, though, as if to cement the fact that I was now a jobbing TV host, a new experience happened to me while I was working on Strictly. For the first time in my TV career, I was offered a new job even before my current one had finished. The job was another BBC3 companion show to a big BBC1 project. The BBC1 series was called Fat Nation and it was an ambitious project attempting to deal with the national obesity in the UK. It would be based in a typical street in Britain and the whole series would be filmed and broadcast from there. It was a bit more of a serious kind of show than I'd ever done before. I thought that might be interesting. I knew my mum would love it. She always thinks I should try to do something more serious.

So I was quite excited by this Fat Nation.

The job meant that I had to visit Birmingham every Thursday for nine weeks. Whilst I was doing that job, hosting Fat Nation live from Handsworth Wood, Strictly was immediately recommissioned and, unbelievably, series two of it started that same year and in fact at the same time as I was working on Fat Nation in Birmingham.

That was a kick in the guts for me. I wanted to be part of Strictly, but instead I was part of a show I didn't really enjoy very much. The problem with it for me was that it was like a cricket bat to the head of larger people. It was basically saying to them, 'You're fat! You're fat and you shouldn't be!'

It was all perfectly well intentioned, of course. They were trying to get the nation fit – watching their calories and wearing pedometers – and they were doing it from a street in Birmingham. But it was a preachy show. And preachy is not my style at all.

So I didn't want our show, which went out after the BBC1 main show, which was beating fat people round the head with a bat for an hour, to be so heavy-handed. My way of dealing with it was to be silly. One time I did my pre-titles tease, basically the trailer before the show that tries to get people to watch it before the titles sequence, by saying, 'Don't eat fruit, it gives you cancer.'

Before the series even started we had to go to a community evening in which the locals could hear how this big series was going to affect their lives, because the BBC was essentially taking over a few streets for the duration of this nine-week show. There was almost a fight. One lot of residents complained about the noise and inconvenience that this huge production was causing and someone else slagged off those people because they had to put up with the noise from their barking dogs! It was pandemonium.

We filmed the show in the freezing cold November. I went shopping one time with the wardrobe lady who was lovely but who looked like Julie T. Wallace in Life And Loves Of A She Devil and she advised me to buy corduroy trousers, fleeces and walking boots. When we got back and I showed my new wardrobe to the producer he knew it wasn't really my style. I was dressed as if I was presenting Country File. But I wasn't John Craven. I wish I was John Craven. But I wasn't. In those days I still wasn't confident enough to challenge that kind of decision-making process. I wouldn't stop the wardrobe lady and tell her we were shopping for stuff that just wasn't me. I went along with it. I didn't want to cause any problems.

The whole show was a chore more than anything. We had some very strange guest bookings. It couldn't have been easy to book guests on the show. We had to ask them to come to Birmingham on a cold, dark, autumn evening, to take part in a BBC3 show spinning off from a series telling people they were too fat.

We had Frank Bruno on one week and throughout the entire interview his nose was running profusely.

Snot was running right down into his mouth.

I thought, 'Why doesn't he seem to be noticing that his nose is running? And what the hell am I supposed to do about it? Can he not feel it? Should I tell him? Can I stop a live interview and ask him if he needs a tissue?!'

So I just let it run, so to speak. But it was really off-putting. I've no idea what I asked him that evening while his nose was running.

Another booking was Debbie McGee. I had to interview Debbie, and, brilliantly, Paul Daniels came with her to the show. But she was the one who was booked. Just her. In fact, Daniels came on the show with her. But the booking was McGee! I went to see Debbie in the Green Room and was surprised to see Paul Daniels, who I'd never met before in my life. He was quite a hero of mine when I was a kid watching his magic shows on TV. So I was excited to meet him and talk about magic. He took out a pack of cards and demonstrated to me two or three sensational David Blaine-style card tricks. But we'd booked Debbie McGee.

One minute we would have Shola Ama on the show and I had to conduct quite a serious interview with her about her former cocaine addiction. The next minute we had a big Michael Jackson skit in which all the residents on the street did the dance routine to Thriller. Another time I had to try out a bucking bronco. No idea why. And on one show, I had a guy called Lorenz on who was a Dreamboy stripper. He was about to release a single. We got him to strip off but he could barely speak English. What were we doing? What was the show?!

For the majority of the time I had no idea what the hell was going on. It became a huge effort for me and I didn't enjoy it in the end. My way of dealing with the fact that I didn't enjoy it was to go completely over the top and make it fun for myself. It was either that or I'd be stabbing myself in the eyes.

That would be the case for a lot of the early shows I did. I couldn't sit back and relax because I didn't really have confidence in the format of the actual show. The pauses and silences in shows that are not going well can be interminable. I hate it when a show doesn't go anywhere. I hate it when they get slow and uncomfortable to watch. So my response is to go a bit nuts. And I know that attitude of mine divides people and I don't blame them.

There's one incident that sums up people's attitude towards me.

One night a homeless bloke stopped me in the street in Bristol while I was hosting Flipside and he said, 'Hey, I've watched you on that late-night thing where you change channels and talk about what's on TV … '

I said, 'Oh yeah, Flipside … '

And he said, 'Just chill out, man.'

I get a lot of homeless people telling me they watch me on TV but he was the only one who gave me a critique. And while I get his point, I would also defend myself because on that show, as on other shows I've done, if I hadn't been constantly 'on', constantly talking and working at trying to make it funny, then they would have been interminable.

So, no, Mr Homeless, I won't chill out! At least not when I'm hosting a bit of a rubbish show.

I suppose after Fat Nation, I was a bit down again because I had ended doing a job that I didn't enjoy and that just wasn't me. It wasn't like I was working a rude cat puppet or anything, but in some ways it wasn't far off.

Thankfully, a show soon came along that made me happy again.

Later that year I had meetings with a production company about hosting a one-off show called Bring Back ... Spandau Ballet. It was based on a VH1 series called Bands Reunited which was a big hit at the time. The idea was that a presenter would try to reunite the members of once popular bands for a one-off show. They did A Flock Of Seagulls, Frankie Goes To Hollywood and Kajagoogoo (in which I seem to remember that they all gave Limahl a hard time). So we were going to adapt this show for the UK and call it Bring Back ... and we were going to start with Spandau Ballet.

In preparation for this show, they gave me a huge folder, a dossier if you like, on Spandau Ballet. It was a huge Spandau dossier. By the time I read everything in this folder I knew everything you could ever want to know about Spandau.

A few weeks later, while I was at Xfm, I got a call telling me that Bring Back ... Spandau Ballet had fallen through. They were in such conflict with each other that they were never going to reunite for a

Channel 4 TV show hosted by a long-haired Bristolian. So it was going to be a big, expensive waste of time.

They decided to try OMD instead. Orchestral Manoeuvres In The Dark. But OMD only consisted of two members. Andy McCluskey and the other guy. So that wasn't going to work.

I started to think it wasn't going to happen at all. I started to think we weren't going to Bring anyone Back.

Then they had the idea of bringing back Grange Hill, or more specifically Bringing Back the 1986 period of Grange Hill when the cast released the song Just Say No as part of the big US/UK anti-drug campaign.

I thought it was a good idea.

So we made a programme in which I tried to track down the cast members who sang on the single Just Say No.

It was the first of what has since become an occasional series of eight Bring Backs.

But that first one about Grange Hill was exciting because none of us really knew how it would pan out, as I ran around trying to find Zammo, Roland, Ziggy Greaves and the rest. The first ambush I did was Lee MacDonald, the actor who played Zammo, in his key-cutting business in Carshalton, Surrey. I ran into his shop and he had no idea I was coming. He was great about it. I waited at Waterloo station to ambush Ziggy. He seemed to think I was some kind of Roger Cook figure about to shop him for something.

Yet I couldn't quite work out if it was going to make for a coherent TV show. It was hectic stuff. I couldn't quite see it. But in the end it worked.

Although the reunion itself was dicey.

It was held at the Hammersmith Palais in London at one of their School Disco nights. We arranged for all the Just Say No cast members to arrive at the venue and sing Just Say No from the stage. It sounded perfect.

But there was a flaw in our plan. The kind of people who went to the School Disco night turned out to be in their late teens or early twenties. They'd barely been born when Just Say No came out. So when I interrupted their fun night of dancing and having a good time by coming out on stage in front of thousands of them and stopping their music and introducing old members of Grange Hill, they were understandably disgruntled. And they started pelting me with bottles of piss. They weren't happy.

The saving grace was that some members of the cast, like Roland – aka Erkan Mustafa – gave it their all and just about calmed the crowd down, although they certainly didn't enjoy it.

The show went out on Channel 4 in May 2005 and it did really well, thankfully.

Off the back of Grange Hill, Channel 4 decided to make more Bring Backs. We were in talks about doing a co-production with Granada in which we were going to do Bring Back ... The World Cup Penalty Takers. I was going to reunite the England and Germany penalty takers from Italia 90 to see if we could beat them at penalties the second time around. That was going to happen, which would have been brilliant. But Stuart Pearce and Chris Waddle had some kind of advertising contract which meant they couldn't do it. So that died a death. We couldn't have done it without the key people who took the penalties.

After that we discussed other possibilities of shows we could Bring Back. They asked me to make a list of all my favourite American TV shows from when I was growing up. What an opportunity! I told them Knight Rider, The Fall Guy, Magnum, Miami Vice, The A-Team.

From that list, Channel 4 chose The A-Team, which was by far my favourite, so I was thrilled. It was the show with the action figures which my mum bought me to try to help me stop wetting the bed.

Bring Back ... The A-Team turned out to be the best thing I had ever done and the most fun I had ever had working in my life.

I couldn't believe I was doing it. It was a pinch-me-I-can't-believe-it moment. The two-week shoot in Los Angeles was one of the best two weeks of my life. It was as if someone had said to me, 'Take something you absolutely love and go make a TV show about it and have as much fun as you can while you're at it. In LA. And we'll pay you!'

This was a show I loved when I was a kid. It was my favourite programme on television.

Good times. To say the least.

We had Colonel Decker, the most famous villain in the show. He turned up to the reunion and I interviewed him. Well, I interviewed an actor called Lance LeGault who played Colonel Decker. At one point, I asked him whether Mr T was really scared of flying. Lance didn't answer but instead he very slowly pulled out a knife. And he said, 'Son, I will cut you long, deep and continuously.'

I thought, 'What the fuck?!'

There was no explanation. He just did it to freak me out.

That interview didn't make it into the final show.

Of course the highlight of the show was my interview with Mr T. Originally we couldn't get him. We flew to LA to make this show but he wouldn't agree to do the show. Then the day before we were due to fly home, they managed to negotiate a fee with his people and he agreed to do it. We had access to him in a hotel for about an hour.

I was so excited to meet him, though, because not only was he in The A-Team but he was also in Rocky III, one of my favourite films as a kid.

I wanted to check with him whether the story of how he was cast in Rocky III was true: I was told that Sylvester Stallone had seen him on television tossing a dwarf.

As soon as he entered the room he said, 'Yeah yeah yeah – I never met a camera I didn't like.' He brought a goodie bag with him that had Mr T keychains and other merchandise which he handed out to all of us.

I wondered what to call him.

He said, 'Just call me T.'

Then I asked about the dwarf-tossing story.

'No no no,' he said. 'It wasn't a dwarf.'

'Oh,' I said, 'was it a midget then?'

'No no no,' he said. 'It wasn't a midget.'

'What was it then?'

'I'll tell you what it was – it was a short stunt man.'

It turned out that this show that Sly Stallone had seen was a strong man competition to find the world's toughest bouncer. Mr T was one of the contenders, and one of the challenges was to throw a short stunt man. We might call him a dwarf or a little man, but Mr T called him a short stunt man.

I asked him how far he threw the short stunt man.

He told me: 13 feet.

Another notable interview I did was with Stephen J. Cannell, the creator of The A-Team. It was notable mainly because when we finished our chat with him at his fabulous Pasadena house, Jimmy, our soundman, who had been kneeling down at the feet of this guy, asked if any of us had noticed his erection. Apparently, Stephen J. Cannell had been in a state of arousal throughout the interview. Only Jimmy the soundman noticed.

But when he showed up for the reunion event, we did all take a long hard look at his groin ... nothing seemed too amiss.

Bring Back ... The A-Team went out in May 2006. And just when I thought it couldn't get any better for me, Channel 4 asked me to do Bring Back ... Dallas and then the big one – Bring Back ... Star Wars.

The one stand-out moment from Dallas was with JR, Larry Hagman. I spent an astonishing afternoon with him. We ambushed him in Santa Monica where he lives and he invited us back to do the interview in his beautiful apartment on Santa Monica beach with a panoramic view of the surrounds. The thing about Larry Hagman is – he IS JR Ewing. He still wears the ten-gallon hat and has the whole JR look. That afternoon he was showing off these amazing new wireless speakers he'd just bought. They were like large orbs. He was holding them, one in each hand, and he was dancing and singing while blaring out at a huge volume the song Senza Una Donna by Paul Young and Zucchero, while I sat there and looked at him in astonishment.

It was the most incredibly unlikely sight of my life.

The other funny thing that happened with Larry Hagman was that in the middle of the interview he suddenly stopped and asked if we could halt filming. We wondered if something serious was wrong with him, but no, it turned out he had just got his finger stuck in his plastic bottle of water.

Eventually he extracted himself.

But Star Wars is as big as it gets. We're never going to cover anything bigger.

It wasn't an easy shoot though. I was bitterly disappointed that we didn't get Mark Hamill. It was a given that we weren't going to get Harrison Ford because he's a Hollywood legend and huge star, but I thought we'd be able to get Hamill. Who isn't a huge star. But apparently he has no desire to talk about Star Wars. He has significant issues with it. We offered him loads of money and he still turned it down.

But we did get Carrie Fisher, who was wonderful.

I told you a bit about her in the introduction to this book, if you can remember that far back. But lovely Carrie Fisher let us film her in her house in the Hollywood Hills, which used to be Bette Davis's house. It was a wonderful house – very chic, in that shabby, cool kind of way. She gave me a full guided tour. Carrie Fisher's mum Debbie Reynolds lives next door and at one point Debbie Reynolds drove by in her car and said hello to the crew.

My interview with Carrie Fisher is one of the best interviews I've ever done and probably one of the greatest single experiences I've had in TV. Another 'pinch-me' moment. It took the crew a while to set up their equipment in her garden and in that time I got to know Carrie a bit and we got on really well. I thought, 'My goodness me, you are amazing. I could easily fall in love with you. Maybe I have fallen in love with you a little bit. And I've only known you an hour.'

CHAPTER 16

THE ROAD TO ALAN AND ARCHIE...

Meeting Princess Leia is one thing. Having a baby is quite another. That's a rubbish way of saying that my wife got pregnant in 2004 which of course made everything we'd ever done before in our lives pale into insignificance.

She loved being pregnant too.

But while she loved it, I wasn't very good with pregnancy. It did funny things to me. I know that sounds pathetic but it's true. It was a psychological thing and I'm ashamed to admit it now, but I didn't cope with my wife carrying a baby inside her very well at all.

This amazing thing was happening to the woman I love – this life-changing event. But I found it scary. I didn't know what to do. I didn't know how to react and it made me almost feel that I didn't want to be around. I'm not proud of that feeling but I must admit it was there.

Of course in the end I was present at the birth of my gorgeous son Archie and it was the most wonderful thing. But in the build-up to that day, I did find it very difficult.

At least there was one element of the birth I could help with. Archie was a planned Caesarean birth and the nurse at the hospital told us we could bring in our own music to play while the operation was taking place. I thought this was a brilliant idea. So I threw myself into the task of finding the right music to bring along with gusto.

I thought maybe Appetite For Destruction by Guns N' Roses might work – it would be cool if he came out while Sweet Child Of Mine was playing. So I took Guns N' Roses to the hospital. But I thought I should take some alternative options, so I picked out the Footloose soundtrack too.

So there we were in the hospital and I was holding Karen's hand and I put Appetite For Destruction on and I started to wonder if maybe it was too loud and overbearing. I wasn't sure if the doctors were into it. They were performing quite a significant operation after all. So I took off Guns N' Roses and put Footloose on.

And as the Footloose music was playing, just at the point when our little pride and joy came into the world, track two of the soundtrack comes on – Deniece Williams singing Let's Hear It For The Boy.

Archie was born to the sound of Let's Hear It For The Boy. 'My baby he don't talk sweet ...'

And I hadn't even planned it.

My second child Harvey was born to Jethro Tull.

He wasn't really. I'm only joking.

It was hugely important for me that Archie wasn't going to be an only child. I wanted him to have pets too. A cat and maybe a dog. I wanted him to be surrounded by animals and people and family.

But most importantly, I wanted him to have the little brother I never had.

In between the arrival of my first child and a pretty constant stream of TV work, thank goodness, a weird thing started to happen with my body.

I was doing my show at Xfm one day and I noticed a little patch of dry skin just above my right ear. It was itchy and I had to scratch it and it started to get a bit flaky.

In those days I would wash my hair and leave it soaking wet and not dry it. I would go out in all winds and weathers with wet hair. My mum always told me to dry my hair and she'd always follow me out the door with a hairbrush making sure my hair was tidy by brushing the back of my hair.

So I thought maybe my wet hair had given me this dry skin patch.

But within about a year it had spread all over my head, across my hairline on the back of my neck, in my ears. It was all over my head – itchy dry skin. Psoriasis.

It turned out that it runs in the family. My mum's two sisters have got it and my granddad has got it, but he didn't get it until he was in his thirties, like me. There's no cure, it's hereditary and it's stress-related. So I only got it when my career was really busy, when Karen got pregnant and so my head soon got covered in flaky skin.

It also spread to my balls and genitalia and my anus. I would be in bed at night constantly scratching my bum and balls. Karen would be next to me telling me to leave my bum alone. Sometimes I'd even ask her to please scratch my bum for me. She'd say, 'No, I'm not scratching your bum.' But I could live with that. I could live with itchy balls. I'd rather have itchy balls than an itchy flaky head.

The psoriasis is also a control issue. When I'm not in control of something, the first thing I do is to start scratching my head. If it isn't going my way, I'm scratching my head.

Right now, as I write this, because I am the happiest I have been in quite a few years, my stress level is way down and my psoriasis is minimal. There's just a little bit on the top of my head.

It's eighty per cent better. And I'm convinced that the day I give this up, it will disappear completely.

Other than the arrival of a new skin condition, 2005 was full of high points for me.

Perhaps the highest after the birth of Archie was that I got to host The Games on E4. This was the support show for The Games on Channel 4 – a kind of celebrity Olympics held in Sheffield.

To get the job I had an interview with the producers and I think I made it so clear to them that I was such a fan of The Games ever since it was first aired in 2003 that they were quite keen on me. Then I sealed the deal when they told me who would be taking part in the series that was forthcoming.

First, they told me, they'd booked Chesney Hawkes. Now I loved Chesney. Still do. So I told them how much I loved him and we chatted about the legendary song The One And Only for a bit, which they referred to as a one-hit wonder, but I then pointed out that his follow-up single I'm A Man Not A Boy was also a great song, and a minor hit. And then I sang the chorus. They were impressed by my Chesney knowledge. How couldn't they be impressed?

After I left, the producer checked what I'd said about Chesney Hawkes on the internet to make sure I hadn't invented it all.

They gave me the job.

And I absolutely adored it. My co-host was Caroline Flack and I loved her to bits.

My stint on The Games also opened a lot of doors for me on Channel 4.

Afterwards, the then head of E4 told me that I could become Channel 4's answer to Louis Theroux. I considered that to be a huge compliment. And a brilliant idea!

The other show I hosted in 2005 was much less fun than The Games. But it was a great thing for me to do in the end for one reason. Which I'll get to ...

It started when I had a meeting with Endemol in 2004 about a new comedy show for Channel 4 which would be a showcase for comedians and the idea was that they'd give three hosts the chance to present their own late-night show for a whole week. It sounded great. It was going to be called FAQ U.

But what actually happened was that it was a strange format in which the host asked a panel of comedians topical questions and the comedians got to hold forth and try to be funny. My job was just to read the autocue, ask the questions and basically shut up. It wasn't a huge amount of fun for me.

Things like this happened: we did a top five list during each show. One of them was the Top Five Ways You Know You've Bought The Pope's Old Car (because the new Pope had apparently just put his car up for sale). One of the entries on the list was: Does the car smell of Old Pope?

In rehearsal I read this joke and said, 'Shouldn't we say, does the car smell of Pope Pourri?'

Because Old Pope doesn't rhyme with Old Spice but that was clearly what the writers were getting at. So I thought Pope Pourri worked. I wasn't saying it was a great joke, it was just a better one than Old Pope.

But the producer looked at me, entertained my idea for all of three seconds and said, 'No, just stick with what it says.'

I just said, 'Okay – you know better than me so I'll just say it as it is on the script.'

When it came to the actual recording later that evening, one of the guests was comedian Paul Foot, who had appeared with me many years ago on the final of the BBC New Comedy Awards. And he won.

I did the Top Five Ways You Know You've Bought The Pope's Old Car list and I read the line 'Does the car smell of Old Pope?'

It barely got a giggle from the studio audience. Then Paul Foot chimed in, 'Er ... shouldn't that be "Does the car smell of Pope Pourri?"'

Huge laugh from the audience.

I said, 'Yeah, yeah ... that's what it should be.'

That summed up the frustration of my experience on FAQ U.

But I did have an amazing night of appearing on Channel 4 twice when my Bring Back ... Grange Hill was on the same evening as one of my FAQ U shows. I was on the channel from 10pm through to about 11.30. Bad luck if you hated me. But good times for me. I really was being noticed now.

But FAQ U was significant in my life for one much better reason: I got to know a young comedian called Alan Carr.

I'd met Alan a few times before. First of all we met when he was a guest on an episode of Flipside I hosted. I thought he was funny. But a year later when he was on FAQ U with me, he was brilliant. Everything he said was clever and funny and he was also totally likeable. Most of the comedians on the show just did their act, or a variation on their act, which is what happens when you have a group of stand-up comedians on a TV show. Or they will give you pre-planned, written responses that they'd prepared earlier. It's the standard technique on panel shows and the like. Now I'm not slagging them off for doing that, but when you're the host of a show and that's what you're getting from them as guests, I find it pretty uninspiring. It's not real. It's a turn. It's their shtick.

But Alan Carr was different. He was genuinely responding there in the moment to what I and the other guests were saying. He could improvise. He could be funny on the spot. And you could go with him. You could bounce off him. I loved him.

Later that same year in 2005 Al and I did another show together called Law Of The Playground.

It was pure coincidence that Al and I recorded our talking-head bits for this show on the same day.

This was a show in which comedians reminisced about their school days. It was as simple as that. We filmed the show in a school in Acton in London and when I showed up Alan Carr and David Mitchell were there and we filmed a bit together in which Al, myself and David talked about the original government public information Aids campaign from the 1980s – 'Aids: Don't Die Of Ignorance', the very same ad which terrified me as a kid, which I'm sure you remember me discussing earlier in this book.

The producer said to us, 'Have you heard about Super Aids?'

Al said something like, 'Oh god, what's that?'

The producer explained that the HIV virus was becoming immune to the main anti-Aids drug AZT and it was mutating into a kind of Super Aids.

At which point Al put the back of his hand to his forehead in a classic camp gesture and – just like that – said, 'I've only just got over Diana.'

I looked at him and thought, 'Oh my god. Where did that come from? That's genius.'

Towards the end of that year, 2005, I'd filmed an entertainment pilot for Channel 4 called Friday Night Hero which didn't work. But off the back of that failure Channel 4 offered me a job co-hosting the new series of The Friday Night Project.

I was wary of The Friday Night Project because I knew it had loads of hosts for its first series – Alan Carr, Sharon Horgan and Rob Rouse

– which hadn't really worked. But they said they were changing it, simplifying it, having fewer hosts. They were very keen that I agreed to do the show but I had one question and one question only: who would I be hosting this show with?

They said, 'Do you know Alan Carr?'

I told them, 'Yes I do. Brilliant. Where do I sign?'

CHAPTER 17

THE FRIDAY NIGHT PROJECT — GUEST BY GUEST

We've had the most incredible array of guest hosts on the Project, whether it was on Friday or Sunday night. Here are my considered (or not) thoughts on each of them ...

1. BILLIE PIPER

The night before our first ever piece of filming together for The Friday Night Project, Al and I went out for a bonding session together and got absolutely hammered. We ended up in a private members' club in London and got so steaming drunk that Al lost his wallet and I lost my mum's Christmas present – a Louis Vuitton handbag. I'd clearly left it in a taxi on the way back to my hotel.

I spent the next morning calling the lost property department of the London Taxis and couldn't get through. But just as I was about to try to buy a new one, I got a call from my Xfm radio producer saying, 'Did you leave a Louis Vuitton handbag in a taxi last night?'

Apparently a guy had found the bag in the taxi, saw the receipt with my name on it, recognised my name from being on Xfm and phoned the station to tell them, and then took it over there for me. How good is that? What a lovely guy.

The next day Al and I filmed our first bit for the show – we went ice skating with Billie Piper, our first ever guest host – in London for an item we called Doctor Who On Ice. She was wonderful. I love her.

2. LORRAINE KELLY

Lorraine got a little bit upset during the show. It was Phil Tufnell's fault – he made a joke about her growler during the Who Knows The Most About Guest Host portion of the show. He kept mentioning her growler and Lorraine didn't take too kindly to it.

3. CHRISTIAN SLATER

He didn't take his sunglasses off during the entire rehearsal. Eventually one of our producers had to come down to the studio floor and gently ask Christian if he wouldn't mind taking his shades off. He did remove them.

We had a Brokeback Mountain sketch that night. Slater said he was happy to take part in it but he didn't want to be a cowboy. And he didn't want to be gay.

4. DENISE VAN OUTEN

I've always liked Denise but I felt for some reason we didn't particularly click. She clicked with Alan. It wasn't that we didn't get on, but she definitely bonded more with Al. That was quite common in the first few series. They would click with one of us more than the other. But she was great. She came out for that show in a great dress and high heels and she sat on the edge of the desk and she looked sensational.

5. MICHAEL BARRYMORE

Barrymore was a tough one. We didn't really want him on the show. He had just come out of Celebrity Big Brother and we filmed him at the house in Elstree and while Al and I watched him give his interview to Davina we noticed that he couldn't sit still. He was constantly knocking his knees together. He was nervous and he didn't seem quite right.

Nevertheless he came on the show and in those days I would give the hosts nicknames, so I called him Mickey B. It was just one of my silly nicknames, but a critic in the Sunday Mirror slagged off the show and seemed to think I was trying to make him sound cool by calling him Mickey B. But actually I was really making mild fun of him. So I ditched the nicknames after that.

The standout memory I have of Barrymore was a Sven-Göran Eriksson/Nancy Dell'Olio sketch we did. In the sketch Barrymore was supposed to slap Al. The first take we shot, he hit Al really hard. Then we did it again and he hit Al even harder. We shot it for the third time and the director asked him to ease up on the slap and Barrymore agreed to 'pull it'. But he slapped him even harder. He really walloped him.

6. JAMIE OLIVER

I became good friends with Jamie as a result of him appearing on the show. And he's one of only a few people to do the show more than once.

The night before the show, Jamie invited Al and I to have dinner at his restaurant 15. We got drunk and had a fantastic night.

I can't speak too highly of Jamie.

7. JESSIE WALLACE

We filmed a sketch with Jessie in a pub and Al and I played country bumpkins and for some reason I kept asking Jessie to squeeze my nipples. I kept asking her to squeeze them really hard and she did. I've no idea why.

8. TRISHA GODDARD

We had a really eclectic mix of hosts from Hollywood legends to home-grown hosts like Lorraine Kelly and Trisha. And often the Trishas and the Lorraines would be better value. Al and I did a spoof of Trisha's show and we played fighting guests in fat suits.

9. JERRY SPRINGER

He was brilliant. He's a really funny man and Al and I spent a lot of the time laughing. We took Jerry to the Big Brother house and because Big Brother isn't a big deal in America, Jerry had barely even heard of it. So we took him behind the scenes in the camera run of the Big Brother house, the secret spaces behind the glass screens where the cameras film the housemates. Springer was totally fascinated by it. We had to be quiet because the housemates can hear and Springer could barely stop himself from laughing out loud while we watched the housemates waking up. And Springer's laughter was making Al and I laugh too. I bet they heard us in there.

In the Ask Me Anything section of the show, when the host takes random questions from the audience, one person stood up and asked Jerry if it was true that when he was mayor of Cincinatti he was caught paying a prostitute by cheque. There was an intake of breath in the studio because we had no idea this question was going to be

THE FRIDAY NIGHT PROJECT - GUEST BY GUEST

asked. But he dealt with it brilliantly. He said he wasn't mayor at the time but he did make a stupid mistake and he had apologised about it before. Jerry insisted we kept that bit of the show in the final edit. What a great man.

10. PATSY KENSIT

She was adorable. She was quite mumsy with Al and me, making sure we were looked after all the time. I really liked her.

11. ROB LOWE

Rob was a beautiful man. One of the most handsome men I had ever met. And suddenly every woman and quite a few men appeared on set that day wanting to be around the guest host.

We did another football-based sketch in which Al played Sven-Göran Eriksson and Rob played David Beckham. Rob, being an actor, took his part in this sketch quite seriously and he had an issue with the wig he was given. He was confused about whether he was really supposed to look like Beckham or whether he was just a comedy Beckham in a deliberately silly costume. Rob was asking about the intention of this sketch and the producer spoke to Rob about it and tried to explain that ultimately it didn't really matter because the costume was a red England top with Beckham written on the back. But Rob Lowe still had an issue with the wig and said to the producer, 'Have you seen the wig?' The producer said he hadn't seen it yet. So Rob replied, 'Well, you need to see it before you make the call.'

I thought that was probably what it was like working on The West Wing, where you must have a keen eye for every detail. But our show isn't The West Wing.

12. MISCHA BARTON

We went to a premiere in London with Mischa and we had champagne in the back of the limo. I kept filling her flute but she told me she couldn't be seen to be drinking on camera because she was a young teen star of The OC.

After the show, she was attending a huge black-tie ball in London and during our day filming with her, she kindly invited me along to this ball with her. But I'm not really a ball type of person so I felt it would be a bit weird plus I had nothing to wear – just my jeans and T-shirt. I also thought she was just asking me along out of politeness. But after the filming of the show, she came into the Green Room to find me and said, 'So are you coming?' And that was when I realised she was serious about me going to the ball. I said no. I just couldn't go. Some people will think I was mad for snubbing Mischa's invitation to the ball.

13. IAN WRIGHT

We played golf with Ian and I enjoyed it so much. He was a lovely bloke. I'd never played golf before in my life but he made it very enjoyable.

After we played golf with him, some bloke asked if he could have his photo taken with Wrighty and he agreed. Then once the shot had been taken, the bloke tried to be funny by pointing at Ian in the photo and saying, 'Who's that black bloke?' Ian replied, 'Am I black?'

I asked Wrighty how he puts up with idiots like that and Ian told me that he wasn't bothered by them at all, because he'd never see them again and it was a few seconds out of his life. I thought that was a very intelligent philosophy.

14. JADE GOODY

She looked absolutely amazing, dressed in this figure-hugging jade green dress and she'd recently undergone a makeover which was more of a complete physical transformation and it was a triumph. She just looked stunning. She was also great value – totally honest and funny. I thought she was fundamentally a really decent person who'd clearly had a bad time growing up.

Al and I went to her beauty salon in Hertford called Ugly's and she gave us all-over body tans, but mine wouldn't take. The tanning substance wouldn't adhere to my skin and it looked awful.

Her mum Jackiey was in a sketch with us and in it Jackiey had to hide behind this set of a bar and she was crouched down behind me. I started singing randomly, as is my wont, the song I Wanna Wake Up With You. And suddenly I heard Jackiey's deep, throaty voice saying, 'TUNE!'

15. JUSTIN HAWKINS

He gave me his shoes. He was wearing these fantastic blue leather Cuban heel cowboy boots. I told him I loved them and he asked what size I was. I told him size nine. He said he was size nine. And there and then he took the shoes off his feet and gave them to me. They were blue leather Dior boots. And I now have them. Still to this day. I've never worn them.

So we got on well. We exchanged phone numbers in fact, and a few days after we did the show, I started to receive weird text messages from him. Now I'm a huge text addict. I text regularly, frequently, all hours of the day. I love to text. It's my number one form of communication. I don't really like calling people and speaking to them, but I do love to send a text. My phone bills are sky high because of the number of texts I send. So I know a strange text message when I see one, and I saw quite a few from Hawkins.

Then they stopped. I was quite relieved.

A few weeks later I got a new text from him which said, 'I would just like to apologise if you received a few weird messages from me. I was having a difficult time and I had to go to rehab.'

That explained it.

16. RUPERT EVERETT

Rupert's done the show twice and the first time he did it there were certain things he didn't want to do. He's very open about certain things, as you'd know if you've read his memoirs, but he wants to be open very much on his own terms. And who can blame him?

Yet his idea for a filmed bit for the show was to take Al and I cruising on Hampstead Heath. It was quite an experience.

17. CAROL VORDERMAN

Carol was one of my very favourites. We'd wanted her for ages and she had said no to hosting the show a few times but she was great. We asked her about the famous GQ shoot she did in which she looked gorgeous. I told her I enjoyed the picture so much that I had to buy another copy. She loved it.

But one unfortunate thing happened. We went to meet Carol on the Countdown set when she was hosting it with Des Lynam. The Countdown audience is largely made up of elderly people, and I think they bring them in on coaches from nearby homes.

On the day we were there one poor chap soiled himself. And we don't know how but it was all up his back. Somehow it had gone out and up and went vertical. It was most unfortunate. He had to be taken out because in all the excitement he lost control.

That's probably why Des Lynam left.

Because shortly after that, Des O'Connor took over.

18. ROSS KEMP

I got on really well with Ross. He was very keen to make fun of himself and his hard-guy image which we thought was great. We did a sketch where we were in army fatigues and Al and I and Ross were playing very camp soldiers. Ross agreed to take part in the sketch but after the first take he said that we had to make sure we got it the second time round because he wasn't doing it again!

But he was good on the show. We swapped numbers and I've seen him socially since. He's a really nice guy.

19. GIRLS ALOUD

The first time they came on we had Sarah, Cheryl and Kimberly. Sarah was the stand-out for me. She was funny, and warm and open. We got Sarah to dress up as the topical barometer – in a head-to-toe maroon body suit onto which Al stuck the topics. But she was willing to go along with it which we thought was great.

That was the second time I'd met Girls Aloud because I once hosted Top Of The Pops with Fearne Cotton. It was the only time I hosted it and Girls Aloud were on. In my link introducing Girls Aloud I was supposed to name them, so I tried to memorise their names for this link, but Top Of The Pops didn't have an autocue, so I forgot some of them. I think I only remembered three of their names. Westlife were also on that show, duetting with Diana Ross, but Ross was only on a screen. I said, 'Here's Westlife with Diana Ross. They're here. She couldn't be arsed.' They thought it was funny but the producer wouldn't let me say 'arsed' because the show was on at 7pm on BBC2.

The second time Girls Aloud came on the show, they all did it. I think the others had seen Kanye West on the show, and that encouraged the other two to come on.

20. DAVID TENNANT

What a lovely, lovely guy. We had Billie Piper to thank for getting Tennant. She told him what a good time she had, so when he got the call to ask him to come on, Billie told him he had to do it. We also had Amy Winehouse on that show, just before her descent into the troubled period she's in now. She sang Back To Black and was sensational and then she also took part in the panel game section on Alan's team. I had George Galloway on my team. In one of the games we had to recreate sexual positions from the Kama Sutra on a bed. Al and Amy did some sexual positions. But when it came to me and Galloway he didn't seem to realise what was going to happen. Maybe no one had explained it to him. But during one of the positions we attempted, called the Italian chandelier, in which he was sat on the edge of the bed while I contorted my body around him and he was doing nothing apart from thinking, presumably, 'Why the fuck did I agree to come on this show?', he decided he had enough, he'd had a gutsful, so he stood up and got off the bed. Which left me to fall off the bed and so I put my hand out to try to stop myself from falling, and, quite by accident, I touched his groin. At that moment he was looking to walk out but I don't think he knew the right way to go.
I touched George Galloway's penis.

21. TAMZIN OUTHWAITE

Very lovely but very nervous.

22. JAMES NESBITT

I wasn't that keen to have him on, not for any personal reason but I thought I'd seen him on every talk show and entertainment show going. He's a darling of the chat shows. So I thought, 'What can we get out of him? What new stuff can we ask him that hasn't been asked before?' We've all seen the scene from Cold Feet with the rose in his arse-cheeks.

As it turned out he was absolutely fine. He's very affable and likeable and gave us plenty of good stuff.

23. NOEL EDMONDS

The legend. Dad. I absolutely love him. I loved House Party at its height, I loved Christmas Presents, I loved Swap Shop and I love Deal Or No Deal - he does a brilliant job on that show. He was at the top of our wish list.

Before he came on we bumped into him at the Montreux festival where Friday Night Project won the Rose D'Or and we asked him to do the show, and he did.

He did one very nice thing. During rehearsal he was reading a link on the autocue and in the script it said, 'Here are a couple of other legends ... ' i.e. the scriptwriters had him referring to himself as a legend. But he ditched the word 'other'. He wouldn't refer to himself as a legend. I thought that was a classy thing to do, because he is a legend.

24. STEVEN SEAGAL

Quite possibly one of the strangest guests. He's a Buddhist and in his faith he is designated as a lama. He had some kind of harem with him and he had one lady whose job appeared to be to unscrew the top of his water bottle for him. He held it out and she unscrewed it.

We went to see him play with his band too but he didn't seem to want to talk to us after the gig.

I was a big fan of Steven Seagal's films and every time a new Seagal film was released in the cinema I would go on the opening night with my mate Dan. I mean, this is the man who invented the word 'Fucknuts'. He says it in the film Out For Justice. I asked him about it on the show and that was one of the few occasions when he gave me a big smile.

My mum also loves him. In fact she won't hear a bad word about him. She gets upset if I say anything negative. When I told her what he was like on the show, when I told her he was a bit difficult and a bit weird, she didn't want to hear about it. She kept saying, 'Don't say that – he's lovely.'

So I won't say any more for fear of annoying my mum. She still loves him.

25. ASHLEY JENSEN

She was adorable. We did a fashion show and Al, Ashley and I hit the catwalk. Al and I wore orange pants.

26. DAVID WALLIAMS

Without doubt the most nervous guest host we've ever had. I think that was because he wasn't used to doing shows like that. We had him taking part in a big opening production number with vaudeville girls and music and dancing and we decided to do it because we thought it was special and exciting that he'd agreed to do the show, so we came up with that special way of opening the show. But it took a long time to get ready and so David was kept waiting for a long time. He wasn't very happy that there was such a long wait. I said to him, 'Are you okay, Dave?'

He looked at me and just said, 'Hurry up!'

I don't blame him because I knew where he was coming from. He was nervous and he couldn't wait to come out there and start the show.

The wonderful thing about that show, and the moment when it took off, was when his mum appeared on the panel of Who Knows The Most About The Guest Host and his dad was in the audience. His mum was beautiful and lovely. I kissed her and David joked, 'Leave my mum alone!' From that moment on, David completely relaxed and it became a great show.

There was also a sketch in that show which wasn't one of our finest. We all dressed up as Teletubbies and the costumes were awful and it wasn't a great sketch. David looked at us during rehearsal and asked us if we thought it worked. But when you're working on a show week in week out, you let things go – like the odd weak sketch. So he was right. It wasn't a good sketch!

27. CHRIS MOYLES

He was fantastic. He was relaxed and comfortable and at the end of the show he told me how happy he was to have found a TV show he enjoyed doing.

We became good friends as a result of him doing the show.

28. SHARON OSBOURNE

I absolutely love her. She's fascinating. I adore her. I love Kelly. I love Jack. I love Ozzy. She was a dream guest because she was so open and honest. The wonderful thing about her is that she's very clever and smart. She doesn't try to be wildly controversial for the sake of it, for effect. She's just honest. Fiercely honest. I wish that I was a rock 'n' roll star in the 1980s so I could have married her. I love her to bits.

29. MEL C

We wanted a Spice Girl. We went to Majorca to bond with her, which was great. The day after we filmed the show, it was announced that the Spice Girls were getting back together, and we even asked her about it on the show, but she wouldn't and couldn't say, because it was all planned to make the big announcement the next day. We missed out on a huge exclusive. She sent a nice note afterwards, explaining that she couldn't tell us about the reunion for the contractual reasons.

30. LILY ALLEN

She makes me feel quite old, because she's so young. She's lovely and hugely talented. We wrote a song to perform with her and it ended up on YouTube and it went round the world. She revealed that she had a third nipple and showed us and that clip was a huge YouTube phenomenon.

The highlight though was when we got a runner called Ed to take part in the game show at the end. Lily told us she had to fart and she said, 'Shall I do it on him?' and she did. I helped her up and she squatted down on Ed the runner's face and farted on him. I assumed she knew him. But she didn't. She didn't know him from Adam.

31. PAULA ABDUL

She thought Al and I were special needs.

We did a dance routine with her, which she choreographed and we went into the dance studio dressed absurdly with headbands and figure-hugging T-shirts and lycra shorts and stuff, and we acted the goat a bit. She took one look at us and saw how we were behaving and asked someone on the production if we were retarded. She wasn't being funny or cruel – she genuinely thought we were simple.

32. BETH DITTO

I liked the Ditto. But on one level, and I mean this with the best will in the world, she was a bit difficult. Despite this image we have of her of being above all things to do with appearance and image and vanity, she in fact took an age to get ready and kept everyone waiting for a long time. It was just a bit of a surprise.

But the song she sang – Standing On The Edge Of Control – was amazing. It was a phenomenal performance. One of the best ever musical performances in the history of the show. She blew us all away.

33. JOHN BARROWMAN

The dream host. He's quite happy to expose himself. He gives. He'll do almost anything and ask anything.

During the rehearsal he burst into a bit of a cappella song and I thought he was pitch perfect. I said as a joke, 'You're so much better than Michael Ball,' and he said, 'You have to say that during the show.'

34. JOANNA LUMLEY

She was stunningly beautiful. The camera loves her, more than anyone I've ever seen. She looks great in the flesh, but on camera – amazing. She was a lovely person too. She was really funny. Kooky, offbeat and always thinking laterally. I loved spending time with her. I'd like to spend more time with her.

35. DAVID GEST

We first met him when he was at this theatre rehearsing a stage show which was all about his relationship with Liza Minnelli, who was played by a drag artiste. And her version of Liza was always drunk, with a bottle in her hand. There were dwarves who he called The Little People Of David-land. He intended this show to go on tour, but strangely it never happened.

He also very kindly gave Alan and me gifts from Tiffany. I opened up my box but I had no idea what my gifts were. They looked like matching bulbous door handles with holes in each end of these handles. I could not work out what they were. Alan told me they were candlestick holders.

But weirdly, mine looked kind of used. One of them had a dent in it. A friend of Al's wondered whether David Gest was re-gifting us his wedding presents.

36. KANYE WEST

A huge booking. At that time he was one of the biggest music stars in the world. We also had Tim Westwood on the show, and Kanye gave Westwood an awful lot of respect. Clearly he's got kudos in the hip-hop world.

We also shot a spoof pop video with Kanye and during it I told Kanye that Al liked cock. He didn't say anything.

37. KIM CATTRALL

For our bonding session with Kim, we went shopping in Harrods. She was in such amazing shape, and she took a silvery dress off the Dolce and Gabbana rack and tried it on and she emerged from the fitting room looking perfect in this dress. It fit her like a glove. And it was off the rack.

She puts twenty-year-olds to shame.

38. CILLA BLACK

We had a ridiculous bonding film with Cilla. Someone thought it would be a good idea to take her to the Notting Hill Carnival. We took a pensioner to the carnival. On a Bank Holiday Monday. It was insane! We couldn't move. We were on a float, a rubbish two-tier truck and poor Cilla had to climb a ladder to get up there. She must have wondered what the hell she'd let herself in for. Her shoe fell off and someone spilled a can of Coke into it.

Luckily we just made sure there was a lot of champagne for Cilla and she was fine.

39. ELLE MACPHERSON

She had no idea who we were. She kept getting Al and me mixed up. I doubt she knew our names at the end of the show, let alone at the start.

40. MARIAH CAREY

She took us to dinner after the show, because on that day she found out she had her thirty-eighth Number One, or something, in America. So she was celebrating. Her manager, who was called something like Benny Branco from the Bronx, invited us to this back room in a swanky restaurant. And we proceeded to have dinner with Mariah.

You hear a lot about her diva demands and stuff, but she was absolutely fine with us.

Matt Di Angelo was also on that show, and she took quite a shine to him.

41. ELIJAH WOOD

One of the loveliest people I've ever met on the show. Just a sweet, kind, good-natured man. He was adorable.

42. GERI HALLIWELL

I received a Christmas card from her following her appearance on the show, with a picture of her kids' character Eugenie Lavender on the front. Inside the card she'd written, 'To Justin, thanks for all your support.'

I looked at it for about six minutes, wondering, 'What did I do?'

But whatever I did, I'm glad it worked out for her.

She gave me a present too – a Mason Pearson hairbrush. Which was very high end, not that I know much about hairbrushes.

But if I ever run into Geri again, I would like to say one thing to her: the bristles are far too soft.

She also got us into a huddle before the recording. One of those Madonna-style huddles where you pray or whatever. All of a sudden it was like we were in the Spice Girls.

She's also big mates with George Michael, of course. So Al and I asked her to ask him to do the show and to forgive us for making fun of him, which we've done a few times. We're still waiting ...

43. GOK WAN

Gok was brilliant. He'd appeared earlier that series in the game show bit of the show and had been so good, we thought we had to ask him to host the whole thing, and he did and he was great.

44. KATIE AND PETER

Peter was a very nice man.

We met them on this beach in Essex and filmed a Wife Swap-style video at a nearby huge house.

In a break during filming, Peter looked at me and asked if I had psoriasis. He told me his brother has it and that he'd recently started using a cream you could get on the internet and that it had done wonders. He offered to give me the details, which I thought was a lovely gesture.

I think he is brilliant for her because he balances her. I like her as well. I hope they work things out.

I never used the ointment though.

45. PAMELA ANDERSON

She was convinced Al and I were a couple. Nothing we could say would convince her otherwise. So she gave us a present afterwards: a toaster. I think Al's still got it.

She would only do one take. So we had to film the rehearsals and pretend that we were just rehearsing but we were also filming. After each take she'd just say, 'We're done!'

46. MARK RONSON

I love him and we got on so well we became friends afterwards. We spent a day with him at his apartment in New York. He seemed quite reserved at first but the more we got to know him, the more his dry humour came out.

He's a very cool guy, in the proper sense of the word. He's not trying too hard. He's just got it.

47. BOYZONE

We performed live on stage with them in Glasgow. I ripped my trousers off and threw them into the crowd and I was gyrating in my pants in front of 15,000 Boyzone fans.

48. DAVID HASSELHOFF

We recreated a few classic, romantic Hollywood scenes with him - the potter's wheel from Ghost, Richard Gere picking up Debra Winger in An Officer And A Gentleman. But he wouldn't do the spaghetti-eating sequence from Lady And The Tramp. He thought it would come across as gay. He said he didn't have a problem with people thinking it was gay, but he was concerned about the clip ending up on YouTube. The weird thing was that he picked out Lady And The Tramp to be worried about, and not Ghost or An Officer And A Gentleman.

The funniest moment was when he was about to lift Al up in the An Officer And A Gentleman spoof. He stood there looking at Al and asked how much he weighed. He was worried about picking him up. The producer came down to the floor to run through what the Hoff was supposed to do, to pick Al up, and the Hoff just said, in all seriousness, 'I *can't* pick him up!'

49. BARBARA WINDSOR

We had a tour of the EastEnders set and had a drink in the Woolpack. She loved doing the show and at the end of it she said to me, 'There's very few like you in this business … ' Which I thought was lovely.

50. WILL YOUNG

I think he liked me. In that way. He was very nice, surprisingly nice perhaps. And he bought me two vintage T-shirts, which is a considered gift. He clearly knew my style. I still have those T-shirts. They're nice. One of them is yellow.

At the end of that show, which was the last in that series, I was booked to go on holiday with Al to Vegas, including tickets to fly over the Grand Canyon and tickets to see Bette Midler live. We always went on holiday together at the end of each series. But I had an awful ear infection. They got a doctor to come and see me. I asked him if I would be able to fly the next day. He told me I could go, but if I did, I could be in excruciating pain. I thought, '"Excruciating" is quite a word to use.'

I didn't go to Vegas with Al.

51. TOM JONES

The Legend, the Voice. I've seen him live twice, first at Colston Hall in the early 90s when I was still at Filton College and then Christmas 2007 I took my dad to Vegas to see Ricky Hatton fight Floyd Mayweather Jnr and we saw Tom perform at the MGM Grand and he was sensational.

But of course the highlight of the show was getting to perform It's Not Unusual with him. It was one of the highlights of all the TV shows I've ever done. I sang Delilah at Papillon's nightclub. Then I did the show called Convention Crasher where I became a Tom Jones impersonator at the convention for celebrity impersonators in Florida, where the leading celebrity impersonators agent told me I could be the leading Tom Jones impersonator within a year. He'd been a key figure in my life.

I told Tom Jones the story about the convention and he said, 'Oh right!'

The other funny thing that happened during that convention was that I met a few Liza Minnelli impersonators, one of whom I met on camera. I told her I do Liza Minnelli as well, which I do. I started to sing the song Losing My Mind which Liza did with the Pet Shop Boys. This Liza impersonator looked at me and literally walked away. She didn't say a word. But that was nothing to do with Tom Jones.

52. SIMON PEGG

I love him and that was one of my favourite shows we've ever done.
During the first break, he was already sweating profusely and he
looked at Alan and me and said, 'God, it's just like free-falling!'

Because it is a hectic show to do. A knackering, non-stop show.
It moves at quite a pace.

After the show, we talked about having a night out in Bristol,
because he went to college here. I asked if he knew the pub called the
Highbury Vaults, which he did. But he didn't know the fact that it was
the first pub in Bristol to introduce outside patio heaters. One day
soon we're going to have a night out there and I can't wait.

53. PHIL AND KIRSTIE

Al said to them while we were filming that I was always going on about
living in Clifton and Kirstie said it always had been a hot-bed of a
desirable location. They're like brother and sister – they have a lovely,
natural relationship. They were funny and warm and endearing.

54. JAMES CORDEN

We filmed a music video with him called Moobs. I was jealous that he
had better moobs than I did. It was a better music video than the one
we did with Mariah Carey. It got millions of YouTube hits.

55. CATHERINE TATE

I got on very well with Catherine. I like her a lot and she's very sexy.
She was also very excited that Martin Sheen was going to be hosting
the show after her and she was a massive fan of Sheen and The West

Wing and she asked if she could come on that show the following week to take part in the panel game bit. I thought that was great.

56. MARTIN SHEEN

One of the best shows. What an incredible man. A Hollywood legend and yet he went along with every stupid thing we asked him to do, including a silly spoof called Apocalypse Wow and a West Wing spoof in which he wore Village People-style leathers!

He threw himself into it all with gusto. He completely entered into the spirit of our silly, daft show, which is the key to being a great guest host. Our show is Saturday morning TV for adults. And he totally went with the silliness. He was an absolute delight.

57. DAVINA MCCALL

One of our most successful shows. I am a huge fan of hers and have been going way back to her earliest days when she hosted shows like her first ever show on MTV. I was just a fan watching her on TV and my first job was at MTV and I used to ask around about her. One guy at MTV told me she was one of the sexiest women you could ever meet and that when she walked into a room, every head would turn. And she still does.

I think she does a brilliant job on Big Brother. She holds the whole thing together.

58. BIG BROTHER SPECIAL

That was our worst show ever. We had about ten or more old Big Brother housemates co-hosting and it was a total ball-ache. I don't mind having an evictee wearing our coat of cash, that's fine. But hosting the show? Ten of them? No! At one point I reached the end of my tether with Charley Uchea, who threatened to walk out because the audience was baiting her. I told her to be like a rock in rushing waters. Then I lost it with her and said, 'Shut the fuck up, Charley!' Needless to say that was cut from the show.

I love watching Big Brother. I've even watched them sleeping at night. But I don't want them guest hosting our show. Never again!

CHAPTER 18
NAILING IT

As I write this last bit of the book, I'm giving myself a little scratch on my head where I've still got a little bit of psoriasis but not nearly as much as I had a mere matter of months ago when I was still tense and anxious about things. Maybe I'm feeling particularly calm and at peace because I've just finished filming my first ever chat show series. That's a dream come true right there. I've loved David Letterman, the American chat show legend, for years now. I used to watch Jonathan Ross hosting The Last Resort with my mum on a Friday night. I love the idea of the pure chat show – a host behind a desk, with guests and conversations. That's what we tried to do with The Justin Lee Collins Show and while I wouldn't ever dare compare myself to Letterman or Ross, I have really enjoyed the experience of at least trying to do an old-fashioned, no-nonsense chat show.

I've also just filmed some shows for Sky in which I try out Mexican wrestling, star in a West End show (Chicago), attempt proper competitive diving (I punctured my eardrum but it's on the mend), ten-pin bowling across America (like The Big Lebowski, one of my favourite films) and surfing. Amazing experiences. I can now actually stand on a surfboard and surf. I don't wear the Hawaiian shirts much any more, but I can now properly claim to be a surfer dude. And perhaps most ridiculous of all, two songwriters have written a song for me, and we've recorded it. It's like a cross between Tony Christie and Tom Jones. It's a deep grime/rap crossover obviously. Imagine me becoming a recording artiste. It could happen!

The real star of these Sky 1 shows, by the way, is my son Archie. He steals every scene he's in. He's a star already and he's only four.

So without wanting to sound smug, it's all going ridiculously well as far as my TV career is concerned, which is especially difficult to believe because, as you've read (unless you skipped the middle of the book to get to this bit), not so long ago I didn't have enough money to buy frozen Chicago Town pizzas and the only job I could get in TV was to have my hand up a puppet cat, annoying celebrities.

These days I barely have a day off. One minute I'm interviewing Whoopi Goldberg or singing with McFly on my chat show, the next I'm diving from a ten-metre board and bursting my eardrum, and then a few hours later I'll be in the recording studio trying to 'lay down vocals', as they say, on this song called 'You Had Me At Hello' written specially for me. Not forgetting the time I've been spending grappling with a transvestite Mexican wrestler who slapped me round the face as some kind of induction ritual into the weird, wonderful world of the Lucho Libre wrestling scene. And it bloody hurt too.

Despite the occasional painful slap from a transvestite wrestler, I feel unbelievably lucky. In the end, it's all come right for me when it could all have carried on going as wrong as it did when my lovely wife Karen was supporting me because I just couldn't get any work. It wasn't so long ago that I was essentially a kept man!

But I have to say I really wouldn't have minded too much if, back in 2003, when I didn't earn any money for months after that one Ski yoghurt ad, I'd have ended up back working in a video shop. I loved it there. And, of course, if I hadn't worked there I wouldn't have ended up meeting Karen. Well, maybe I would have minded deep down. I would have known that I had failed to fulfil my professional dream, but I would have coped with that. I would have been happy with Karen and my family.

In fact, what is really so good about these times I'm enjoying these days isn't anything to do with the glamour of my job or the fact that I get to mingle with famous people and have my picture in the papers, it's that I get to do the job that I love, meet some of my heroes along the way, whether it's singing with Tom Jones, getting Ewok soap from Princess Leia or telling Mr T that he nearly helped cure my bed-wetting, and that it's enabled me to have such a lovely home in Bristol with Karen and my beautiful boys.

I still live in Bristol because I love it here. It's the best. There's no greater pleasure for me than to sit having a nice Americano coffee (I used to drink full-fat lattes all the time but I've been trying to lose weight) while looking over at the Clifton Suspension Bridge – surely one of the finest sights on the planet – knowing I've got everything a man could possibly want.

I'm lucky enough to have had success in my chosen field of TV, so much so that I suppose I could have lived some people's dream and moved to London and gone to loads of showbiz parties and premieres and all that shit. But I've never even thought about doing that. It's never appealed to me in the slightest. In fact the whole idea of a showbiz party makes me feel mildly sick.

Karen would hate it too. She's not keen on London, and both our families are here, who have supported us all the way, whatever we've been doing.

Why would I want to spend time at a swanky bar or club in London, when I can sit here in Clifton on a rare day off, watching Ghostbusters on DVD with my little Archie?

Of course I hope I'll still get to do loads more exciting TV shows and, luckily, it seems like there are people in TV still willing to pay me to do the kind of programmes I love. But I'm under no illusion that it will carry on like this forever. I'm not sure I want it to carry on forever. I can't see myself making TV shows when I'm in my fifties and sixties. I'm not sure if I've got the stamina. And I doubt people will want to see my stupid face for decades to come.

When I sit here thinking about what the future might hold, I'd love it if I did get to carry on doing a chat show for a while. I love being the host behind the desk, meeting interesting people.

But I'd also be happy with a low-key little local late-night radio show, playing the music I like, talking nonsense.

I'd be equally happy if I wasn't even in 'the business' (shit, I've used that phrase – shoot me in the face now!). I'd love to open my own video shop, although, as I said before, I doubt if people will be going into video shops much what with the internet and downloading and getting DVDs in the post and stuff. Maybe I'll open my own bookshop in Bristol. I'd love that.

People look at the likes of me and assume we must love the fame. But that's never been a factor for me. Honestly. I just enjoy performing. I enjoy the attention, obviously, while I'm there in a studio or in some exotic location and I love knowing that someone somewhere might be amused and entertained by me. I love getting a response from an audience. There's nothing better than seeing audiences laughing and smiling at something I've said or done. But that's it. I don't need people to recognise me wherever I go, even though they're always lovely to me when they do.

All this stuff I've been so lucky to have been able to do has really been about fulfilling my dream to do the only thing I've ever been interested in.

I'll tell you one final job and two subsequent final moments which crystallise everything for me, everything that's important to me, and it goes back to my mum and that awful failure on my part to invite her to come and see me on Strictly Come Dancing.

Four and a half years later when I opened in my role as Amos Hart in the West End production of Chicago for a show I filmed for Sky, I told my parents that I would love them to be there to see me at one of my performances. This job was part of this series where I'm being challenged to do all these difficult tasks, from surfing to Mexican wrestling. But this was the best one for me. The ultimate: taking part in a show, a musical show, in the West End. I was only going to do three performances, but by god they were the kind of thing I dreamed of doing since I was a little boy.

And on the opening night, my mum and dad did come and see me. It was a triumph. It could not have gone any better. After the show I came to see them at the private bar, and I hugged and kissed my wife and my dad and my mum.

And my mum very quietly leaned into me and, with the biggest smile on her face, whispered in my ear, 'You nailed it.'

Her saying that to me, in her quiet, understated way, was one of the greatest moments of my life.

Then a few months ago, as I write this now, Karen and I sat down at home to watch a finished DVD of that West End Star show and in it, before my eventual triumph on stage in Chicago, there's a scene during my early musical theatre training in which I pathetically tried to join the chorus of a local theatre group production of The Pirates Of Penzance. And I was half a second behind everyone else.

It was a ludicrous sight. I was rubbish. And my wife Karen sat there in hysterics, crying with laughter at my rubbishness.

I hadn't seen her laugh like that in ten years. It was wonderful to see.

It made me realise all over again that I'm a very lucky man.

I have nailed it.

Good times.